C000133185

R

# Fasting for a Miracle

It is my privilege to endorse this book because in 1985, as the story in this book relates, I was miraculously healed as a result of the prayers of Dr. Jerry Falwell, Elmer Towns and 5,000 Liberty University students. Your reading of *Fasting for a Miracle* will give you faith to pray for others whom you think can be healed.

**Vernon Brewer**
Founder and President, World Help

From the day of Dr. Elmer Towns's salvation until today, he has lived his life through the miraculous dimension that most people can only dream about. God answers his prayers! When you read *Fasting for a Miracle,* you will learn how to fast and pray in a manner that moves the heart of God for the miraculous to be unleashed in your life.

**Dr. James O. Davis**
Founder, Cutting Edge International
Co-founder, Billion Soul Network

I believe God answers prayers supernaturally, because I was fasting and praying when God led me to my future wife. I know that fasting works, and I want you to read the stories in this book and to fast for a miracle.

**Daniel Henderson**
President, Strategic Renewal

I praise God for this book that tells the miraculous story that I am alive. Because of the prayers of my father and Dr. Jerry Falwell, I lived through one of the worst accidents imaginable. Today, I lead the prayer ministry at Liberty University. Read my story and the other great stories in this book.

Charles Hughes
Prayer Pastor, Liberty University

# ELMER L. TOWNS

# FASTING
## FOR A
# MIRACLE

### HOW God's Power CAN
### Overcome THE Impossible

**BETHANYHOUSE**
a division of Baker Publishing Group
Minneapolis, Minnesota

Published by Bethany House Publishers
11400 Hampshire Avenue South
Bloomington, Minnesota 55438
www.bethanyhouse.com

Bethany House Publishers is a division of
Baker Publishing Group, Grand Rapids, Michigan

Bethany House edition published 2015
ISBN 978-0-7642-1597-1

Previously published by Regal Books.

Printed in the United States of America

Library of Congress Control Number: 2015950591

Unless otherwise indicated, Scripture quotations are from the New King James Version. Copyright © 1982 by Thomas Nelson, Inc. Used by permission. All rights reserved.

Scripture quotations labeled ELT are from the Elmer L. Towns Version (paraphrase from the author).

Scripture quotations labeled KJV are from the King James Version of the Bible.

Scripture quotations labeled NLT are from the *Holy Bible*, New Living Translation, copyright © 1996, 2004, 2007 by Tyndale House Foundation. Used by permission of Tyndale House Publishers, Inc., Carol Stream, Illinois 60188. All rights reserved.

Scripture quotations labeled TLB are from The Living Bible, copyright © 1971. Used by permission of Tyndale House Publishers, Inc., Wheaton, Illinois 60189. All rights reserved.

Note: The fasts suggested in this book are not for everyone. Consult your physician before beginning. Expectant mothers, diabetics, and others with a history of medical problems can enter the spirit of fasting while remaining on essential diets. While fasting is healthful to many, the nature of God would not command a physical exercise that would harm people physically or emotionally.

# CONTENTS

## Part V: Fasting for the Deepest Miracles

## Appendixes

# FOREWORD

When Elmer Towns writes, earnest Christians read! We do so, among other reasons, because of his *sensitivity to the times*—a hallmark of his ministry. Elmer is solidly anchored in God's Word, yielded to His will, and attuned to His Spirit. For decades Elmer has proven to be a steadfast servant of Jesus Christ and His Church.

My friendship with Elmer Towns goes back 20 years. It began with an interview I was humbled to have him request of me while he was writing his book, *America's Ten Most Innovative Churches*. That was when I discovered that whenever he spent a weekend in the Greater Los Angeles area, he attended The Church On The Way, where I was then the senior pastor. As our friendship grew over the years, I came to know more about this man who is far more than an effective writer—indeed, today, many see him as I do: a strong and stabilizing influence and a statesman in the Body of Christ.

What many people do not know is that Elmer Towns co-founded Liberty University—and partnered with Dr. Jerry Falwell in leading the rise of that great institution. As a man with a pastoral heart, Elmer teaches the Pastors Bible Class at Thomas Road Baptist Church in Lynchburg, Virginia. At the same time, his love for the whole Church has won him a multitude of friends across the spectrum of Christ's Body, including all who welcome the Holy Spirit's ministry as well as a sound Word-centered evangelistic ministry. He passionately espouses the desire that the *whole* flock of Jesus' Church unite our hearts, moving forward as one.

Here, Dr. Towns has written a book on *Fasting for a Miracle*—a work he brings us as the capstone of his writing ministry on spirituality. More than 15 years ago, he wrote the book, *Fasting for Spiritual Breakthrough*, and sent me one of the first copies. After reading it, I placed an order for 2,500 copies and called our people to read it together over a period of eight weeks. It was a trying time in our nation's life, and as I joined a preaching series to the content of Elmer's book, I witnessed a dynamic knitting together of our hearts as a congregation.

The wisdom and truth of this key to spiritual health and ongoing release of God's grace among His people helped cultivate a lifestyle for The Church On The Way. For decades, I led the congregation to fast from Sunday evening through Wednesday noon preceding Thanksgiving each year. During these days, we focused on intercession for God's blessing on our nation, as well as fasting for local and personal breakthrough as we approached our national day of thanking God for His goodness and grace upon us as a people.

Elmer's book on *Fasting for Spiritual Breakthrough* continues to be a perennial bestseller—used by many churches and individuals in every circle of Christian life. Which brings us to the present companion volume: a book to help individuals fast personally and devotionally unto dynamic outcomes. This book will not only prepare you to fast with a clear spiritual focus on the truth of God's Word about fasting, but also equip you in the practical steps—the techniques of how to go about *Fasting for a Miracle*.

My thanks go to my brother, Elmer Towns, for this book. I pray that Father God will use it in the life of innumerable individual believers. Now, as you take it in hand, I urge you to read—and then, to reach out to God; in doing so, you will discover that as you fast, seeking Him, God Himself will extend His strong arm—reaching out to you!

Sincerely, your brother-in-grace,

Jack W. Hayford
Founding Pastor, The Church On The Way
Chancellor, The King's University, Los Angeles, California

# INTRODUCTION

# Hungry to Touch God

As I wrote this book of true stories about fasting for the greatest—even the impossible—needs in our lives, I fasted for God to do a miracle in the life of you, the reader. I yearn for you to experience God as you read these pages. After you've read every story in this book, I want you to hunger for God—more than you hunger for bread. I want you to hunger in your soul as you hunger physically during a fast.

As I shaped each practical application in this book, knowing that real people with real problems would really be fasting, I talked with God. Now it's your turn to talk with Him as you read. Sometimes I talked out loud; sometimes the conversation was internal—subvocal talking. I interacted with God as I interacted with words and sentences on the page.

I heard God talking to me as I wrote this book. And I reached out to touch Him. No, not with a hand or a finger. But it was the same as touching someone with a hand. I knew inwardly what I experienced. I touched God. Will you reach out to touch Him as you read?

More importantly than my touching God, He touched me. The God of the universe came to me. I could feel His atmospheric presence, although I could not see Him with my eyes. I knew He was there, just as surely as I know my wife sits across from me when we eat a meal. I experienced God's presence as I wrote.

Will you be sensitive to His presence? Will you ask Him for a miracle in your life? Before you begin reading these true stories of fasting, will you pray, *Touch me, O God?*

Written from my home atop Liberty Mountain

Elmer L. Towns
Co-founder, Liberty University

# PROLOGUE

# When Charles Needed a Miracle

The doctor didn't offer even a sliver of hope as he broke the news: "Charles won't make it; he's as good as dead."

Robert Hughes's jaw dropped. He had rushed across three states to be at his son's side. How could this be? Charles's head crushed in an accident? Almost no chance of survival? The likelihood that if he did hang on, he would be in a vegetative state the rest of his life? It didn't seem possible.

Just a few hours earlier, Charles—a bright senior in college and a gifted preacher with seemingly limitless potential—and three other fine young men from Liberty University had climbed into a van and headed off for a weekend adventure packed with opportunities to preach the gospel. Now Charles lay almost lifeless. Would he even make it through the night? It was a turn of events impossible to fathom.

"We'd like you to sign papers so that we can harvest his vital organs to save the lives of others," the doctor gently prodded.

"No!" Robert Hughes objected. His voice reverberated up and down the hospital's corridor. "Absolutely *not!*"

\* \* \* \* \*

Late on Friday, March 17, 1978, Charles Hughes, Mark Lowry, David Musselman and Dick Bernier departed Lynchburg, Virginia. It was chilly—in the mid-30s—but there was no hint of snow. The foursome planned to travel through the night to upstate New York, where Charles was scheduled to speak at a Word of Life basketball marathon on Saturday. Mark would sing, and David would play keyboards. Also on the weekend slate were a youth rally and church services.

The van they rode in had been donated to Liberty University by businessmen from Alabama and Michigan, customized with swiveling captain's chairs up front, a bed in the rear and extra storage space. As each young man took his place for the journey, Charles noticed that Mark sat with his head facing toward the back of the vehicle rather than toward the front. "Don't you get claustrophobia?" Charles asked.

"If we wreck, I'd rather hurt my legs than my head," Mark explained, having no idea what lay ahead of them that night.

Dick drove as everyone chatted and some rested, Mark facing backwards all the way. The weather mostly held steady as they rambled through Virginia and Maryland. In Southern Pennsylvania, two inches of snow had fallen that day, and the temperature hovered just above freezing. On a dark winding highway near the city of Carlisle, the driver of an 18-wheel truck lost control. His gigantic vehicle slid down a steep incline and slammed into the Liberty van, smashing it against a mountainside.

The van's four passengers were transported to a nearby hospital. David was not seriously injured, though it was originally feared that his hands might be mangled. Mark, who would go on to gain notoriety as a member of the Gaither Vocal Band, had 11 broken bones. Dick had a punctured lung.

Charles, who hadn't fared as well, was rushed into surgery. The force of the impact had slung his skull against metal on the inside of the van. His head was crushed, resulting in an open gash. His spleen was ruptured (and had to be removed), and he was comatose.

Within hours, Liberty University President Jerry Falwell and Robert Hughes arrived in Carlisle, and they went directly to the hospital. Instead of agreeing to sign papers that would have effectively ended his son's life, Hughes asked where the prayer chapel was. Although aging, Hughes almost ran down the hallway. "God gave us Charles when we couldn't have children," he told Falwell, who was following him. "God told me that Charles was going to be a great preacher of the gospel . . . He's *not* going to die."

The physicians couldn't dissuade Hughes. Falwell didn't even try. He respected the father's convictions and knew of the family's steadfast faith—for many years Hughes had served alongside Falwell at Liberty as a dean.

In those days there were no cell phones, but Falwell carried a large mobile telephone. He dialed my number.

"Elmer," he said. "Quick, Charles is about to die, and we must pray to hold back the pressures of death. He's in a coma."

Charles needed a miracle, and fast . . .

*(continued in the postscript)*

# PART I

# The Miraculous Power of Extreme Faith

*The most incredible thing about miracles is that they happen.*
G. K. CHESTERTON

# I

# Fasting . . .

In the spring of 1994, I put together a list of five potential books for my publisher, Regal Books. I was a consultant to the company, and my expertise was primarily in the areas of Sunday School and church growth, not spirituality. As I sat in an editorial meeting, discussing my ideas, Bill Greig III, president of Gospel Light, saw on the list my suggestion of publishing a book on fasting. "Wow," Bill said, "someone needs to write a book on fasting." Then he went on to ask, "How long has it been since anyone has written a significant book on fasting?"

"Over 100 years," I answered.

Someone suggested that Regal ask Bill Bright to write the book on fasting, because he led a conference on fasting and prayer through Campus Crusade for Christ. I had served on the planning committee for that event, so I knew all about the conference. But Bill was not available because of his other projects.

Kyle Duncan, editor of Regal Books, said, "Jack Hayford would be the perfect person to write this book, because he calls his church to fast." But Hayford was not available either, because he was involved in a different writing project for Regal. The discussion languished, and a little frustration set in. Finally I sheepishly raised my hand and said, "I can write your book on fasting."

"What do you know about fasting? You are a Baptist!" someone said. I don't remember who made the comment, but it was a common assumption that Pentecostals and charismatics fasted, while fasting was not a Baptist practice.

I answered, "Every year I teach a course on fasting to our RAs (resident advisors) at Liberty University in preparation for the school year." Then I added that Thomas Road Baptist Church and

Liberty University had a fasting lifestyle, and that many great answers to prayer came through fasting.

"Let Elmer do it," someone said, and the group moved on to other topics.

When I got home, I began to outline a few ideas for the book, but nothing was coming. I looked up every reference to fasting in the Bible, and then I wrote a summary of what we could learn about fasting from each verse. But all I had was a legal pad full of isolated facts—nothing resembling the glue that held a book together.

I talked to my wife, Ruth, about the problem, telling her that I didn't have any idea how to bring a book on fasting together. I was really not asking her for help, but her perceptive answer was brilliant in its simplicity.

"Since you are writing a book on fasting," she reasoned, "why don't you fast about what you should write?"

Later I realized her answer came supernaturally from God.

The following Monday, I fasted for God to give insight about the book. I usually fast on Mondays using a *Yom Kippur* format. I don't eat a meal on Sunday night, and I skip breakfast and lunch on Monday. During this type of fast, I drink orange juice in the morning, and I also sip on a cup of coffee—from early in the morning through the afternoon. I end the fast at sundown on Monday. The Jews count a day from sundown to sundown, the way God described it: "So the evening and the morning were the first day" (Gen. 1:5).

That Monday evening, Ruth and I went out to the Crown Sterling, a fine white-linen restaurant, to break my one-day fast. As we sat, she asked, "What did God say to you about fasting?"

"Nothing." I shook my head in discouragement. "I spent the day filling my legal pad with more isolated facts, but there's no glue to hold them together." Then my answer came through the next thing I said—or started to say: "All I have is one sermon on fasting with nine points that I preach to the Liberty students at the beginning of every new school year."

That phrase, "All I have is one sermon on fasting with nine points," seized me. My hand froze in mid-air, and I stopped speaking in mid-sentence. For a few seconds I stared into space, and a deep smile crept across my face.

"Nine points."

Instantly I knew that God had answered my prayer, and I saw nine chapters unfold before me. Each point of my sermon was a practical suggestion for fasting; I'd write a book with nine practical chapters on how to fast.

I grabbed a napkin to begin outlining the nine points, each of them coming from Isaiah 58:6-8.

I decided to teach one of the nine points each week in my Pastors Bible Class at church. It would take nine weeks to teach the lay people how to fast. It would take nine weeks to write the book. I decided to fast each week on Monday, which would be the day when I prepared lessons for the following weeks. That way I would not be hypocritical; I would continue to fast for God to give me insight about fasting.

Around halfway through the nine weeks, after my Monday fast, Ruth and I again went out to the Crown Sterling Restaurant. She asked, "How is your writing coming?"

It was an idle question, but I was excited. So I read to her the chapter titles.

"Those titles sound too academic. . ." Her words trailed off into nothing. She's not a negative person, just extremely practical. So she added, "Your titles sound like a term paper or something for a master's thesis, not for a popular book on fasting." I agreed with her, but I thought the list I had was the best I could do. So Ruth said, "Why don't you fast and ask God to give you the right titles?"

"Excellent idea."

So on the following Monday, I fasted looking for chapter titles. During that day, I scratched out several lists of titles, each time not satisfied with what I wrote. Again that evening I broke my fast as we went to the Crown Sterling Restaurant. I had to confess to Ruth that I was nowhere closer to titles than I had been previously.

She noted, "Too bad you can't use something like our church choir." She explained, "They are following a Daniel fast to save money for a mission project."

*"Did you say a Daniel fast?"* I blurted out. That was the answer I was looking for. Right there at the table, God gave me nine popular titles. Again, I grabbed a napkin and began writing. I have polished those nine titles with time, but they have remained the same ideas in essence for the past 15 years. Each fast has a different name, accomplishes a different purpose, and follows a different prescription:

1. The Disciple's Fast: to break sin's addiction.
2. The Ezra Fast: to solve problems.
3. The Samuel Fast: for revival and soul winning.
4. The Elijah Fast: to overcome discouragement and despondency.
5. The Widow's Fast: to care for the needy.
6. The Saint Paul Fast: to make decisions and gain insight.
7. The Daniel Fast: for healing and physical health.
8. The John the Baptist Fast: for testimony and influence.
9. The Esther Fast: for protection.

## Seeking Divine Insight

Many times we pray for understanding or divine insight. God gives us the Holy Spirit to help us find His will. He also leads us through the Scriptures and through our experience. Therefore, God will show us His will and give us divine insight as we:

1. Attend church services and Bible studies where we hear the Word of God (the first step in finding God's guidance for our lives is hearing the Word of God taught and preached);
2. Personally study the Bible and carefully analyze its meaning;
3. Memorize Scripture and hide its truth within our hearts (see Ps. 119:11); and
4. Meditate on the Word of God and mull over its truths in our minds to gain further insight (see Ps. 1:2).

After this biblical preparation, we must pray for spiritual insight: "Open my eyes, that I may see wondrous things from Your law" (Ps. 119:18). Then God is able to speak to us by showing us divine insight as we wait before Him in prayer and fasting. The following steps can make a fast more effective:

1. *Write down the purpose for the fast.* Be specific. When praying and fasting for the miracle or revival, for example, don't just write "revival." What part of your life needs revival? What do you want to accomplish with revival, and in what areas are you asking God to send revival? Ask the same questions if you are praying for a miracle of healing, guidance, financial breakthrough or whatever you need. You must ask the Lord to focus your mind on how you will fast and for leadership in your fasting. The more focused you become, the more specifically you can pray for the answers you seek. This will compel you to pray more strategically.

2. *Before you begin, determine the type of fast and what food or drink you will eliminate.* There are many different kinds of fasts (see appendix A for descriptions of the six ways to fast). Ask yourself some pointed questions before you make your decision and write down your vow to fast.

3. *Determine how long you will fast before you begin.* You may fast for one day or three days, or perhaps longer. I always suggest that beginners start slowly, beginning with a one-day fast. As you become more accustomed to fasting, you can build up to longer times. Never start with a 40-day fast; you will probably fail and kill any future desire to fast. If you have a giant request, then vow to fast one day a week for 40 weeks. Think of all you'll learn in those 40 weeks.

I strongly suggest you write down when you will begin your fast, and when will you end. I have included a fasting checklist at the end of this chapter to help you with this extremely important step. Make an agreement with God about when you will begin and end the fast, and don't let circumstances change your mind. If it's a three-day fast, plan the first meal that you will eat after the fast is over. That's important. It gives you a target. Don't just stop fasting! Conclude your fast with victory, including prayer and a spiritual benediction.

One of the worst things to do is to come to the end of a three-day fast and decide to stretch it to two or three more days. That may not be the Spirit of God speaking to you. It may be your unsure heart that's controlled by your emotions. Keep your vow to God. Begin on time and end on time. Often I receive letters from people who have passed 40 days of fasting and don't want to stop. If they ask me what to do, I tell them, "Stop immediately! Eat and break your fast." If it's truly a biblical fast, keep the vow that you originally made with God.

## Guidelines for Fasting

Fasting involves much more than going without food. Genuine fasting requires planning and preparation, and it also demands an intentional and complete commitment to seeking the Lord throughout the fast. Below are several steps you should take if you desire to fast effectively

### Plan Your Prayer Time
*Determine how much time you will spend each day in prayer and study of God's Word.* Obviously none of us can pray all day, although some can stay in a spirit of meditation and worship. However, most Americans have jobs, family commitments, and other responsibilities that require our time and attention. When I'm in a one-day fast, I begin each day, as I would a normal day, with prayer. Beyond that, I begin my fast by not eating my evening meal and giving the mealtime—usually about an hour—over to prayer. In addition, I keep my regular evening prayer time. Time praying for fasting needs to be an addition to your regular devotions, not a replace-

ment for them. The next morning, I use breakfast time—generally around 30 minutes—for prayer. I usually take an hour or an hour and fifteen minutes for lunch, so when I'm fasting, I close the door to my office and spend that time praying instead of eating.

### Take a Spiritual Inventory Before Fasting

When you fast and pray, you are giving up food to discipline your body. Make sure you do the same thing with your attitudes and thoughts. You want to bring all parts of your life under the discipline of Jesus Christ. Make a list of sins or weaknesses in your life. Yield them to Christ—especially for the time of your fast—and ask God to keep you holy. Pray for victory (see 1 Cor. 10:13).

### Confess Every Known Sin (see 1 John 1:9)

Acknowledge every sin, repent, and be done with it. If we are repeatedly confessing every little sin, we are living on the edge of defeat. Instead of mulling over every way you have failed God, accept His forgiveness and live victoriously in the spirit of 1 John 1:7: "But if we walk in the light as He is in the light, we have fellowship with one another, and the blood of Jesus Christ His Son cleanses us from all sin."

### Engage in Identificational Repentance

Identificational repentance means confessing the sins of our nation and the Church. It involves confession of the sins of those who came before us as well as those who are currently around us. Technically, God does not forgive them as a result of our repentance or confession. God only forgives those who confess their own sins. But in confessing the sins of our nation or others, we are asking God to withhold His punishment or the consequences on society of their sins.

Daniel confessed the sins of his forefathers that had resulted in the Babylonian captivity: "I set my face toward the Lord God to make request by prayer and supplications, with fasting, sackcloth, and ashes. . . . We have sinned and committed iniquity, we have done wickedly and rebelled" (Dan. 9:3-5).

Similarly, Nehemiah entered into identificational repentance when he said, "I pray, LORD God of heaven. . . . We have acted very corruptly against You, and have not kept the commandments . . . which you commanded" (Neh. 1:5-7).

### Check Your Relationships to See If You've Offended Anyone

If you have wronged another person, you must go to them and ask for forgiveness (see Matt. 5:23-24). But I urge you to go a step farther. There might be someone who has offended you. How do you pray for them? You pray for them as you pray the Lord's Prayer: "Forgive us our trespasses as we forgive those who trespass against us."

You must forgive anyone who has offended you (see Mark 11:25-26). Keep your spirit right and your prayer honest. You don't forgive someone for their sake; you forgive them for your sake—your spiritual growth and relationship with God. This sounds counterintuitive, but it's the way God works. In fact, Scripture even calls on us to bless our enemies (see Luke 6:27-28).

### Ask God to Teach You the Word as You Study and Fast

Remember, there is a measure of spiritual blindness in each one of us, so we must ask for the Holy Spirit to teach us (see John 14:26), and we must ask the Holy Spirit to take away our spiritual blindness (see 2 Cor. 4:3-4).

### Ask God to Fill You with the Holy Spirit

The more you know about the Holy Spirit, the more you can give Him control of your life. And the more you walk with the Holy Spirit, the more He can exercise His influence through you. Remember the exhortation of Paul: "Be filled with the Spirit" (Eph. 5:18).

### Yield Yourself Fully to the Lord Jesus Christ

Paul instructs us: "Present your bodies a living sacrifice, holy, acceptable to God, which is your reasonable service" (Rom. 12:1). This exhortation means that we must give God our physical bodies: our hands, feet, eyes, ears, mouth, nose—everything. Once we have yielded the outer body, we must then yield the inner person: our attitudes, desires, and even failures. Give everything to God. It's that simple.

## Ask for Faith

You must be like the young father in the Bible who confessed his weakness to the Lord Jesus: "I believe; help my unbelief!" (Mark 9:24). The first step toward stronger faith is developing an expectant heart for the things for which you are praying (see Heb. 11:6).

## Be Aware of Spiritual Opposition and Temptation

Remember that there is an enemy. Peter describes him this way: "The devil walks about like a roaring lion, seeking whom he may devour" (1 Pet. 5:8). The devil will do everything possible to destroy your fast, and then to destroy your faith. He will place subtle thoughts in our minds. He will discourage us by any failure in our lives. Sometimes we give up or give in to sin because we are discouraged. We must learn to "[pray] in the Holy Spirit" (Jude 20), and to keep our thoughts on God and His Word.

## Fill Out a Fasting Checklist

Just as a pilot goes through a checklist before he attempts to fly a plane, so should you complete a fasting checklist to make sure you're not leaving out anything. Fill out the following checklist, and then sign it.

# Fasting Checklist

Purpose: _____

Fast: What you will withhold _____

Begin: Date _____

Time _____

End: Date _____

Time _____

***Vow:*** *I believe that God is the only answer to my request, and that prayer without fasting is not enough to get an answer to my need. Therefore, by faith, I am fasting because I need God to work in this matter.*

Bible Basis: My Bible promise _____

_____

_____

_____

Resources: What I need during this fast _____

_____

_____

_____

***Vow:*** *God being my strength and grace being my basis, I commit myself to the above fast.*

Signature: _____

# . . . for a Miracle

I believe in miracles. Jesus did miracles when He was here on earth, and God still does them today.

Why do I believe God does miracles? It is simple. The Bible declares that miracles will happen. I have also seen for myself the hand of God at work in my life and in the lives of others. In this book, I tell stories of big miracles and everyday miracles—yes, miracles can happen every day.

When we think about miracles, we usually think first of the big, dramatic ones where someone is physically healed: Lazarus is raised from the dead, a blind man sees, and a lame man walks again. As you will read, miracles can not only be for our physical needs but also go far beyond that. A miracle can include divine guidance, deliverance or financial breakthrough. The greatest miracle of all is salvation.

Every time a soul is saved, God does the miraculous. Every answer to prayer is supernatural, and it's a miracle every time the Holy Spirit enlightens the mind of a believer to understand the Scriptures. Any time the spiritual world affects the natural world, that's a miracle.

Those who deny miracles think like the naturalists, who say the universe is a closed box. The laws of nature run everything in the box, and there is nothing outside the box—no God, no angels, no spiritual world. The naturalist claims that the things inside the box control our world or universe; if there is a god, that god does not influence our present-day world.

Carl Sagan was a functional atheist who was controlled by his naturalism. He believed that the *cosmos* is all that is, or ever has been, or ever will be. Sagan, like all naturalists, does not believe in miracles, because his worldview says there is no God that is influencing life today.

As C. S. Lewis said in his book *Miracles*, "The word *Miracle* [means] an interference with Nature by supernatural power."[1] No one denies the laws of nature or other laws that control life.[2] But given that there are laws, isn't it self-evident that there must be a Law Giver? And can't the Law Giver interpret His laws for His purpose? Or, can't He make a higher law? In heaven and outside our universe, God has laws that we humans don't even know about.

In essence, a miracle is the *work of God*. According to the *Holman Christian Standard Bible*, "A miracle is defined as God's working at just the right time, in just the right place, in just the right degree to produce a redemptive outcome."[3] You can't really believe in the God of Scripture if you deny the supernatural and the existence of miracles.

Mir-a-cle \ *mir-i-kel* \ fr. Latin *mirari*—to wonder at. (1) An extraordinary event manifesting divine intervention in human affairs. (2) An extremely outstanding or unusual event. (3) A divinely natural phenomenon experienced humanly as the fulfillment of spiritual law.[4]

The believer who says there are no miracles today has probably been influenced by naturalism, or by the influence of evolution. With evolution being so widely taught in public schools, it is no wonder so many reject the miraculous. Even some Christians who reject evolution have been affected by the influence of naturalism. They have thrown out the prostitute, but kept her baby, i.e., these Christians throw out evolution, but still reject the supernatural.

Then there are some Christians who have convinced themselves that "the day of miracles has passed." These are called cessationists, i.e., people who believe miracles have ceased. Some are cessationists because of their view of Scripture; perhaps others haven't seen the power of God in their lives. They experienced the miracle of conversion, but like the disciple who began walking on water (also a miracle), they have begun looking at the threatening waves of this world and have started to sink. They need to cry out to the Lord as Peter did. Jesus rescued Peter, and He will do the same for anyone who prays, "Lord, save me!" (Matt. 14:30). Of course, the Lord also rebuked Peter: "O you of little faith, why did you doubt?" (Matt. 14:31).

## Types of Miracles

Technically, there are different kinds of miracles. While each kind is different in nature, all bring glory to God.

First, there were *creation miracles* where God brought matter, energy, laws and life into being by His spoken word. This was a miracle *ex nihilo* (out of nothing). The creation miracle falls into the category of one-time events that will not be repeated. They ceased because the reason they were needed was accomplished; therefore, they are no longer necessary.

- Creation of the world (see Gen. 1–2)
- Universal flood (see Gen. 6–7)
- Animal sacrifices (see Heb. 10:1-18)
- Virgin birth (see Matt. 1:18-20; Luke 1:35)
- Perfect life of Jesus (see 2 Cor. 5:21; 1 Pet. 2:22; 1 John 3:5)
- Sacrificial death of Jesus (see Heb. 7:26-29; 9:26-28; 10:10)
- Resurrection of Jesus (see Rom. 1:4)

Second, there are *providential miracles*. This is God's loving care whereby He preserves, governs and exercises His will over all things that He has created. The word providence comes from the Latin *providere*, which means "to foresee." God has foreknowledge or foresight and works all things according to His divine plan. The eternal Law Giver uses His laws to accomplish a divine purpose, and He works through His laws to give a solution to a human problem. In response to prayer, sometimes God does not bend or interfere with His laws; rather, He works behind the scenes and uses His laws to deliver an answer.

Providence is God choosing to work in the affairs of people, but remaining anonymous. So we can conclude that there are two epistemological kinds of miracles: those God actively performs (when we pray and fast) and those of His providence.

Remember, God runs the world by His laws. So God directs what happens by His power that is already in place, i.e., the force of the laws of the universe. That doesn't mean there is no chance or coincidence. If there is no chance, that means God is responsible for everything that happens. If there is no coincidence, can we blame God for murders, rapes, diseases and financial reversals? No. God is in control of His universe, but He has an opposing force, i.e., the world and the flesh (see 1 John 2:15-17). The energy behind these forces is determined to destroy everything that belongs to God and serves God. Therefore, there is an unseen battle between God and His enemy: the devil (see Rev. 12:9), who wants to take God's place and become like the Most High (see Isa. 14:12-15).

God is the divine chess player who plans several moves ahead to win a game for those who are yielded to Him. He is the director of a play, and we are the actors on stage. God plans our actions and movements on stage to deliver a magnificent play. But we who are His actors must learn our lines and practice our calling. We must use our abilities and call on His help by fasting and prayer, working with other players to serve God, who is our director and master. Similarly, we can view God as the conductor of a symphony; we are the musicians and instruments that blend our talents to deliver an enjoyable concert.

Third, there are the *signs/miracles of Scripture*. These involved supernatural acts, such as the 10 plagues on Egypt wrought by Moses, or the miraculous supply of manna (food from heaven) that fed Israel as she wandered in the wilderness. Sometimes these were supernatural interventions in the laws of nature; at other times there was a higher law or power that operated above the laws of nature.

Sign miracles are a lot like the signs we encounter as we travel on the highways. Some signs give directions—like the miracle of the burning bush that was not consumed (see Exod. 3:1-9). God used that sign to direct Moses to a mission in Egypt. Some signs warn of danger—such as the 10 plagues against Egypt, which warned Pharaoh to obey God and release the people of Israel. Some signs make an announcement—like the miracles of Jesus that declared He was the Son of God (see John 20:31). Other signs give credibility to the messages of God—such as the miracles by Elijah, Elisha and the apostles (see Heb. 2:1-4).

The fourth group of miracles includes the ones that *Jesus performed to show His power*. In Matthew 8:27, we read, "Even the winds and the sea obey Him." The miracles of Christ authenticated that He was the Messiah the people expected, but even more importantly, that He was God—and that He wielded the power of God:

- Jesus was the Deliverer, because He delivered people from demon possession.
- Jesus was the Healer, because He healed the apparently incurable.
- Jesus was omnipotent, because He exercised power over nature.
- Jesus was omniscient, because He knew the thoughts of His enemies.
- Jesus was the object of worship, because He allowed Himself to be worshipped.

The miracles of Jesus had a purpose. They revealed that Jesus was God, and His revelation demanded a response. Observers of His miracles believed in Him, obeyed Him, grew in faith or worshipped Him. Yet, when His enemies asked for a miracle, because of their unbelief Jesus did not do what they asked. A group of scribes and Pharisees said, "Teacher, we want to see a sign from You" (Matt. 12:38). Isn't that always the response of a rejecting heart? They wanted outward proof. But Jesus told them, "Your words now represent your lack of faith, either your words will make you right; or your words will condemn you" (Matt. 12:37, *ELT*).

*Conversion miracles* involve the work of God by the Holy Spirit in the life of an unsaved person when he or she is born again (see John 3:3-7). First, God's providence may turn the person's thoughts toward salvation: "He . . . sends rain on the just and on the unjust" (Matt. 5:45). Experientially, the Holy Spirit convicts the person of his sin or lack of righteousness and of his potential judgment (see John 16:7-11). This affects his experiences, knowledge, emotions and will. The person understands the gospel, and when he believes in Christ, the Word of God regenerates him (see 1 Pet. 1:23) and transforms him (see 2 Cor. 5:17). When people testify of their salvation, many affirm: "It took a miracle."

The Holy Spirit leads God's children by *guidance miracles*. The believer is directed where the Holy Spirit guides him or does what the Holy Spirit wishes or accomplishes what the Holy Spirit wants (see Gal. 5:16). "For all who are led by the Spirit of God are children of God" (Rom. 8:14, *NLT*). This is an internal work of God that has outward results. God leads through an understanding of Scripture, through prayer, through counsel of others (see Prov. 11:14), and through the rational/common sense of the believer. God leads through open doors—opportunities—or closed doors (see 1 Cor. 16:9). "The steps of a good man are ordered by the LORD" (Ps. 37:23). This supernatural guidance is also miraculous.

Next there are *spiritual gift miracles* where the believer is able to serve God with supernatural results when he properly exercises the spiritual gifts given him. There are two aspects of God's supernatural activity at work in these miracles. First, the believer is given ability for spiritual service (see Eph. 4:7-11). These gifts are not identical in all believers, but God gives different gifts to different believers, with different levels of ability, to accomplish different results (suggesting God's supernatural disbursement). As Paul puts it, we have "gifts differing according to the grace that is given to us" (Rom. 12:6). The second supernatural aspect is when God uses our spiritual gifts to do the work of ministry. "As each one has received a gift, minister it to one another" (1 Pet. 4:10). God super-naturally uses a gifted person to accomplish His purpose.

The area of *prayer miracles* is next. Jesus promised His followers that they could move mountains (see Matt. 17:20; Mark 11:22-24). Most likely, He was referring to the removal of problems or hindrances in ministry; He was probably not talking about moving literal mountains.[5] By prayer we can remove barriers, obstacles or problems that are facing us or our ministry.

At first glance, it seems like Jesus gave an unlimited promise: "Whatever you ask in My name, that I will do" (John 14:13). But a full reading of all the promises Jesus made about asking suggests the following biblical limitations on asking and receiving:

1. Ask according to the promises of Scripture (see John 15:7)
2. Ask because we abide in Him (see 1 John 3:24)
3. Ask when involved in Christian service (see John 15:16)
4. Ask because we are obedient to God (see 1 John 3:22)
5. Ask in faith (see Mark 11:24)
6. Ask persistently (see Luke 11:5-10)
7. Ask because we have repented of former sin (see Ps. 66:18; John 9:31)

## Miracles in Scripture

Miracles are not evenly spread out in Scripture. Moses was a mighty worker of signs/miracles, but David did not experience obvious miracles, although God did give him a victory over Goliath, bring Him safely through battles, and deliver him from the constant pursuit by Saul. In many of his Psalms, David cried out for relief, feeling that God had abandoned him. Why did Moses experience an abundance of supernatural miracles and David didn't get them?

The writer of Hebrews maintains, "God verified the message by signs and wonders and various miracles . . . whenever he chose to do so" (Heb. 2:4, *NLT*). Note that miracles were used to verify God's message and that God did them according to His timing and purpose.[6]

There were miracles in the life of Abraham, when God set one people (the Hebrews) apart for His purpose. Notice the lack of miracles in the lives of Isaac, Jacob and Joseph (although God's providential working was evident). Then Moses saw great miracles when God established the nation of Israel with its laws and the Tabernacle as the center of worship. Notice how many kings did not experience miracles. Then God told the nation to repent or lose its privileged place with Him. To verify this message, God sent Elijah and Elisha working miracles.

Then, in the New Testament, "John the Baptist did no miracles" when he introduced Jesus (see John 10:41). But Jesus came doing signs, miracles and wonders—"and many believed in Him" (John 10:42). So what about us? Should we be doing miracles?

Jesus told us, "He who believes in Me, the works that I do he will do also; and greater works than these he will do, because I go to My Father" (John 14:12). This verse indicates we can do the same works that Jesus did—and if that's the case, we should expect miracles.

## The Power of the Holy Spirit

Remember, Jesus didn't do His works in His own power but in the power of the Holy Spirit. So we need the Holy Spirit's power to expect miracles. Note the four empowerments of Jesus' works: "Jesus [was] filled with the Holy Spirit" (Luke 4:1), He "was led by the Spirit" (Luke 4:1), He "returned in the power of the Spirit" (Luke 4:14), and He said, "The Spirit of the LORD is upon Me, because He has anointed Me" (Luke 4:18). When we are as dependent upon the Holy Spirit as Jesus was, then we can do the miracles He did.

We must come to the place Jesus was when He said, "The Son can do nothing of Himself" (John 5:19). Similarly, He said, "I can of Myself do nothing" (John 5:30) and "I do nothing of Myself" (John 8:28). Just as Jesus relied on the Father and the Holy Spirit to do all He did, so there is nothing in us that can do the supernatural. But God does the miraculous through us.

Look again at what Jesus promised: "Greater works than I did, you shall do." What is greater than healing the deaf, giving sight to the blind, or raising the physically dead? I'll tell you what's greater! It's leading a person to Christ so that he goes to heaven instead of hell. That's the greatest work of all. No—that's the greatest *miracle* of all.

While I was a freshman at Columbia Bible College, I heard a sermon from a beloved teacher on Philippians 4:13: "I can do all things through Christ." In the sermon he said, "I can do all things but fly . . ." Afterward, in the men's lounge, some of the other boys and I discussed and dissected the sermon, as young aspiring theologians are apt to do. There was a boy from the Pentecostal church who maintained he could fly, while we non-Pentecostals said it was impossible. We were discussing flying like a bird, not flying in an airplane. I'm embarrassed to admit that I mocked the young Pentecostal boy in our debate, just as the other non-Pentecostals did. We goaded him, "Go ahead . . . jump off a chair and fly." Of course he didn't try.

Later, when I was not there, the other boys kept badgering him until he stood on a chair, and then prayed to make sure he was yielded and ready. I was told he stepped off the chair to walk on air but fell to the floor. The mockers didn't laugh; conviction came on them, and they apologized deeply. The failure ended up in a prayer meeting. When I heard the story, I too was deeply remorseful for my attitude. I don't know what happened to that Pentecostal boy, but I hope he went on to serve God in a fruitful way. I hope he took some authentic leaps of faith in serving God. Jesus promised we could do greater works by winning souls to Christ—not by flying off of chairs.

Then Jesus promised, "These signs will follow those who believe: In My name they will cast out demons; they will speak with new tongues; they will take up serpents; and if they drink anything deadly, it will by no means hurt them; they will lay hands on the sick, and they will recover" (Mark 16:17-18). Does this verse mean that all "those who believe" should do these signs? Does this include all believers, for all occasions, at all times? Probably not!

Jesus attached these miracles to the Great Commission: "Go into all the world and preach the gospel to every creature" (Mark 16:15). The passage concludes, "They went out and preached everywhere, the Lord working with them and confirming the word through the accompanying signs" (Mark 16:20). Jesus was not promising that all believers would do these sign miracles just because they believed. He was telling His followers that when they preached the gospel, they could expect miracles.

All the illustrations given by Jesus in this passage were fulfilled in the book of Acts, except drinking poison. This promise of miracles is attached to the "greater works" which follow: evangelism and soul winning. The miraculous power of God is displayed to verify the word of God.

Can we conclude that if there is no soul winning, there will be no miracles? Probably not! But when we attempt to win the lost to salvation, we are more likely to see greater evidence of the miraculous power of God than we do in normal church ministry.

## Your Notes

_____

_____

_____

_____

_____

_____

_____

_____

_____

_____

_____

_____

_____

_____

_____

_____

_____

_____

_____

_____

# PART II

# Fasting for the Impossible

*If you can believe, all things are possible to him who believes.*
MARK 9:23

*Oh, for five hundred Elijahs, each one upon his Carmel,*
*crying unto God, and we should soon have the clouds bursting*
*into showers. Oh, for more prayer, more constant, incessant prayer!*
*Then the blessing would rain upon us.*
CHARLES SPURGEON

# 3

# Challenging Cancer and
# Changing God's Mind

In the spring of 2012, construction crews tore down the old gym at Liberty University. They leveled the 3,000-seat facility to make way for a new library building, but they couldn't take away all the memories.

Before the demolition, I visited a small back room where for years University leaders and sometimes guest speakers had gathered to pray before our chapel services for faculty, staff and students. (Sometimes the speakers were with us in the room. At other times they waited in a nearby room while we prayed.) I lingered in that room, remembering when, as senior staff members, we had prayed for presidents Ronald Reagan and George H. W. Bush when they came to speak at Liberty. I could still picture us praying with or for guest speakers Billy Graham, Rick Warren, Mike Huckabee, Joni Eareckson Tada, John McCain, Clarence Thomas, Elisabeth Elliot and Ted Kennedy. That's correct, we once invited Senator Ted Kennedy to speak at a Liberty chapel service!

Over the years, we had shared many laughs and shed many tears in that room. I paused as I relived one particular day. On that day, 26 years ago now, we received some grave news only minutes before the chapel service was to begin. Our friend and colleague, Vernon Brewer, had been diagnosed with cancer.[1]

To this day, I clearly recall each moment of that fateful morning, almost in slow motion. Upon hearing the news, I grew very quiet, and a grim question tumbled through my mind: *Vernon is one of my best friends, and he makes one of the greatest contributions to the spiritual life at Liberty . . . why is God letting* him *die?*

## "We Must Change God's Mind"

Nearby, three or four Liberty vice presidents commiserated about how terrible it would be for Vernon to go in this way. Our president and chancellor, Jerry Falwell, was seated at a small desk in the corner of the room, listening but at first saying nothing. Finally he spoke: "We can't let Vernon die; we must change God's mind."

I didn't immediately jump with joy, even though Vernon was a great friend. Rather, my initial response was theoretical. The conservative theologian in me thought, *How can we change God's mind? God never changes.*

"Forget the program," Falwell said as he arose to walk from the small side room to the chapel service. "We'll sing one hymn and have special music, but we won't have our usual sermon." He emphasized what would be our focus that day when he said, "We'll pray."

Laughing and talking among themselves, students took their usual places in the folding chairs and bleachers in the gym. Of course, they had no idea that once chapel began, their laughter would turn to mourning and then to prayer and fasting. The chancellor started the service and got right to the point.

"Vernon Brewer has Hodgkin's disease and has been given six weeks to six months to live," Falwell announced.

From my seat on the platform, I could see shock and grief ripple through the audience. But that didn't slow our chancellor down. He repeated to everyone what he had said to us in the small room: "But we're going to fast and pray to *change God's mind.*"

My human mind reeled and argued that Vernon's healing was impossible. But my spiritual mind made the leap, knowing how God's miraculous power accompanies fasting and praying.

Falwell was at his best that day, instantly conceiving a plan and putting it into action. With a simultaneous sense of calm and urgency, he promised us that if we would join him in fasting and praying, our lives would be changed. I listened closely to his words. He did not say, "If God heals Vernon." Nor did he say, "We hope that God will heal him." He said we *would* see God heal Vernon Brewer.

Under my breath I whispered, "Lord, I want faith that strong. Please give me faith to believe You for a miracle."

Falwell's instructions were more powerful than any sermon we could have heard. He asked us to begin fasting that evening, and to not eat breakfast or lunch the next day. He went so far as to say that the school's dining hall would be closed during the normal meal times so we could fast.

In addition to foregoing food, everyone was asked to pray for one solid hour during the next 24 hours. We couldn't count time spent jogging as prayer time, nor could students sit in a class and pray rather than pay attention. "Don't add up short periods of time until you get one hour," Falwell said. "I want everyone to pray for 60 minutes without stopping." He punctuated his instructions with the words of Jesus, who asked His disciples, "Could you not watch with Me one hour?" (Matt. 26:40).

Falwell noted that 60 minutes is the only specific time allocation for prayer in the Bible and drove home his point with a personal story. Many years earlier, as a freshman at Baptist Bible College, he had determined to spend time with God. An empty dorm room was available and quiet. His intention was to pray after lunch was over at 1 PM until the evening meal started at 5:30 PM—and to do it every day. On the first day, after praying for just 20 minutes, he had covered everything on his list. Tenacious in his desire to keep the afternoon prayer time in focus, Falwell went to the library and checked out a pile of books. Over the course of the next few weeks, he read one Christian classic a day, including *Power Through Prayer* by E. M. Bounds, *The Christian's Secret of a Happy Life* by Hannah Whitall Smith, *Abide in Christ* by Andrew Murray, *The Pursuit of God* by A. W. Tozer, and *The Pilgrim's Progress* by John Bunyan.[2]

Falwell's story illustrated how difficult it would be to pray for a whole hour without stopping. So he suggested we congregate at the prayer chapel and spend our prayer time there. To make sure we understood the challenge, he instructed, "Begin five minutes before the hour, and go at least five minutes past, so you know you have fulfilled your one-hour vow."

At about this point in the chapel service, a staff member came onto the platform and whispered a message into Falwell's ear. As soon as the exchange was complete, the chancellor announced that it was wrong to close down the dining hall completely, even for a spiritual discipline such as a fast. He said some people had medical conditions, such as diabetes. A few needed their scheduled meals as much as some people need their medicine. There are about 30 pathologies that require people to eat on a disciplined regimen, or they could face serious physical repercussions. To provide for anyone with medical needs, as well as any students who chose not to commit themselves to the fast, at least one food line would be open in the dining hall, and those students could also raid the kitchen refrigerator.

With the preliminaries out of the way, Falwell divided us into groups of two or three people. He asked each person to pray, and reminded everyone of Matthew 18:19: "If two of you agree on earth concerning anything that they ask, it will be done for them by My Father in heaven."

The challenge was clear: We were to agree in prayer for Vernon's healing.

Nothing of eternal importance is ever accomplished apart from prayer. —Jerry Falwell

## "There Is Value in the Volume of Prayer"

There is great power when people unite in common intercession. Jerry Falwell had a slogan he used often, and he reminded us of it that day. That slogan was: "There is value in the volume of prayer." By "volume" he did not mean how loud our prayers were, but the total number of people interceding together. At the chapel service, he looked out over the audience of 5,000 people and said, "God will not resist the unified prayer when all of us pray together in faith."

Falwell also quoted one of his favorite verses: "Without faith it is impossible to please Him, for he who comes to God must believe . . . that He is a rewarder of those who diligently seek Him" (Heb. 11:6). He challenged us:

> Remember that God exists and that He hears prayer; and if we diligently seek Him, we will get the answer we seek. Faith is not getting things from God—even Vernon's healing. Faith is recognizing the presence of God in your life. When you know that you are talking to God, and you know that He hears you when you diligently ask for anything, God will give us Vernon's healing. One more thing about faith: If we have faith as a grain of a mustard seed, we could say to the mountain, "Be moved," and we will get what we want.

Falwell described the mustard seed as one of the smallest perceptible things in creation—so all we had to do was have the smallest perceptible amount of faith to move a mountain (see Matt. 17:20). "Perhaps you might have the smallest amount of faith, smaller than anyone else in the gymnasium this morning," Falwell said, "but your small faith might be the power that leads to the healing of Vernon Brewer."

When Falwell said that, I wondered, *Lord, are you talking to me? Can it be my faith?* From the overwhelming response that followed, no doubt others asked the same questions of themselves.

The students divided into small groups. The 10 Liberty University vice presidents on the platform also prayed together. I just happened to be seated next to Vernon, so it was my privilege to pray with him while everyone else was praying for him.

As I turned to pray, I heard an inner voice as clear as if it were audible. The voice said, *Lay your hands on Vernon's head and pray.*

These words were not loud or demanding. The voice I heard was probably the same type of voice Elijah heard on Mt. Sinai—a still, small voice that spoke quietly. It was gentle and clear, but I began to rationalize. The laying on of hands was something Pentecostals did, and I was a Baptist at a Baptist university. Because I had Pentecostal friends, some people already speculated that I might be a closet Pentecostal even though I didn't speak in tongues and didn't interpret the baptism of the Holy Spirit the way some Pentecostals do. *No, Lord*, I countered. *Everyone will think I'm a Pentecostal if they see me laying hands on Vernon's head!*

Instantly, I recognized my mistake. I had spoken a terrible oxymoron: two opposing ideas placed together. A person can't call God "Lord" and at the same time tell Him "no." Either God is Lord of your life, or He is not.

When I had said, "No," I was telling God that He was not the Lord of my life, and therefore my prayer would have been self-sabotaged. Thankfully, I saw my error right away.

*Forgive me, Lord*, I prayed sincerely, almost crying in fear that God would not hear anything else I said. Two or three times I repeated, *Forgive me Lord; I believe in Your power, and I believe You can heal.*

Then, in front of the whole student body, I placed my hands on Vernon's head and prayed in the name of Jesus, "Lord, heal Vernon Brewer miraculously."

Mine was not a commanding prayer, nor was it a fleeting one; it was a simple prayer of belief that God can heal. Instantly I had a certainty that I had rarely felt before. I knew that God would heal Vernon. I did not feel an electric shock on my hand, nor did I notice anything tingling or warm in my body. There was no excitement or ecstasy. Rather, I sensed a strong inner confidence that God was going to heal Vernon. There was power not just in my prayer, but in the volume of prayer coming from the students, faculty and staff, who all loved Vernon and wanted to see him healed. Were we changing God's mind? From that moment on, I never doubted.

After we had prayed for some time, Falwell called us back together as a group. He pointed to a large cream-colored wall more than 30 feet tall and as wide as the gym. "Before noon today, I want someone to construct a huge sign [picturing] a clock on the wall, showing the 24 hours of a day beginning at sundown today." This would be a prayer clock. Every person was to sign his or her name and commit to pray at a specific time.

Falwell suggested that we all go to the prayer chapel to pray. That seemed a little funny to me, as the prayer chapel seated about 80 people, and Falwell was telling more than 4,000 students to go pray there.

I signed up for the 2:00 AM to 3:00 AM slot, because I thought fewer people would pray at that early hour.

When I arrived, a full moon illuminated the prayer chapel grounds. To my surprise, hundreds of people were there. Someone had set up a portable sound system. The microphone was in the chapel, but the speakers were outside, permitting the 200 or so people gathered on the lawn to join in the prayers being led from inside. On the east and south sides of the chapel, others prayed silently or in small groups.

I went inside to the microphone. I read a few verses of Scripture to challenge everyone to pray. Then I asked students to line up to lead in actual prayers. The line formed immediately, and I prayed first. I remained in the prayer chapel for the hour until the next faculty member came to lead group prayer. As I prepared to depart, I walked between the small groups toward my car. Someone stopped me and said, "Dr. Towns, come pray with us." Then another person requested that I join their group. I prayed with one group after another, until the sun began to come up around 6:00 AM.

For the entire day, we fasted, prayed, and believed that God would change His mind.

## Closing Thoughts

Every year now, on April 25, I phone Vernon to say to him, "Ain't it great to be alive!" That's poor English, but a sound spiritual admonition.

Each year he tells me, "I just had my yearly check-up, and there is no trace of cancer in my system."

*Jehovah Rapha*—the Lord heals.

While God performed a miracle in response to praying and fasting, He also used some of the latest in medical technology. The physicians operated and removed a five-pound mass of cancer from Vernon's heart and lungs. He also went through both radiation and chemotherapy treatments. That should have left him weak and his energy depleted. But Vernon works as hard now as he did before God healed him.

Vernon founded and leads World Help, a humanitarian organization that works in emergency relief efforts, church planting endeavors, and other projects around the world. He has nearly 200 Liberty graduates on his staff. They raise literally millions of dollars and have sent supplies to needy people in the aftermath of almost every major disaster over the last 20 years. World Help raises more than $300 million each year and is listed among the largest charities in the world. God had a plan for Vernon, and it involved 4,000 students who prayed and fasted for him to be healed.

## Your Notes

_____
_____
_____
_____
_____
_____
_____
_____
_____
_____
_____
_____
_____
_____
_____
_____
_____
_____
_____
_____

# 4

# Fighting for Finances and Seeing the Biggest Miracle Ever

Jerry Falwell was serious about fasting. He was so serious that in 1996 he fasted for 40 days—twice. The fasts didn't cover 80 consecutive days, but they were fairly close to each other. When God told Falwell that he could fast a second 40 days for finances, those of us close to him knew the health risk of going without food, and we were concerned. Sure enough, after the second fast, Jerry suffered a heart aneurism but lived through it.

"Jerry, you could have died because of that second fast," I lectured him once.

"Yes, I would have gladly given my life for Liberty University," he replied.

Years later, Jerry recorded the story of how he fasted and prayed for God to perform a miracle during that time of crisis.[1]

> For many years I raised money on television and by direct mail. People responded very well. Without difficulty, we had enough cash to build Liberty University, the fastest growing Christian school in the world. Each year, donations exceeded $27 million of needed cash. In 1986, Liberty University had no long-term debt on its property and easily covered our operating expenses.
>
> Everything changed in the late 1980s. After Jim Bakker and Jimmy Swaggart fell to sexual sins and drew massive media attention, it became clear that we could no longer

raise money through television appeals, or support the University financially by direct mail. . . .

I often compare television ministries to what happened in the savings and loan industry. When the bad ones began falling like dominoes, many good savings and loans were wiped out in the tidal wave.

Likewise, many strong evangelical media ministries such as ours were permanently hurt. Giving declined substantially to our ministry and other ministries. Contributions to the "Old Time Gospel Hour" and Liberty University dropped about $25 million a year, which was about twenty-five percent of our total revenue.

We had a university. We had $250 million invested in facilities and students on campus, but suddenly found ourselves unable to raise money to pay bills. After four consecutive years of $25 million deficits, our debt reached $100 million to $110 million.

The first thing I did was get out of the political ring and start spending most of my time in Lynchburg so that I could concentrate all of my energies on Liberty University. For the first time, I moved my office onto campus.

Through days and nights of fasting and prayer . . . we raised enough to pay our electric bill and meet salaries. Restoring the school to financial stability was a monumental task. From 1991 to 1996, I practiced fasting and prayer as never before in my personal life. Survival was the name of the game. Finally, at the end of the fiscal year, June 30, 1996, by God's enablement, the debt had been reduced from $110 million to approximately $52 million.

Though progress was made, a double-barreled shotgun was pointed at our head with both hammers cocked. In addition to the financial debt, Liberty University's regional accreditation was threatened. The Southern Association of Colleges and Schools (SACS) would not reaffirm accreditation for a university that had such precarious indebtedness as ours.

Liberty had to reduce its debt before it could continue its accredited status. SACS put Liberty on probation in December 1996. Without accreditation, I didn't think very many students would attend the university. Facing this crisis, I planned to fast, and fast seriously.

The Lord impressed upon my heart in the summer of 1996 that it was time to do the unthinkable, that is, personally go on a 40-day fast.

On July 15, 1996, I went to Dr. Gregg Albers, my doctor, and told him I was thinking about a 40-day fast. He said I had to have fluids. I told him I was going to use water only, but he said, "I would recommend that every few days you take a small glass of fruit or vegetable juice," so I chose V-8.

From July 20 to the first of September, I fasted and prayed that 1997-1998 would be the year when God removed Liberty's debt burden. About every third or fourth day I would drink an 8-ounce glass of V-8. Every day I drank a lot of water—a lot of water! To me it is not a fast if you're drinking blended food or drinking any kind of food value. I also took one Centrum, a vitamin tablet, every morning. After about 10 days, the hunger pangs subsided and about the thirty-fifth day they returned. The last five days were the hardest struggle.

I fasted 40 days and saw mighty things begin to happen internally, but no financial breakthrough. In that first fast, I kept asking God for money, but He impressed upon my heart that I needed to get close to Him, to listen to Him and to trust Him. God was telling me, "Stop looking for My pocketbook, find My heart!"

As I ended that first 40-day fast, I felt I had learned what God wanted to teach me. But I didn't have an answer about money. I began eating normally. I tried to do everything else SACS asked, but still couldn't pay off the debt.

Twenty-five days later, God told me I could now ask Him for money. So I went on another 40-day fast that began September 25 and ended on November 4. The first fast was easy; the second was excruciatingly difficult. I fasted for 80 days out of 105 days during the summer and fall. I broke the fast with a light meal after preaching at Two Rivers Baptist Church in Nashville, Tennessee. The results came quickly. First, we received a cash gift large enough to pay off our long-term mortgage debt. Second, we replenished the cash flow of Liberty University with several million dollars. Third, God sent Liberty a new president, Dr. John Borek, a Ph.D. in business administration, who had been the chief financial officer at Georgia State University. Without him we might not have been prepared for SACS's accreditation visit. Fourth, when SACS visited and then evaluated Liberty, they removed all sanctions and recommended Liberty University for 10 years of reaffirmation, which is the bottom line of why I fasted.

Liberty University received over $50 million because of those two fasts.

## Results of the Fast

After his first 40-day fast, Falwell began to fulfill everything that SACS required of Liberty to keep its accreditation. SACS prohibits one-family domination of the Board of Trustees, and university employees cannot set policy. Therefore, Falwell's wife and sons dropped off of Liberty's Board of University Trustees. In addition, several board members who were also vice presidents resigned. I was a vice president and had to resign.

A couple of weeks after the second 40-day fast ended, I got a phone call. "Come to my office immediately," Falwell said, his voice trembling. "You're going to see a miracle that you'll never forget."

Falwell had summoned several senior staff members and close friends. Just a few minutes after we got there, a courier arrived, unzipped a small leather pouch, and handed Falwell a check for $27 million. I had never seen that much money at one place in my life.

"Let me hold it," I quipped.

"No!" Falwell laughed, gripping the check daintily by its two upper corners. "No one touches it until I hand it to the teller at the bank."

It had been years since Falwell had personally made a bank deposit for the university, but he was resolute. I never asked whether he gave the check to a teller or to the bank president, but a photocopy of it is still in the university's financial offices.

The big check covered only half of the $52 million we owed. To deal with the remainder, other practical steps were taken. A benefactor of the university arranged for his various industries to assume our indebtedness. Creditors had been fearful of never being paid what was owed to them if the university went bankrupt, so they cooperated and agreed to extremely low- or no-interest loans on outstanding balances. SACS agreed to these unusual financial arrangements, and Liberty was debt free.

## An Even Bigger Financial Miracle

After Liberty's debt was paid off, everything swiftly came together. Our enrollment and reputation grew each year. With the growth came opportunities.

David Green, a Christian philanthropist and owner of the Hobby Lobby chain of craft stores, has long been a generous supporter of Liberty. At one point, he offered to donate an 80-acre parcel of land in the Chicago area. Valued at $90 million, the property included a 300,000-square-foot building and a large parking deck. We were tempted, but a secondary campus 700 miles away didn't fit into our long-range plans. Liberty's leaders wanted to consolidate operations in Lynchburg.

Falwell respectfully declined Green's offer, but the stage was set for a gift 10 times greater. Lynchburg is home to about 75,000 people and lies at the heart of Virginia. Falwell was born here, and it was here that he founded Thomas Road Baptist Church in 1956 and served as senior pastor until his passing in 2007. The university sprang out of the church, and the two have always worked in tandem, even after Liberty acquired its current campus several miles away from where the church met at the time. This wasn't ideal, but Lynchburg is a small town, so we managed—but God had better things in mind for us.

For years, the Ericsson telecommunications company had operated an 880,000-square-foot assembly factory on 113 acres next to Liberty University. The building was not simply large; it was huge. A hallway stretched half a mile from one end to the other. During the plant's heyday, Ericsson manufactured cellular telephones there. However, those jobs went to China, and the Lynchburg property went up for sale.

Immediately, Jerry Falwell placed a $2 million bid to purchase the property. Ericsson rejected the offer as too low—the facility was valued at $100 million.

Falwell wasn't deterred. He called everyone at the church and university to fast and pray. Perhaps God was going to give us the biggest miracle in the history of Liberty. If so, the miracle of Ericsson would eclipse the miracle of $52 million received after Falwell had fasted alone.

Ericsson received no other bids for the property, and the huge building sat empty. Lynchburg city leaders feared that they were not going to get another occupant that would contribute to the tax base and help them meet their budget. Eventually, Ericsson contacted Falwell to ask him to submit another bid, but this time they wanted a credible offer.

"No," Falwell replied. "Liberty will not bid unless you open up an absolute auction." An absolute auction would mean that the seller had to accept the highest offer made on the spot. Falwell didn't want to keep raising his offer, allowing Ericsson to keep rejecting it in order to land at a higher price. With few options, Ericsson agreed.

Jerry Falwell submitted a bid for $10,200,000. There were no other bidders. Liberty won the absolute auction.

Ericsson's attorney advised Liberty that they wanted to close the deal on February 14, 2003. That quick turnaround didn't allow much time for a fundraising campaign.

The university and Thomas Road Baptist Church gathered every bit of cash from every possible source. The total from checking accounts and reserve funds was a little more than $4 million. Carter Bank and Trust Company—the university's bank—agreed to loan the difference.

On the morning of the deadline to close, February 14, the in-house attorney for Liberty University received an e-mail from Ericsson's lawyers asking for a seven-day extension. Falwell was traveling on the following day. En route to California, he stopped in Oklahoma City for lunch with David Green and his family. During their conversation, he told them about the Ericsson property and the fact that the closing had been postponed until the following Wednesday.

"Let me buy that for Liberty," Green said.

He explained that Hobby Lobby would purchase the property and donate it to the ministry for a tax receipt. Instead of going $10 million into debt, Liberty University acquired the Ericsson plant without spending a dime.

"I found myself almost stunned at what a glorious and sudden thing our Lord had done for us," Falwell said.

## Exclusive Because of the Greatest Miracle

The ink on the contract was barely dry when the transformation of the Ericsson facility began. We added five new basketball courts, a weight room, a cafeteria, and an NCAA regulation-sized swimming pool. In the large south wing, we spent $5 million on classrooms and offices for the new Liberty University School of Law. We even constructed an exact replica of the United States Supreme Court trial room.

Acquiring the Ericsson plant was just the beginning of our 2004 miracle. Money began to flow in for other projects: new dorms, new buildings, paved parking lots, a million-dollar tunnel, paved roads, ball fields and more.

Someone once said when it rains it pours, and when God is pouring blessings on you, it seems like they never stop. Tim and Beverly LaHaye's grandson had attended Liberty, and he was an ice hockey enthusiast. As a result, the LaHayes donated $4 million to

Liberty for a new ice hockey complex. At first there was discussion about a large plastic dome over a sheet of ice, but that idea was dropped. The next brainstorm centered on a very crude steel building. Finally it was decided to erect a complete ice complex that would enable Liberty to compete in NCAA Division I hockey. The first year Liberty fielded a team, it was ranked seventh in the NCAA.

Just when it seemed there couldn't be another miracle, Thomas Road Baptist Church decided to move. The church signed a $20 million contract with Kodiak Construction Company from Charlotte, North Carolina, to build a new 6,000-seat sanctuary—right next to the Ericsson plant. The north end of the plant would be converted to Sunday School classrooms and would house the church's K-12 Christian school with more than 1,000 students in attendance.

The gift of the Ericsson facilities to Liberty University at the beginning of 2004 was indeed miraculous. But God had much more in store for us that year. Liberty received an additional $55 million in gifts, grants and loans for dormitories.

Attendance at the university doubled from nearly 5,000 students to almost 10,000 students that year alone. Enrollment at Thomas Road Baptist Sunday School jumped from 4,000 to almost 8,000. Church attendance grew from approximately 5,000 to more than 10,000.

This all happened as an answer to fasting and praying.

## Examine Your Priorities

In these tough times, many people have enormous financial needs. You may be one of them. Before you jump into a fast for a miracle, please carefully consider two factors.

First, make sure what you are asking for falls within God's priorities. When you take the time to consider your motives and His goals, your fast won't be just about getting something from God. Millions of dollars came in to Liberty in our greatest financial miracle only because we had right priorities. We trained young champions for Christ who were going out to plant churches, capturing their towns for Christ,[2] or to build great entrepreneurial businesses—but no matter their destinations, they were going to be great soul winners. We also taught our students to fast and pray. Liberty's priorities reflected God's priorities. Our approach followed God's pattern.

God's priority is people. He loves us. Jesus died for us and wants us saved. So we, too, should prioritize winning souls to Christ. Why? Because we are made in God's image. Our inner person is a reflection of God and His desires. Remember, "The Lord is . . . not willing that any should perish but that all should come to repentance" (2 Pet. 3:9).

We can—and at times should—pray for money, buildings and other material items. But we must always make sure that we seek possessions that will help carry out the Great Commission to win people for Christ. Christians have often fallen prey to wrong motives when it comes to money and possessions. We get fixated on the dollar signs or the size of the building when we should be fascinated with how the money and property can be used to build God's kingdom. Some Christians pray for money just because they want it, or even because they legitimately need it. Others seek to get their finances in order, but do so just for the sake of order. Nothing is wrong with balancing the books—we should. But we shouldn't balance the books just so we can feel secure or proud; we should balance the books so that we can be effective for God with all that He has given us. Without a focus on people and God's purpose, we will suffer in our spiritual growth, and probably will not receive what we seek. When we pursue and get close to the purpose of God, He will open up the treasure houses of this world to supply our needs.

Second, realize that God is not going to answer every giant prayer request we make. Paul thought it was important that God heal his "thorn in the flesh," and he prayed for deliverance on three occasions, yet God did not free him from his pain or restrictions (see 2 Cor. 12:7-9). We don't know what Paul's "thorn" was, but the apostle no doubt considered it a hindrance to his ministry. Yet God said no.

Moses is another example. God told him to speak to a rock to bring forth water. When Moses disobeyed and smote the rock,

God decided that Moses would never enter the Promised Land (see Num. 20). After spending almost 40 years leading the unruly mob of Israelites through the wilderness, Moses would not get the privilege of going with his people into the land.

Moses thought God had a short memory, so right before Israel was ready to enter the land, he had a conversation with God: "Then I pleaded with the LORD at that time, saying: 'O Lord GOD, You have begun to show Your servant Your greatness and Your mighty hand. . . . I pray, let me cross over and see the good land beyond the Jordan, those pleasant mountains, and Lebanon' " (Deut. 3:23-25). This seems like a simple request. It's a prayer I might have said had I been in Moses' shoes. But God told Moses, "No!"

The Lord was angry with Moses and told him to keep quiet. "Enough of that! Speak no more to Me of this matter" (Deut. 3:26). We can't expect a favorable answer to every big request, and we can't move every mountain blocking our way.

## Closing Thoughts

In 1996, Liberty University almost entered into bankruptcy, owing more than $52 million. Jerry Falwell took the unusual step of his two 40-day fasts. Did God look down from heaven and honor Falwell's actions because he was willing to die for Liberty? Did God respond as though Falwell were already dead? (Remember, we are to die to self.) Because of Falwell's fast, God did more than give the university $52 million; perhaps it was more than a billion dollars. Fifteen years later, Liberty has one of the strongest financial statements of any accredited university in America. Over the course of approximately 20 years, we went from facing a $100 million debt to enjoying a financial worth greater than $1.2 billion. A bond agency has ranked Liberty at AA+, higher than the United States government.

Christians have always prayed (and many have fasted) for money and other material needs. These requests have taken many forms. Some have prayed for food, some for property, some for buildings, some for foreign missionary support, and some for funds to pay for an evangelistic endeavor. And of course, many have simply prayed for a salary.

God blessed Liberty University because its purpose is close to His heart. But then again, aren't all Christian training institutions close to His purpose? Probably yes! But we had a founder and president who loved God, served God wholeheartedly, and believed God wanted him to build one of the greatest Christian training institutions in the world, if not the greatest of all time. Jerry Falwell had faith big enough to see things that were not as though they were. Toward the end of his life, he often quoted Hebrews 11:6: "Without faith it is impossible to please Him, for he who comes to God must believe that He is, and that He is a rewarder of those who diligently seek Him."

Before we begin a fast, we need to ask ourselves what our priority is. Then we need to believe that God is big enough to deliver on His promises. When we start our fast from this position, we have set the stage to fight for the greatest financial breakthrough ever (or whatever answer we need) and to see God bring about His blessings.

## Your Notes

_____

_____

_____

_____

_____

_____

_____

_____

_____

_____

_____

_____

# 5

# Confronting Terror and Prevailing Over Danger

The Philistines went up against the armies of Israel, defeated them, and stole the Ark of the Covenant. That's right, the enemy of God's people took this important piece of furniture from the Tabernacle. The Ark was revered by the Israelites because the Shekinah Glory cloud—the presence God—sat on its lid. It was called the Mercy Seat.

The stealing of the Ark no doubt angered the Jewish people. God responded with harshness, too. He judged the Philistines because they had desecrated His holy presence. While the Ark was returned, the Jewish people were still stinging because of their military defeat. Samuel, the priest and prophet, knew the reason for Israel's loss in battle. He challenged them, "If you return to the LORD with all your hearts, then put away the foreign gods and the Ashtoreths from among you, and prepare your hearts for the LORD, and serve Him only; and He will deliver you from the hand of the Philistines" (1 Sam. 7:3).

Upon hearing these prophetic words, the people of Israel repented, disposed of their foreign gods, and gathered themselves in Mizpah, historically the place where the Tabernacle and the Ark of the Covenant had been kept. It is also the location where God's people came to make sacrifices. So what did they do? "They gathered together at Mizpah, drew water, and poured it out before the LORD. And they fasted that day, and said there, 'We have sinned against the LORD'" (1 Sam. 7:6).

This verse gives evidence of Israel's remorse. They repented outwardly by throwing away the graven images of false gods they had been collecting. They repented inwardly by fasting before the one true God. First Samuel gives this unusual description: "They drew water, and poured it out before the Lord." Theologians throughout history have interpreted this "pouring out of water" to mean the shedding of tears. The Old Testament Jewish scholars translated it, "They poured out their hearts in repentance as water before the Lord." These references point to the truth that the Israelites were experiencing heartrending repentance. *And it was accomplished through their fasting.*

The problem was that the Philistines heard that the children of Israel had gathered at Mizpah, and they came with a mighty army, ready to attack. "They [Israel] were afraid of the Philistines" (1 Sam. 7:7).

Israel's leaders said to Samuel, "Do not cease to cry out to the LORD our God for us, that He may save us from the hand of the Philistines" (1 Sam. 7:8). Samuel complied by offering a sacrifice of blood to cover the sins of Israel as they went to battle. What happened? This time Israel's forces drove back the Philistines (see 1 Sam. 7:11). The victory was so decisive that the enemy fled Israel's territory altogether, never to return, and the Jewish people regained control of the cities that had been taken in the previous battle (see 1 Sam. 7:13-14).

*What a difference fasting and praying makes!*

## Lessons from Old Testament and Historical Fasts

When we face danger or a battle, can we fast like the Israelites fasted and be guaranteed to prevail? No! We cannot codify fasting. What the story of the Israelites does show us is that fasting is a reflection of our heart. As God's people called upon God for victory, fasting was a symbol of their sincerity. It has worked this way for believers throughout the ages, and it works the same way for us today, no matter what threat we face. God will send victory, but He always sends it in His own way.

Threats come in various sizes and are delivered in numerous ways. They can be subtle, demanding or life-threatening. Sometimes we fear loss or bodily harm—even death. Threats can be personal, made against our family, directed toward our nation, or hostile to our walk with Christ.

Sometimes we know exactly what to do when threatened. We fight back, flee, get help, or plead for mercy. At other times, we can be frozen, without a clue as to how to respond. What do we do when we don't know what to do? When we're at our wits' end? When we're scared and fear great harm?

Threat- \thret\—(1) An act of coercion or danger or injury imposed upon a person. (2) An act that elicits fear or other negative response. (3) A communication of intent to harm a person physically, or mentally, or psychologically. (4) An indication of impending damage or a menace to normal reactions. (5) Punishment.

The Psalmist declares, "Whenever I am afraid, I will trust in You" (Ps. 56:3). How can we trust God in the face of a threat? We can pray! If we are really serious, we can also fast.

Perhaps we want more than rescue from the threat. We want more than a return to peace and equilibrium. We want victory, and we pray that the threat is so thoroughly defeated that it doesn't come back. We want to conquer our threat and conquer evil. We want to destroy the danger of sin so it won't attack us or anyone else again. This kind of mountain-moving faith does not prevail except by prayer and fasting (see Matt. 17:21).

When we have a big request or need, it takes serious, prolonged and intense fasting to deal with it. It usually requires many people to pray and fast—sometimes even an entire nation. We can learn to fast in this way from those who have gone before us—those who have made the sacrifice and as a result have seen great exploits from God.

There is value in a vast number of threatened people who fast!

## Israel's Fast for Unity

One of the first fasts described in the Bible came in the aftermath of another devastating military defeat. There were 12 tribes of Israel—God's chosen people. Eleven of those tribes assumed that they were in proper fellowship with God when they were not. One day those 11 tribes took up a fight against Benjamin, the smallest tribe (see Judg. 20:23-25). It was a mismatch of numbers and force. But to everyone's surprise, the Benjamites defeated the much larger army.

While the 11 vanquished tribes weren't in full fellowship with God, they were alert enough to know that their military demise had spiritual implications. How did the losing side respond? "Then all the children of Israel, that is, all the people, went up and came to the house of God and wept. They sat there before the LORD and fasted that day until evening; and they offered burnt offerings and peace offerings before the LORD" (Judg. 20:26).

In this verse, we see frightened people who had come to the end of their wits. They went into the Lord's presence to repent. Fasting was again a demonstration of their utter sincerity. Eventually God gave them a military victory, and the tribe of Benjamin was brought back into the fold of the 12 tribes of Israel.

## Jehoshaphat's Fast for Survival

Jehoshaphat was a mediocre king, but he knew the power of fasting and praying.

One day, Jehoshaphat faced a threat against his kingdom: "The people of Moab with the people of Ammon, and others with them besides the Ammonites, came to battle against Jehoshaphat" (2 Chron. 20:1). The enemy forces were described as "a great multitude" (2 Chron. 20:2). What did Jehoshaphat do? He "feared, and set himself to seek the LORD, and proclaimed a fast throughout all Judah" (2 Chron. 20:3).

The king knew that this great army could annihilate his kingdom. Of course, he didn't want to be defeated, but there was more than that at stake. Remember, Jehoshaphat's Southern Kingdom of Judah contained the messianic line through which Christ was to come. This threat could cut off the coming Messiah.

Jehoshaphat called a fast and pleaded with his followers to pray. It seems that he understood Ecclesiastes 9:11: "The race is not to the swift, nor the battle to the strong." He also knew the truth carried in 1 John 4:4: "Greater is He that is with us, than he that is with them" (*ELT*).

Jehoshaphat began his prayer by asking a rhetorical question of God: "Oh LORD God of our fathers, are You not God in heaven, and do You not rule over all the kingdoms of the nations, and in Your hand is there not power and might, so that no one is able to withstand You?" (2 Chron. 20:6). The king went on to confess his sins, and to call upon God for deliverance. He finally ended his prayer with a plea: "O our God, will You not judge them? For we have no power against this great multitude that is coming against us; nor do we know what to do, but our eyes are upon You" (2 Chron. 20:12).

What is one aspect of true fasting? Worship! After fasting and praying, "Jehoshaphat bowed his head with his face to the ground, and all Judah and the inhabitants of Jerusalem bowed before the LORD, worshiping the LORD" (2 Chron. 20:18). The king was so sure he would triumph that he appointed singers to march out before his army (see 2 Chron. 20:21).

Jehoshaphat didn't have to raise a sword, sound a trumpet, nor engage the first enemy soldiers. God worked His providence to do the supernatural—and gave Jehoshaphat a great victory that day (see 2 Chron. 20:22-23).

Do you see the role of fasting? In the face of a dire threat, Jehoshaphat exercised great faith—not faith in his ability to pray or his worthiness, but faith in God who could deliver him. Jehoshaphat probably did not know how victory would come, but he had confidence that God would do something. How did fasting lead to the victory? It was a demonstration of faith, sincerity and repentance.

### Ezra's Fast for Safe Travels

Ezra was another Old Testament hero who turned to fasting for a miracle.

After Persia had defeated Babylon for good, the Persian king allowed the captive Jews to return to their home in the Holy Land. Ezra the priest—who had been living in exile—was permitted to return home to Jerusalem. He traveled with approximately 4,000 people and brought many valuables to rebuild the house of God. Many miles lay between Babylon and Jerusalem. On those dangerous roads, Ezra and his entourage faced tribes that were hostile against the Lord—and others that were simply bloodthirsty thieves. The enemies along the way would attack, loot, kill and, if possible, wipe out Ezra's entire group.

What did Ezra do about the danger that lurked ahead? With the river Euphrates behind his back, he looked out over the desert. His confession is actually a little humorous. He said, "I was ashamed to request of the king an escort of soldiers and horsemen to help us against the enemy on the road, because we had spoken to the king, saying, 'The hand of our God is upon all those for good who seek Him'" (Ezra 8:22).

It was time for Ezra to put his bold claim (and faith) into effect. He mulled over the logistics and risks of the grueling trip, and then he decided to fast for protection (see Ezra 8:23).

When Ezra arrived safely in Jerusalem, he wrote, "The hand of our God was upon us, and He delivered us from the hand of the enemy and from ambush along the road" (Ezra 8:31).

### The Lollards Fast Against an Invading Force

In the sixteenth century, Pope Sixtus V urged King Philip II of Spain to send a naval armada of 151 ships, 8,000 sailors and 98,000 soldiers to capture England. Why would there be a war between the two most powerful nations in the world at that time?

King Henry VIII had thrown the Roman Catholic Church out of England. That's why. The loss of England was a monumental defeat to the Roman Catholic Church. The pope wanted Spain to help recapture England.

For centuries, each time Protestants had taken over a nation in Europe, there had followed a long, bloody war resulting in thousands of deaths on both sides. But in England, a different scenario unfolded. A new Anglican Church (English Protestant) was established, and the government took over all of the property owned by the Roman Catholic Church—without battles, wars, or the massive loss of life.

Philip, the Spanish king, thought his wife's half-sister, Queen Elizabeth of England, was a heretic because she was a Protestant. History tells us that Philip supported several plots to have her overthrown. The Spanish monarch was trying to replace Queen Elizabeth with his cousin—Mary, Queen of Scots—a Catholic. In a classic power play, Mary was imprisoned, and she was executed in 1587.

Undaunted, Pope Sixtus V proposed a plan. If Spain would send an Armada and transport the Spanish army to the shores of England, he would pronounce the invasion a holy crusade and throw all the weight of the Roman Catholic Church and other European nations behind it.

To make sure the plan was carried out, the pope allowed King Philip to collect crusade taxes from Spanish citizens as well as others. The pope also permitted all of the soldiers indulgences: Their sins would be forgiven because they were on a holy crusade.

Spain marched 30,000 soldiers to Gravelines, in the Flanders district of France. Large barges had been readied to convey the troops across the English Channel. Once they had made the crossing, the Spanish-led force would invade London and all of England.

Word that an invasion was afoot reached Queen Elizabeth. In a bold step of faith, she called for prayer and fasting. The Queen proclaimed, "We shall shortly have a famous victory over the enemies of my God, of my kingdom, and of my people."[1] The people of England complied, fasting and praying sincerely—not just because they feared an invasion, but also because they had become

Bible-believers. It is said that by the sixteenth century, one out of every two Englishmen had been converted to protestant Christianity, mostly in a reformation movement called Lollardy. The Lollards were disciples of John Wycliffe (1320-1384) and later William Tyndale (1492–1536). They translated the Bible into the English language of that day. They also took the Great Commission very seriously. Lollards went out two-by-two to all the farms, villages and cities of England to share the Bible with the common people. Each Lollardy group had only a portion (or book) of Scripture. In the evening, they would read that section of the Bible to a small group of people and explain its meaning. When they finished, they went to another house and repeated the teaching. Families were eager to receive the next group of Lollards so they could learn more of God's Word. This house-to-house training prepared the people to live out their faith.

So when Queen Elizabeth called the British nation to fast and pray, the people were ready. They begged God for deliverance and went without food so that their country might be delivered from military destruction and from the re-establishment of Roman Catholicism. They knew that if Spain and the Catholic Church took over England, many people would be martyred.

On April 25, 1588, there was an official blessing of the Spanish fleet by the Catholic hierarchy in the harbor of Lisbon, Portugal. The Armada was so large it took two full days for the fleet to catch a tide to leave port. The Armada anchored off Calais in the English Channel and waited for the British to challenge them. A fierce five-day battle ensued.

The Spanish invaders unleashed a proven military strategy. They rammed and then boarded British vessels, attempting to wrest control. Queen Elizabeth's force was ready with a new battle plan. British troops surprised their enemy with smaller and swifter vessels. They darted in, fired at the Spanish, and then retreated before being rammed.

At night, the British dispatched eight fire ships to spread fire through the Spanish fleet. King Philip's troops attempted to escape into the Northern Atlantic Ocean, hoping to sail around the

British Isles and return home to Spain. It was a good plan of retreat; however, they never made it. A violent hurricane rolled through the region and ripped apart the Spanish Armada. The final tally was 4 Spanish ships lost in battle, and 59 vessels sunk by the bad weather. More than 7,000 Spaniards died from sickness; many more were lost when the fleet of boats went down. On the other side, not one English seaman was lost.

As a result of prayer and fasting, the Protestant reform movement in England survived, and Lollardy thrived. Certainly, this wasn't God's endorsement of everything that the British Crown did. Nor was it an indictment of every Roman Catholic or the Vatican as a whole. Rather, the victory was His response to the heart cry of a people who had preached the Word and applied their faith.

**Americans Pray and Fast**

At the start of the Revolutionary War, the United States Congress called for a day of prayer and fasting. It recommended that July 20, 1775, be set aside as "a day of publick [sic] humiliation, fasting, and prayer for . . . success to our Arms . . . strictly forbidding all recreations and unnecessary labor."[2]

President Zachary Taylor issued a proclamation of Fasting and Prayer for August 1, 1848, because of a devastating nationwide plague. President Taylor decreed that "all business . . . be suspended . . . [and] that people gather in their respective places of worship . . . to implore the Almighty . . . to stay the destructive hand of cholera which is now lifted up against us."[3]

In the dark days of the Civil War, President Abraham Lincoln issued a proclamation for fasting and prayer on March 30, 1863. Perhaps this call for national repentance only four months before the Battle of Gettysburg was the reason the tide of the war was turned. This was Lincoln's appeal to the war-torn nation:

> It behooves us, then, to humble ourselves before the offended Power, to confess our national sins, and to pray for clemency and forgiveness. . . . I do by this my proclamation designate and set apart Thursday, the 30th day of

April, 1863, as a day of national humiliation, fasting, and
prayer. And I do hereby request all the people to abstain . . .
from their ordinary secular pursuits, and to unite at their
several places of public worship and their respective homes
in keeping the day holy to the Lord . . . that the united cry
of the nation will be heard on high and answered with
blessings no less than the pardon of our national sins and
the restoration of our now divided and suffering country
to its former happy condition of unity and peace.[4]

As a young boy growing up in the South, I ignorantly lamented
the South's loss in the Civil War. But my loyalty was wrong for many
reasons. If the South had been the victor, our nation would have
been divided into two, and we would still see institutionalized
racism. As a divided nation we would probably be squabbling with
one another to this day, rather than recognizing that all people are
equal under God. Two small, bickering nations would never have
had the worldwide Christian missionary impact that a strong united
nation has had. True, the more-populated and better-financed North
should have won. But united prayer by Christians contributed to
the victory.

## How to Pray As a Nation

Between 1789 and 2011, various presidents of the United States
of America called the nation to prayer, humiliation and fasting
137 times. The reasons for these fasts have been varied. But turn-
ing to God has been a centerpiece of the American story since our
nation was founded. Our longevity can in great part be attributed
to our being "one nation under God."

There is power when large numbers of people come together
to seek God for help. This applies to churches, and it also applies
to nations. The Bible verse best associated with national survival
is 2 Chronicles 7:14:

If my people, which are called by my name, shall humble
themselves, and pray, and seek my face, and turn from

their wicked ways; then will I hear from heaven, and will forgive their sin, and will heal their land (*KJV*).

When a sanctuary-, arena- or stadium-sized crowd fasts and prays, the participants enter into what the Bible defines as corporate prayer. Obedience to God in this way unleashes a palpable energy. No doubt some of the vigor arises simply because of the number of people who come together in agreement at one physical location. A sense of this dynamic can also be achieved when people at various locations across the nation or around the world unite in praying and fasting. But God doesn't merely respond to the number of participants; it's about the sincerity of the people. It's about faith, as we have already seen.

## Corporate Prayer

God has promised to hear the prayer of unity (see Matt. 18:19). Whether that united prayer is offered by a whole nation, a church (see Acts 12), or a few individuals, God delights to answer when interactive faith recognizes His existence, and people corporately call on Him for deliverance.

An Old Testament story demonstrates the power of corporate praying and fasting even when only a few are involved. King Nebuchadnezzar had surrounded Jerusalem and threatened to destroy it. To stave off the invasion, the Jewish people gave great amounts of treasure to the Babylonian leader and promised to send him taxes each year. To further appease Nebuchadnezzar, Israel dispatched a number of select young men to Babylon to be trained in the Babylonian way of doing business. These young men were interns who would return home as civil servants.

Daniel and three of his friends were among those young Israelites sent to Babylon. When they arrived, they were probably placed in dormitories, and they were assigned to take their meals at the king's tables, which meant their food would come from the same kitchen that supplied the king's food. Daniel, however, decided that he wouldn't defile himself by consuming royal delicacies (see Dan. 1:8).

Why did Daniel decline to eat the king's food? It could have been that such an action violated Jewish ceremonial law, or that the food had been offered to foreign idols, or that the meal included alcohol, which would numb his senses. Whatever the reason, Daniel suggested to his overseer "a ten-day diet of only vegetables and water" (Dan. 2:12, *TLB*).

Daniel was unyielding. He did not say he would eat the king's food if his and his friends' health failed, or that the Babylonians could punish him if their health failed, or that they could kill him if their health failed. Instead Daniel put God first and yielded to His will. Daniel was willing to put God on the spot.

There was a second test for Daniel's three friends. Apparently Daniel was away when the Babylonians gave Shadrach, Meshach and Abednego a choice. They were to bow before an idol—probably a statue of King Nebuchadnezzar, who was supposed to be treated as a god—or they would be thrown into a fiery furnace.

The young men refused to honor the statue. Instead they yielded themselves to God, saying, "If it be so, our God whom we serve is able to deliver us from the burning fiery furnace, and he will deliver us out of thine hand, O king. But if not, be it known unto thee, O king, that we will not serve thy gods, nor worship the golden image which thou hast set up" (Dan. 3:17-18, *KJV*). "But if not . . ." Three small words packed with meaning. In that statement, Daniel's friends acknowledged that God might not deliver them, and that they were willing to die for their convictions.

The end of the story is well known. God protected the young men. When King Nebuchadnezzar looked into the furnace, he declared, "I see four men loose, walking in the midst of the fire; and they are not hurt, and the form of the fourth is like the Son of God" (Dan. 3:25). Nebuchadnezzar realized that these three young men were different from the others he had captured. They had yielded their bodies, that they might not serve nor worship any god except their own God. Like these three young men, we must cede everything to God if we want to see our prayers answered. Moreover, there is power when two or three of us come together in corporate prayer and fasting, as there was for Daniel and his three friends.

## A Solemn Assembly

When Israel faced an epidemic of locusts that threatened the nation's very survival, Joel called for extreme faith. The people were to turn to God with all their hearts, with fasting, weeping and mourning (see Joel 2:12).

Joel gave a directive: "Blow the trumpet in Zion, sanctify a fast, call a *solemn assembly*" (Joel 2:15, *KJV*, emphasis added). Many of the newer Bible versions call Joel's meeting something else. But it was indeed *solemn*. Throughout history, dedicated Christians have moved the heart of God by a solemn assembly. This type of purposeful gathering still occurs today.

Throughout history, dedicated Christians have moved the heart of God by a solemn assembly.

During a season of corporate fasting, Christians can come together for a solemn assembly—not to worship, preach the Word, or rejoice together, but to confess their sins. During these meetings, they repent—not once or twice. Rather, they beg God continually to take away the threat against them. Usually, one believer after another rises to pray audibly, confessing the sins of the Church or the nation. They continue in intercession until God gives a spirit of assurance that He has heard and will answer. Sometimes a solemn assembly continues every night for many consecutive nights.

A solemn assembly is also known by the term "humiliation." Participants confess their personal sins as well as the corporate sins of their nation. Some people feel that God will not answer until everyone has confessed and repented, and everyone has begged God for His mercy upon them.

Sometimes a group of believers will also practice what is called identificational repentance. During these times of intercession, they take on the sins of others (sometimes those from generations past) and repent. These are sins that they didn't personally commit, but that they recognize as wrong. They seek God's forgiveness and restoration. (See chapter 6, "Repenting Leads to Revival," for a full discussion of this practice.)

**Corporate Repentance and Restitution**
It's probably useless for a person to ask God's blessing until his or her heart is empty and willing to be used by God. Even when a believer has completely confessed all known sins and sought God's holiness, that doesn't mean God will automatically use him or her. The confession only means that the individual is clean and ready to be used. Scripture makes it clear: "If we confess our sins, He is faithful and just to forgive us our sins and to cleanse us from all unrighteousness" (1 John 1:9).

Once a person has been cleansed, he or she can pray as Joel instructed: "Spare Your people, O LORD, and do not give Your heritage to reproach, that the nations should rule over them. Why should they say among the peoples, 'Where is their God?'" (Joel 2:17). Before granting victory, God always does a work of renewal in His people: "I will pour out My Spirit on all flesh; your sons and your daughters shall prophesy, your old men shall dream dreams, your young men shall see visions. And also on My menservants and on My maidservants I will pour out My Spirit in those days" (Joel 2:28-29).

## Closing Thoughts

While the skeptic may not believe that God does miraculous things for a nation in answer to prayer, and the unbeliever explains away the enemies defeated, people with the eye of faith tie together the outpouring of sincere prayer and fasting with the eventual victory. If God sent a lightning bolt from heaven to destroy all the enemies in a flash, many people might then believe that He sent the victory. But they would not have saving faith—their priorities would not be God's priorities. They would only experience relief because the danger had come and gone.

Second Chronicles 7:14 is often quoted to describe our hunger for revival and our pursuit of an outpouring of God's Spirit. It's worth looking at again here: "If My people who are called by My name will humble themselves, and pray and seek My face, and turn from their wicked ways, then I will hear from heaven, and will forgive their sin and heal their land."

This passage makes it clear that the scope of revival depends on how serious we are in calling upon God for His spiritual intervention in our lives—and in the circumstances that demand revival.

Many people turn to God when faced with a great threat. But God doesn't just want the world to believe that He can prevail over danger; more importantly, He wants them to know His mercy to forgive sins, and His power of salvation that is offered to all who will accept His Son, Jesus Christ. While an army may be felled—or a danger to a country overcome—God's heart is always to love the people. When we fast and pray for our nation, that should be our heart as well.

## Your Notes

_____

_____

_____

_____

_____

_____

_____

_____

_____

_____

_____

_____

_____

_____

_____

# PART III

# Fasting for the Greatest Miracle

*And now let me address all of you, high and low, rich and poor,*
*one with another, to accept of mercy and grace while it is*
*offered to you; Now is the accepted time, now is the day of salvation;*
*and will you not accept it, now it is offered unto you?*
GEORGE WHITEFIELD

# 6

# Repenting Leads to Revival

In the eighteenth century, God moved through historic revival movements in North America and Europe. The powerful preaching of Jonathan Edwards and George Whitefield shook the 13 colonies of the United States in what was called the Great Awakening. At about the same time, thousands of people turned to Christ in England, influenced by the preaching of John Wesley. In Austria, revival stemmed from Herrnhutt, the estate of Count Zinzendorf. Christians came to Herrnhutt from all over Europe, seeking refuge from religious discrimination and persecution.

Perhaps the greatest precursor of the first Great Awakening was Jonathan Edwards's sermon, *Sinners in the Hands of an Angry God*, preached on Sunday, July 8, 1741, in Enfield, Connecticut. We often hear that Edwards read his sermons in a monotone style and how, despite a dry presentation, the Holy Spirit moved people to spontaneously repent of their sins. We don't hear as much about one of the spiritual disciplines that undergirded the revival: Edwards fasted.

At the time of the Enfield sermon, Edwards was on a three-day absolute fast (no water, food or nourishment of any kind).[1] The fast was scheduled to end after Edwards preached. The sermon that day was on the horrors of hell; the topic had been selected to shake up the religiously comfortable so they would see themselves standing before God, facing judgment.

Not long before Edwards was to speak, the unthinkable happened. He began to cough and gag. He couldn't stop. If Edwards drank some water and violated his fast, would God bless his sermon? Technically, a fast is a vow to God to abstain from certain foods or liquids for a divine purpose until the time is completed.

When Edwards concluded that he could not preach the sermon in his condition, and the message seemed lost, he relented
and drank some water. That night, Edwards climbed into the pulpit with a 20-page manuscript (his sermon was written out) in one
hand and a lantern in the other. He began to read his sermon:

> The God that holds you over the pit of hell, much as one
> holds a spider, or some loathsome insect, over the fire, ab-
> hors you, and is dreadfully provoked; his anger is as great
> towards them as to those that are actually suffering the
> executions of the fierceness of his wrath in hell, and they
> have done nothing in the least to appease or abate that
> anger, neither is God in the least bound by any promise to
> hold 'em up one moment.
>
> The devil is waiting for them, hell is gaping for them,
> the flames gather and flash about them, and would fain
> lay hold on them, and swallow them up; the fire pent up
> in their own hearts is struggling to break out.
>
> That world of misery, that lake of burning brimstone
> is extended abroad under you. There is the dreadful pit of
> the glowing flames of the wrath of God; there is hell's wide
> gaping mouth open; and you have nothing to stand upon,
> nor any thing to take hold of: there is nothing between
> you and hell but the air; 'tis only the power and meer pleas-
> ure of God that holds you up.
>
> You are held over in the hand of that God, whose
> wrath is provoked and incensed as much against you as
> against many of the damned in hell: You hang by a slender
> thread, with the flames of divine wrath flashing about it,
> and ready every moment to singe it, and burn it asunder.[2]

Men in the audience could not constrain themselves. Feeling as
if they might literally fall into hell, they ran about and grabbed
posts in the sanctuary. God used this graphic message as the cata-
lyst to engage a generation for the gospel because of the *usability* of
Jonathan Edwards. He was broken over breaking his fast by drink-

ing water. His broken vow broke his pride—and God used his brokenness. It's not the beauty of our sermons that God uses, nor is it the theological correctness of our sermons that He uses (though correct doctrine is important). God uses us when we are completely empty of self, disposed of pride, and filled with God. God uses us when we can say, like Paul, "Not I, but Christ" (Gal. 2:20, *KJV*).

## The Layman's Prayer Revival of 1859

Prior to 1859, America had boundless optimism. The Gold Rush of 1849 had brought immense wealth to the United States. Railroad construction was booming. New tracks were being laid everywhere, connecting every large city to every small town. Manufacturing and farm production both doubled. Railroad mileage tripled in 10 years. New York City grew from 500,000 people to 800,000 people during the decade. Immigrants were pouring into the United States at a rate of 200,000 a year, and many of them stayed in New York. The assets in the New York banks were the highest in history.

But there was a cancer in New York City: It was filled with filth, crime, disease and vagrancy. It was estimated that there were 3,000 homeless children on the streets; many of the young girls were prostitutes. There was an alarming mortality rate of one death for every 29 babies—double the death rate of babies in London. A cholera epidemic in 1849 and another in 1854 incited widespread fear. The population of New York had shifted from middle class families to poorer immigrants. As problems increased, middle and upper class families moved to better areas, and so did their congregations. The lower part of Manhattan was left largely without churches.

In 1857 a bank panic shocked the public. The Ohio Life Insurance Company failed on August 30, followed by their branch bank in New York City. Many banks called in their loans and suspended their lines of credit. The New Haven Railway failed, and by mid-September, 29 banks had ceased to operate in New York City alone. Interest rates rose to 5 percent a month, which was high in those days. Factories were closing, and in 1859 alone, 10,000 New York City workers lost their jobs. On top of all these problems, there was the disagreement over slavery with the South, and a constant threat of war.

When the future of America seemed bleak, and it appeared that the government could do nothing for the business community, God changed everything with a revival. Church historian, J. Edwin Orr, called the Layman's Prayer Revival "the most thorough and most wholesome movement ever known in the Christian Church."[3] The large crowds were reported in the secular press daily under the heading, "Revival News." The newspapers of America helped spread the good news.

Jeremiah Lanphier, a city missionary at the Old Dutch Church on Fulton Street in lower Manhattan, did not know how to carry out his ministry. He called for a Friday prayer meeting to be held on September 23, 1857, in a back room of the second floor of the church. By noon of that day no one had come, so Jeremiah prayed alone with a heavy heart. Failure does that to all of us. About 12:20 PM he heard the soft footsteps of someone coming up the back stairway. Another person came at 12:35. The people told Lanphier that they had to eat lunch before coming to the prayer meeting.

The challenge of Jesus to His disciples was applied to believers in New York: "Could you not watch with Me one hour?" (Matt. 26:40). Lanphier asked people to give up their noon lunch on Fridays and come to pray for God to send revival.

The next Friday, the room was filled. So many people started coming to the prayer meetings that the church had to expand them to another room on the second floor—and then a third room. Finally, they ended up in the main auditorium. Hundreds of men—it was primarily a male working world in those days—gave up their noon lunch to come and pray.

In February 1858, editor George Bennett of the *New York Herald* newspaper was looking out the window of his second floor office when the church clock began to strike twelve. Instantly, men ran out of stores and places of business. Some zipped one way, while others hurried in the opposite direction. It was as though they were all at the starting line of a race when someone yelled, "Go!" Almost as quickly as the men had rushed into the street, they disappeared, and the street stood silent and still.

Bennett was flummoxed as to why so many people would go to church in the middle of a weekday, so he sent a reporter to investigate. The journalist dutifully wrote an article that appeared on the newspaper's front page, reporting that nearly 1,000 people had participated in the prayer meeting. The next day the number jumped to 2,000, and then it jumped to 4,000. Before long, there were 25,000 men praying in all types of churches throughout the entire city. Because of time constraints, men had to run to the closest church, theater or auditorium. It was a nonsectarian revival.

*The New York Herald* was shipped to other major U.S. cities. When people in those places read the stories, prayer meetings broke out there, too. There were reports of men gathering at noon for prayer in Albany, New York; Cleveland, Ohio; Baltimore, Maryland; and Savannah, Georgia. The revival spread across the prairies to Seattle, Washington, and San Francisco, California. According to reporters, by May 1859, 50,000 people had been saved as the result of the midday prayer meetings.

The use of revival tents began when factory workers outside of town couldn't leave their factories and reach their places of worship to pray for an hour during the workday. Owners constructed tents adjoining their factories, where workers could go pray for one hour.

Pastors did not control this revival, nor did they drive it with sermons. Rather, laymen prayed. Sometimes all of the men prayed out loud together. Yes, God in heaven hears each individual intercessor through the noise of many praying out loud at the same time. It's not an unintelligible cacophony to God; rather, He enjoys the music of their prayers as one would enjoy a concert, where many instruments are playing in harmony. Hence, this type of corporate prayer is called a prayer concert.

In some churches, everyone prayed silently. At other churches, men prayed one after another while standing in the pews, leading out in passionate intercession to God.

How did people get saved in this revival? As one man would begin praying out loud for salvation, others would hear him and also pray the sinner's prayer. Usually a number of intercessors would gather around the repentant man, praying for him, encouraging him, and rejoicing with him.

Like other great revivals that are cut short by a war, the Layman's Prayer Revival was stifled by the declaration of war between the states on April 12, 1861. While everyone hates to see a great movement of prayer end, we can rejoice that at least 50,000 young men were converted to Christ during the Layman's Prayer Revival before they went to face the enemy's guns in the Civil War. And it all began when a young pastor challenged his congregation to join him on Fridays for one hour of praying and fasting.

## Revival at Liberty University

Sometimes fasting leads to revival; other times, revival is poured out on God's people, and they simply don't have time to eat. That's what happened in a revival in Lynchburg, Virginia.[4] In October 1973, there were 600 students at three-year-old Liberty University. The school had few facilities of its own, instead using the buildings of Thomas Road Baptist Church, renting a hotel downtown, and housing students in dormitories at the church camp on Treasure Island. Classes were taught in an abandoned public school building. Being spread out across town meant there was no place for the students to fellowship or enjoy an easily accessible common room. Instead, they just hung out in the auditorium at Thomas Road Baptist Church.

After one regularly scheduled Wednesday night prayer meeting, about 35 students lingered in the auditorium, chatting and studying together. A young man walked up to the pulpit. Through his tears he began, "You all know me. You think I am a Christian..." Then he began to confess his sins of cheating and other problems in his life. "I made a profession of faith in my home church, and I was baptized as a boy, but I'm not saved..."

The microphone was off, and the platform lights were darkened, so few people noticed him at first. But then the young boy knelt and began to weep uncontrollably. Quickly, several fellow students gathered around him to pray with him and for him. Two or three other small groups throughout the room stopped talking and began praying, too.

When the young man had prayed through his repentance to salvation, there was rejoicing on the platform stairs. Then a second young man climbed up to the pulpit and repeated almost the same story. He confessed his sins, told how he had been baptized as a boy, and then asked for prayer, telling the group, "I'm not saved . . ." Several students gathered around him for prayer, and he too was converted.

Next a young woman made almost the same confession and the same request. After a while, when the rejoicing settled down, a reverent spirit filled the auditorium; people knew God was present. He was working in the young people's lives.

Someone went to the piano, unlocked the keyboard, and began to play. The music continued without interruption from approximately 10:00 that Wednesday night until 9:00 Saturday morning. There were always three or four pianists waiting on the first row to slide onto the piano bench and keep the music going. Someone was playing the organ during the 59-hour stretch as well.

Young people spontaneously began lining up to the left of the pulpit to request prayer for salvation, or to give a testimony of what God had done in their lives. Around midnight on Wednesday, phone calls went out to pastor Jerry Falwell and the deacons: "Get down to the church, fast; revival has broken out." They got there as quickly as possible because the Lord was in the house.

By 6:00 the next morning, more than 2,000 people had flooded the auditorium. No one went to work that day. Mothers got together to babysit for one another, and businesses closed down. Schools cancelled classes. The Lord's presence was being experienced in Lynchburg, Virginia.

The first meal served at the University after the revival began would have been breakfast on Thursday morning. I don't know— and no one else remembers—if anyone went to the kitchen to prepare it. Did anyone go to the dining room to eat breakfast? That same question could be asked about lunch, dinner, and every other meal until the revival was over. No one remembers what was happening in the kitchen or dining room; everybody remembers that God was moving at Thomas Road. No one wanted to leave, because they would miss what God was doing. When students could no longer stay awake, they slept under the pews or on the floor alongside the walls of the foyer.

Some student called for a pizza to be delivered. When it arrived, everyone seemed embarrassed to realize it was there, or to take credit for ordering it. The pizza sat on top of a waste paper receptacle, and shortly was thrown into the trash, uneaten. People were feasting on the Bread of Life, and God was satisfying empty spiritual stomachs.

High-emotion moments take away one's hunger. Imagine you were called to the hospital because your spouse or child was in the emergency room. You would dash there as quickly as possible. Even if it were noon, you wouldn't stop on the way for a hamburger. Eating at such a critical time is not important. We lose our appetite in times of fear, excitement or anticipation. We don't want to eat until it's over.

In those early days, Liberty University experienced a miraculous revival where many young people met Jesus Christ and surrendered to full-time Christian service. While fasting was not the cause of the revival, it was an outgrowth. Perhaps many fasted during this time of revival because they had been part of a church-wide fast before this. For others, it was their first experience with fasting and praying during a revival.

## Baptists Fast for Revival

Revival came to the Southern Baptist Annual Convention in 1995. Pastor Ronnie W. Floyd of First Baptist Church in Springdale, Arkansas, had been elected to preach the message on fasting. Knowing ahead of time that he would present this important message to the entire denomination, he went through that year seeking the Lord's guidance.

During that year of preparation, he fasted often. He even went on a 40-day fast, petitioning God to send revival to America—and to use the Southern Baptist Convention as a vehicle. "I continually asked God to put His power on that sermon," Floyd said. "I preached a message from Joel 2 calling them to repent, fast and pray for God's blessing on America and our churches. I asked each pastor to fast and pray for spiritual power to influence their churches and through their churches to influence our nation. In that sermon, I described my fasting journey."[5]

During the message that morning, God's presence fell on the audience. Revival is defined as "God pouring His Spirit on His people." When Floyd gave the invitation, there was a supernatural intervention of God. Longtime Southern Baptist pastor Adrian Rogers came to Floyd afterward, hugged him, and told him that this was the revival for which many people had been praying. More than 5,000 people came forward in response to Floyd's message. The aisles were jammed, and people couldn't get to the altar—so they knelt and wept right where they were.

Afterward Floyd led his church of 10,000 members on an extended fast, and he wrote the book, *The Power of Prayer and Fasting*.[6] Floyd told *The New York Times*, "These are desperate spiritual moments in the life of our nation." He strongly believed that Christians must lead the way in humbling ourselves before God. He explained that the most dramatic sign of repentance is going without food. Floyd added, "We deny the most natural thing that our body desires, which is food, in order to persuade God to do something supernatural in our lives."[7]

## Your Notes

_____

_____

_____

_____

_____

_____

7

# Kneeling with Soldiers
# and Praying for Salvation

Not long after I started following Christ, I went off to Columbia
Bible College in South Carolina as a zealous new disciple, trying to
do everything possible to serve the Lord. As soon as Saturday night
evangelistic street meetings were organized, I showed up to help.

Usually, eight or nine students gathered in a college room for
prayer, and then we ambled over to the corner of Main Street and
Gervais Street, right across from the South Carolina State House.
The musicians set up a pump organ and organized the literature
to be distributed. The rest of us fanned out onto nearby streets.

The Army's Camp Jackson was nearby. Young men went
through 13 weeks of basic training there before heading off to
other bases. On Saturday nights, downtown Columbia was abuzz
with activity. Soldiers walked the streets, looking for something
to do. Some went to the movies, dances and bars. We went looking
for them.

Whenever we found a group of soldiers, we struck up a conversation and invited them to come with us to our street meeting.
Usually about 20 or 30 of them came along. At the meeting, we
sang five or six hymns. One of us would give a testimony. Someone
else would preach a short message. A gospel invitation for salvation was always given, and when soldiers responded, I personally
relished the opportunity of leading them to pray to receive Christ.

My soul-winning activity was not for a Christian service, an
assignment, a class project, or anything else official. I did it because as a conscientious servant of Jesus Christ I wanted to see
others come to know Him.

ELMER L. TOWNS

Each weekend, different students would preach when we went on the streets. Usually the most mature and senior class students went first. When everyone had had a turn, they started through the cycle again. But they left me out.

"Hey guys," I inquired, "When do I get to preach?"

"Next time around," they promised. I knew I was just a freshman, and they knew I was inexperienced. Not putting me in the rotation right away was their way of not embarrassing anyone.

My turn finally came in February of 1951. It would be my first time to preach anywhere. Gladdie Kreimann was scheduled to be the song leader that night, and it was his first time to lead music. Gladdie and I were excited, but we also knew we needed God's help. We decided to meet for prayer at lunchtime each day for five days before the street meeting, giving up our midday meal, too.

I didn't consider the absence of food a fast. True fasting involves a specific vow and a pledge to pray, trusting totally on God for breakthrough. We simply wanted to see many soldiers come to Christ at the street meeting, and lunchtime was our best time to pray. So we gave up eating for a few days.

The calendar finally rolled to Saturday. Gladdie and I were eager, but also nervous. All day long, my thoughts ran to that evening, when finally I would stand before a crowd of soldiers and preach my first sermon.

The weather didn't cooperate. As nightfall approached, a brisk wind whipped down Main Street, and there was a hint of moisture in the air. Only three college students showed up for the street meeting: Gladdie, the organ player and myself. However, nothing could dissuade us, so off we went to Main and Gervais.

We could only muster up a crowd of five or six soldiers that night. They stood with their hands stuffed in their pockets and shoulders hunched up to protect them from the wind.

Gladdie had planned to sing five or six hymns, but we could barely hear the organ. Also the wind howled so loud that we couldn't hear each other sing. After only a couple of songs, Gladdie turned the meeting over to me. It was time to preach.

I started with a passage from the traditional *King James Version* of the Bible:

Enter ye in at the strait gate: for wide is the gate, and broad is the way, that leadeth to destruction, and many there be which go in thereat: Because strait is the gate, and narrow is the way, which leadeth unto life, and few there be that find it (Matt. 7:13-14).

After I read this Scripture aloud, I launched into my sermon with the passion of a Billy Sunday. Soldiers were going to come to know Jesus that night! Within three minutes, I was finished. I had said everything I had prepared. When I had stood before a full-length mirror in my dorm room and practiced the sermon two or three times, it had taken me 10 minutes. But with a live audience, I quickly ran out of things to say. I panicked. *A three-minute sermon is not enough!*

What did I do? I preached the entire sermon again ... and then looked at my watch. Only six minutes had passed since I had begun the sermon the first time. With the determination of a man on a mission from God, I launched into the invitation—or altar call, as some call it. The soldiers joined in as we sang:

*Just as I am without one plea,*
*But that Thy blood was shed for me,*
*O Lamb of God, I come, I come.*

It was embarrassing. The soldiers stood no further than five feet away, and I was asking them to come forward to get saved. The music was pathetic, the preaching was superficial at best, and everything was much too short. After crawling our way through a couple of verses, I showed mercy on everyone. I lifted my hand to pray a benediction, and pronounced, "Amen!"

I turned to gather the literature we had brought, so that we could make a quick escape back to our dorm room, but I was interrupted.

"MAY I SAY A WORD?" a voice louder than the wind boomed. I looked up to see a man almost seven feet tall, with broad shoulders and greasy, black hair combed straight back. He looked like a Native American.

"MAY I SAY A WORD?" he repeated as he stepped to the front of the small gathering. He proceeded to preach on heaven, first quoting Isaiah 2. As I think back on it, his exegesis of the passage about heaven was really about the last days. But I didn't care that he had mixed up the metaphors; what mattered was that he reached into the hearts of the young men and talked about where they were going to spend eternity.

Next he quoted Isaiah 11, and now he was preaching on his tiptoes. He moved closer to the men, standing less than a couple of feet from their faces. Then he stepped backwards, drawing the crowd with him toward a building—a perfect shield from the wind.

A larger crowd started to form. It seemed that everyone who walked by on the sidewalk was compelled to stop and listen. People in nearby cars double-parked and rolled down their windows so that they could hear.

Within 10 minutes, the crowd had grown to 30 people—the most I had ever seen at a street meeting. The loud evangelist continued his tiptoe routine; he moved close to the people, and then he backed up, pulling them into a tight crowd so others could join.

Twenty minutes into his sermon, the crowd had grown to 50. No one anywhere near Main and Gervais could ignore his booming voice. Everyone wanted to know what he was saying. Once they found out that his message was about God and heaven, they stayed to hear more. Finally he gave an invitation.

"KNEEL," he instructed, raising his finger first toward heaven, then dropping it in an arc and pointing at the sidewalk.

"KNEEL," he repeated his command.

The soldiers, who were used to obeying orders, readily followed the invitation. Several stepped a few feet forward and dropped to their knees; many of them wept.

I knelt beside a young soldier, opened my Bible to the book of Romans, and showed him—using the Romans Road to Salvation passages—the basic steps to eternal life with Jesus.[1] Then I led him in the sinner's prayer to receive Christ. I walked on my knees to the next soldier, and I repeated the process.

The command to kneel kept echoing in the background. Each time the tall evangelist said, "Kneel!" more people came forward to receive Christ. After I had prayed with three or four soldiers, the wind suddenly died down, and there was silence. From my kneeling position, I glanced around to locate the evangelist. He was gone. People were conversing in hushed voices as they started to disperse. Some soldiers remained on their knees, and all three of us college students went from one soldier to another, leading each one in the sinner's prayer.

## Closing Thoughts

Was this unusual turn of events a miracle? Think about the timing. When it finally came my turn to preach, I prayed and asked God to do something big. Gladdie and I were asking God to work in a supernatural way. Obviously, every soul won to Christ is a miracle. Now, 60 years later, I am not sure if there were 10 or 20 soldiers who prayed to receive Christ that night. Even if only one was saved for all eternity, it was a miracle.

Do you see God's supernatural hand in how the street meeting unfolded? The Lord controlled the weather that contributed to my failure. Perhaps He saw my pride and decided that He wouldn't use a tainted vessel that night. Maybe the problem was my lack of skills to preach as a young, immature novice. But there was also sincere prayer—so sincere that we gave up our meals to ask for God's blessing. We didn't call it a fast, but did that really matter? Maybe God can't ignore that type of dedication.

Maybe God in heaven looked down as if to say, "I'm going to answer that prayer, but I'll use someone else to get the conversions for which he prays." So God supernaturally guided a mature evangelist to the street corner at the right time, with the right message, to get the right response. That, to me, makes the evening a miracle.

ELMER L. TOWNS

# Your Notes

_____

_____

_____

_____

_____

_____

_____

_____

_____

_____

_____

_____

_____

_____

_____

_____

_____

_____

_____

_____

_____

_____

_____

_____

_____

_____

_____

_____

_____

_____

# 8

# Witnessing to Mr. Smith, a Dying Atheist

In 1952, I was a 19-year-old weekend preacher at Westminster Presbyterian Church in Savannah, Georgia. The steeple and bell tower in the Colonial-style structure reflected the building's glorious past, but the neighborhood around it had transitioned from upper class to working class over the years, and the church had been closed.

A young, inexperienced ministerial student, I had been allowed to re-open it for ministry. There were three Smith families in the church, so learning everyone's last name was not too tough.

One Mr. Smith did not come to church—ever. I was told he was a skeptic or an atheist. His wife had salt-and-pepper hair, wore an ever-present white apron around her rather rotund middle, and kept one of the cleanest houses in the neighborhood. Dozens of potted plants graced her front porch, and many more filled every free spot in her living room. The house smelled like a florist's shop; walking through it felt like walking through a nursery. Mrs. Smith never invited me for a meal; I just made pastoral visits, which always took place in the living room. Mr. Smith had never been home when I visited, so I had never talked to him.

Mrs. Smith was the quietest of all the women at the church. So it was all she could muster the one time she meekly requested, "Please pray for my husband. He doesn't believe in God."

*Hum,* I thought to myself. *How do I present the gospel to an atheist?*

Mr. Smith worked nights and slept days. I occasionally saw him around town. He always wore a white shirt, with sleeves rolled up past the elbow, and a straw hat. He was neither fat nor skinny, but had a Churchillesque protruding middle.

Usually I took the young people of the church to Youth for Christ meetings on Saturday nights. It was a good means of encouraging them to grow spiritually. After one such meeting was over, we lingered and talked a little longer than usual. Silla Hair was a member of our church. When I saw her walk in through the back door, her face told me immediately that something was wrong.

"Mr. Smith is in the emergency room at the hospital," she told me. "He had a heart attack. He's not expected to live. Mrs. Smith and the family are there now."

I told Mrs. Hair I would get there as soon as possible.

"You can lead him to Christ," Mrs. Hair expressed with great faith—much greater than mine.

I felt compelled to go to the hospital. Was I prodded by guilt because I had not witnessed to Mr. Smith? Was I moved by compassion because he lived in the neighborhood? Or did I feel an obligation as a pastor? I didn't know the reason. I simply knew that I had to do something.

I rode my English racing bike to the hospital. As was my usual practice, I hid it at the back of the hospital building and locked it to a gas meter. Once my bike was secure, I strolled to the front of the hospital, holding my Bible in my hand. I feigned confidence, wanting to appear as dignified as any other clergyman visiting St. Joseph's Hospital—but my heart was pounding like a snare drum in a marching band. I had no clue what I should do.

The hospital was a multi-story, dark brick building located in downtown Savannah. It was big, old and foreboding. Dark green linoleum covered old wood floors, and as I walked through the hallway, the noise from my leather shoes reverberated off the walls: "Tap . . . tap . . . tap . . ."

There was no doubt I was entering an infirmary.

## A Young, Intimidated Preacher and the Family of a Dying Man

The Smith family heard me approaching, for I was the only other visitor in the hospital's Cardiac Arrest Center that evening. When I reached the family waiting room, I saw Mrs. Smith surrounded by approximately a dozen people, none of whom I knew. These were her grown children and their spouses.

At 19, I was the youngest person in the room and probably the most immature. I wore a white shirt, a tie and a suit jacket, and I carried a big Bible. I boldly entered the dimly lit waiting room, walked around, and shook hands with each man, introducing myself as Mrs. Smith's pastor. It was almost midnight, and they had been there since suppertime. They were tired and irritable, and many of them did not want to coddle a young preacher. No doubt they thought I had little to offer to them.

Finally I went over to greet Mrs. Smith, not knowing what to say.

"He's not going to make it through the night," she said seriously. "The doctor doesn't give him much of a chance."

The news of Mr. Smith's imminent death compounded my problem. I did not have the slightest idea of how to prepare a person to die, nor did I have a clue about how to prepare a wife and children for the death of a husband and father. In fact, I didn't know how to prepare myself.

For some reason, I felt that it would be my fault if Mr. Smith died—or at least, it would be my fault if I didn't say all of the right words before he passed. Today, I realize that a pastor must detach himself from the problems of his people, so he can minister grace from his strength. If he emotionally identifies too closely with people, a pastor tends to become neurotic. It can actually become a codependent relationship in which he abdicates any help he may be able to provide. As a young pastor, I did not understand the nuances and risks. I just threw my heart into the family waiting room, walked in as one of them, and tried to help.

*But who was going to help me?*

Not only was Mr. Smith on the brink of death, but I also saw another deep problem. As I glanced around the waiting room from one unshaven face glazed with anxiety into the eyes of the next, a question crawled into my mind that froze me. How many of the Smith children and in-laws were atheists, too? Mrs. Smith was a delightful woman, but she was not the dominant force in her home. I

did not know about the strength of her husband's atheism, or how
much had filtered through to each person in the room.

### Prayer in the Waiting Room

"Would you like me to lead you in prayer?" It was all I could think
to say. My voice was shaky, and so was my plan. Everyone in the
waiting room knew it. There were a few seconds of tension, as one
middle-aged sibling exchanged glances with another.

Finally, one son said, "Mother would like that."

"Before I pray, I would like to read Scripture," I added, quickly
breathing a silent prayer that no nurse would interrupt me, and
that everyone would understand the full scope of what they were
hearing. Slowly I read of Jesus telling Nicodemus, "You must be
born again" (see John 3:1-8).

I carefully explained what it meant to be born again. This family all lived in the Christianized culture of the South. They could
sing hymns and recite religious-sounding jargon. They understood
the Christmas message that Jesus was born of a virgin, and they had
heard the Easter message that He had died for the sins of the world.

I had a deeper question for each of them, however: "Are *you*
born again?"

Although I was young, and intimidated by the possibility that
everyone in the room except Mrs. Smith was an atheist, that
evening in the hospital room I boldly proclaimed the necessity of
new birth. I explained that church membership was not enough,
nor was faithful attendance at worship services. I emphasized that
simply believing in Jesus wasn't even enough.

I pressed home the claim: "You must be born again." I probably overdid it a little—but what is a young preacher supposed to do
in a room full of atheists?

Then I prayed. When you don't perceive yourself as a spiritual
intercessor who can rattle the windows of heaven, how do you pray?
I only knew one way, and that was simply to open my heart to God.
My words were unsophisticated, undignified and ill framed. Nev-
ertheless, I prayed from the deepest place in my heart, because I felt
responsible for Mr. Smith's healing, and for his recovery.

"God, heal Mr. Smith and raise him back up," I prayed boldly in front of everyone. It was not a prayer to show off my theology, but an honest desire for Mr. Smith to live. The rest of my prayer was couched in typical ministerial language: "If it be Thy will . . ." "Thou art the Great Physician . . ." and "We commit him into Thy hands."

### The Pastor Persona

After the prayer, I left the family waiting room and walked to the nurses' station. I introduced myself to the head nurse and told her I wanted to see Mr. Smith.

"I'm his pastor," I said in a ministerial, authoritative way.

The nurse, wearing her starched white cap, dipped her head and looked over the top of her glasses with squinted eyes. She said simply, "Hm-m-m-m-m-m . . ." Her tone told me that she didn't think much of my ministerial persona.

"He's not expected to live, and he's unconscious." She spit the words out in crisp syllables. "He wouldn't know you even if we let you in."

They weren't even letting his wife see him. That's how close he was to the end.

For a few minutes, I lingered in the waiting room with the family. No one talked much, and most of the men smoked—this was long before today's aggressive anti-smoking laws were in place. I was uncomfortable, not knowing what to say. By nature, I was not good at small talk with men who had little in common with me. So I just sat there, wondering why I was there.

*I ought to go home and get some sleep so I can be fresh for my sermon tomorrow,* I thought.

The Smith family wondered why I wasn't on my way home, and I wondered the same thing. But I did not budge.

## Prayers for a Dying Man

At approximately 1:00 AM, the head nurse who had looked over her glasses saying "Hm-m-m-m-m-m . . ." informed us that she was going home. She introduced her replacement, a much younger nurse who knew how to smile.

I again explained that I was a pastor, and that I wanted to see Mr. Smith. I told her that he was an atheist, and I did not want him to slip into eternity without knowing God.

"I go to a Baptist church," the young, smiling nurse said to me. She indicated an understanding of my spiritual dilemma. "I'll see what I can do."

I slipped back into the waiting room. Whereas the previous hours had been filled with anxiety and frustration, now for the first time that evening I was hopeful. I thought, *This young Baptist nurse understands why I am here, and she is going to let me in to see Mr. Smith.*

My faith was rewarded when the smiling nurse stuck her head into the waiting room and said, "You can see Mr. Smith now."

Then, to the surprise of some family members, including a few obviously non-approving in-laws, the nurse added, "Even though he's not conscious, you can pray over him."

I thought, *That's a strange expression: "to pray over someone."* When I entered the Intensive Care Unit, Mr. Smith was lying in bed.

## At Mr. Smith's Bedside

In the 1950s, a heart-attack victim was kept in a clear plastic oxygen tent that covered the entire bed. Air was pumped into the tent, not directly into the nostrils. The dimly lit table lamp was the only light in the room, and dark shadows in the corners added a mystical effect to the setting. The slow hiss of oxygen streaming into the tent compounded the foreboding ambiance. A large red "NO SMOKING" sign seemed unnecessary.

The night sounds of a hospital tell an eerie story, and only those who've been there in the dark know what they mean. The gurgle of the IV, the beeping of the monitor, the echo of footsteps in the hall, and the faint whispers from the nurses' station all confirm that life is scarce and may be slipping away.

The smiling Baptist nurse had seen Catholic priests administer last rites on many occasions, so I guess she wanted me to give the Protestant equivalent. She stood at the foot of the bed and bowed her head slightly, waiting for me to do my ministerial thing. I didn't have a clue what Protestant last rites were, and I had never observed Roman Catholic deathbed rituals. Not knowing how to proceed, I did what I had done in other hospital rooms when I had visited other patients, albeit ones who were more alert.

"Mr. Smith, can you hear me?"

His eyes were closed, his body deathly still. Then he slightly moved an arm and, to the shock of the nurse, nodded his head. I explained to him that while waiting outside, I had prayed for him to be healed.

"Do you understand what I have done?"

He nodded his head again.

Then, opening my Bible again to John 3:7, I told him what Jesus had said to Nicodemus: "You must be born again." Just as I had done dozens of times in hospitals and homes in West Savannah, I explained what it meant for a person to be born again.

At the end of each part of the explanation, I asked, "Do you understand me?"

Each time he nodded his head.

"Do you want to be born again, Mr. Smith?"

He nodded.

"Will you pray these words in your heart?"

He nodded again.

"*Dear God, I believe in you. I believe that Jesus was the Son of God. I believe He died on the cross to save me from my sin.*"

After I had said each sentence, I waited for Mr. Smith to nod.

Then I asked him to say in his heart this prayer: "*Dear Lord, forgive me for my sin. Forgive me for my smoking and drinking. Forgive me for my cursing. Forgive me for not going to church.*" Then again, to make sure, I asked if he had prayed those words in his heart.

He nodded.

"*I pray this in the name of the Lord, Jesus Christ.*"

He nodded once more.

I briefly explained to him how the thief hanging on a cross next to Jesus went to heaven even though he believed just before death. Jesus promised him, "Today shalt thou be with me in paradise" (Luke 23:43, *KJV*).

I explained to Mr. Smith that he was dying, and the doctors thought he might not make it through the night. I told him that if he had honestly asked Christ to come into his heart, then instantly upon death, he would go to heaven.

I read him one more verse of Scripture: "To be absent from the body [is] to be present with the Lord" (2 Cor. 5:8).

### A Prayer for Healing

Then I thought, *I should pray for his physical healing.*

I shyly asked, "Do you want me to pray for God to heal you?"

He nodded his head one more time.

I cannot recall the specific words of this prayer. I do remember stretching out my hand and laying it on the plastic oxygen tent. I asked God to heal Mr. Smith of the heart attack, raise him up out of that bed, bring him home, and put him into church.

When I returned to the family waiting room, I reported to the family that I had prayed for their father and husband, and that he had heard me. I told them he had nodded his head, indicating that he could hear what I prayed. Because of the enmity I felt from some of the children, I did not tell them that Mr. Smith had prayed to receive Jesus Christ. Neither did I tell Mrs. Smith. I decided I could tell her privately at another time.

As I rode my bicycle home that night, I was mentally preparing myself for Mr. Smith's funeral. I was trying to decide whether I would tell the people beside an open grave that Mr. Smith had prayed to receive Jesus Christ right before his death. I was not sure I should make that announcement publicly, because people might think I was grandstanding. I did not have any way to verify what Mr. Smith had done. I was not sure the neighbors would believe my claim.

The next morning, as I was preparing for my sermon, word was brought to me that Mr. Smith had not died during the night. I was requested to pray a special prayer for him in the morning worship service. Indeed, we prayed for Mr. Smith, but I did not mention to anyone that he had prayed to receive Christ as Savior.

## Mr. Smith Goes Home

As was my weekly routine, I returned to Columbia Bible College on Sunday night. The following weekend, when I was back in West Savannah for my weekend ministry, I asked about Mr. Smith. I wanted to know about the impending funeral and if I had arrived in time to officiate.

"He's much better," someone informed me. "He'll be coming home sometime this week."

My ego played a tug-a-war with me. I wanted to announce to the church that I had prayed for Mr. Smith's healing, and as a result God *had* healed him. I could not bring myself to say that, because I would be taking the glory that belongs to God. On the flip side, if people knew what had transpired that night, their faith would be encouraged. I struggled with my feelings for a week, undecided about what I should tell the congregation.

Three weeks after the heart attack, I visited Mr. Smith in his home. A bottle of oxygen was sitting beside him, and a plastic cup had been placed over his nose and mouth. He was wearing flannel pajamas and sitting in the living room, reading a magazine, when I came in. Mrs. Smith came out of the kitchen to sit with us. She was wiping her hands on the ever-present starched white apron as she sat next to him.

I opened my Bible, and once again read aloud John 3:7, where Jesus told Nicodemus: "You must be born again." I described to both the Smiths where and how Mr. Smith had prayed to receive Christ.

"Did you really mean it that night?" I asked him in front of his wife.

As he had before, he simply nodded his head.

Mrs. Smith was not demonstrative. She did not smile, cry or respond; she just nodded her head in agreement with her husband.

Within a couple of months, Mr. Smith started attending church regularly. He always sat with his wife in the last row. He never went back to smoking and drinking, and the next time we had a baptism service, he was sprinkled.

Mr. Smith never went back to work, because of his physical condition, but he was constantly around the church, helping with small tasks. He became one of our most dependable ushers, and I could often spot him walking the two blocks from his house to the church. I knew it was him, because he still wore a straw hat, and the sleeves on his white shirt were rolled up past his elbows.

## Closing Thoughts

*A sincere decision gives power.* Because of my experience with Mr. Smith, I have always believed that anyone can make an instantaneous decision at a crisis point in his or her experience, and that person's life can be irrevocably changed. Whenever I have heard people say that Christianity is just a philosophy or a psychological reinforcement, I think back to Mr. Smith nodding that he had just prayed to receive Jesus Christ.

He was in an oxygen tent when he repented and turned from his sins—sins such as smoking and drinking, which he might never have an opportunity to commit again, given his condition. He later demonstrated to me the efficacy of his conversion experience—in part because he did have the opportunity to regress into old habits of sin, but he didn't yield to that temptation. I do not know what I would do if I were in a similar situation today. I do know that God responded positively to the outlandish and desperate repentance request I made of Mr. Smith when I thought he was dying. Although damaging our bodies—the temple of the Holy Spirit—is sin, if I asked someone to repent of smoking today, I might come off as legalistic.

What's most important is that it only takes a moment to change a life. I was in Mr. Smith's room for less than 10 minutes—in the middle of the night. Yet through that short conversation, his life was changed forever. Where there's life, there is hope. It is never too late to pray the sinner's prayer. The people around Mr. Smith essentially had given up. They sure didn't give any credence to the prayers of a young preacher. Yet, when Mr. Smith was weakest in body, he was strongest in spirit. Was his decision the basis of his physical recovery? We don't know, but we should never disassociate our prayers from the answer to our prayers.

John Calvin was the founder of Calvinism, which holds the position that God works out all details—even the minor ones—by His power and controlling design. When I was a young preacher, I marveled when little things worked out for the glory of God. Often, with tongue firmly planted in cheek, I would say, "John Calvin strikes again." In the story of Mr. Smith, a Baptist nurse allowed me to enter a darkened hospital room to pray last rites over a person she thought was unresponsive. Yet in the sovereign purpose of God, Mr. Smith awakened just enough to hear me pray. He then responded to Jesus Christ in a deathbed conversion, and from that strength he revived physically and lived for Christ spiritually. Praise God, "John Calvin struck again."

This book is about fasting for miracles, so why am I including this story? Can a prayer to raise up a person from a near-death experience be effective without fasting? I didn't fast because there was no opportunity to fast, and at that young age I hadn't learned the power of the discipline of fasting. Our faith—not the specific act of fasting or sincere prayer—is what moves God to action. But fasting and intercession will stimulate our faith. Mr. Smith's story simply shows that when it comes to God's miracles, there is no formula.

## Your Notes

_____

_____

_____

_____

_____

_____

_____

_____

_____

_____

_____

# 9

# Building Faith and Following God's Call

Al Henson was living a comfortable life. After graduating from the University of Tennessee with an engineering degree and marrying his high school sweetheart, Susan, he had landed a good job with an engineering firm. Al and Susan had three wonderful children, went to church regularly, and bought a nice home in Middle Tennessee. Al was climbing the corporate ladder and enjoyed a round of golf on his days off. Then came the night that changed his life forever.

Al was sitting on the deck at his home, leisurely gazing at the nightscape of Nashville. Without notice, the flickering lights in the distance grabbed his heart. His casual appreciation was suddenly replaced by a heavy burden that overwhelmed him—Nashville needed to be reached with the gospel. Within Al stirred an ardent compassion for his own city that was akin to what Jesus once felt for Jerusalem (see Luke 19:41-42).

Some days later, Al decided to take a huge step of faith. He sold everything; moved his family to Lynchburg, Virginia; and enrolled at Liberty Baptist Theological Seminary. Al later confessed, "God was beginning to teach me daily faith."

With a regular paycheck gone and Al studying to be a pastor, Susan started hunting for—and quickly found—work. Her new boss had read someone else's application and hired her! It was no accident; God was providing.

Like many who come to Liberty, the Hensons made Thomas Road Baptist Church their home congregation. At one of the first services they attended, Al decided to put God to the test. *I want to see a miracle, so I can know that God will provide when I start a new church,* he thought. Al only had $1,057 to his name. He paid a $17 water bill, spent $40 on groceries, and put $1,000 in the offering plate. That left him with an empty bank account and empty pockets. He didn't even tell his wife.

"I was anxious to see what God would do!" Al recounts.

The Hensons became friends with Mom and Pop Morris, an elderly couple who had moved to Lynchburg to help Jerry Falwell build a Christian school that would train students to capture the world for Jesus Christ. Pop Morris built a greenhouse on Liberty's campus, grew all types of plants, and purchased hundreds of trees to line the roadways of the new campus. Before Pop Morris came to Liberty, there was nothing but flat acres of dirt. Today, 37 years later, the University enjoys fully grown, mature trees.

The Morrises also wanted to help a student through school, so they invited the Hensons to move into an apartment in their home. For the next three years, the growing Henson family lived rent-free, and the Morrises purchased many of their groceries.

Al and Susan fasted every Wednesday, and on those afternoons, they went to the Bill Sheehan Prayer Chapel to spend one hour in prayer for their future ministry and the city of Nashville.

After graduation, the Hensons returned to the Tennessee capital. They moved into an apartment complex and used the recreation room to plant a church. Al and his associate, Ken Collins, knocked on 3,000 doors the first month, inviting their neighbors to join them. In 1979, Lighthouse Baptist Church (now called Lighthouse Christian Fellowship) was born.

The first Sunday, 41 people showed up. Nila Miller was converted to Christ that day, and she went on to become a faithful member. There were 38 people present the second Sunday, and 45 people the third.

About two months later, Al was driving on I-25, a few miles from downtown Nashville, when he spotted an old house on a large section of uninhabited property. His heart was stirred. Al contacted the owner, but was informed that the property wasn't for sale. It was being left as an inheritance for the owner's children.

As Al continued to pray for a home for this new church, the property near I-25, which was actually in the suburb of Antioch, kept coming to his mind. It was the perfect location. Thousands of people would see the building as they passed by on the interstate each day. The property itself would be a great advertisement for the gospel.

Finally Al and Susan went to the location, knelt, and claimed the property in the spirit of Matthew 18:19: "If two of you agree on earth concerning anything that they ask, it will be done for them by My Father in heaven."

Al approached the owner a second time. The answer was a much more emphatic "no!" What could the Hensons do? God had tugged at Al's heart. That meant the only thing they could do was to return to the property, kneel again, and pray some more. In fact, they made kneeling and praying at the property a routine. One time, they took off their shoes and walked the edge of the property, claiming it by faith. God had spoken, so the Hensons acted.

Henson also challenged his fledgling congregation. Together they fasted and prayed that God would touch the owner's heart. On the last day of the fast, after Sunday church, Al went to the owner's house and rang the front door bell. No one answered, but he could hear laughter and talking coming from the backyard. Al figured he had come this far, so why not go around back. The family was having a cookout. When the owner saw Al, he jested, "This is the man who wants to buy the property."

Al just smiled. After eating with the family and chatting with two or three of the relatives, Al again shared with the owner about his burden for reaching the whole city of Nashville. He emphasized that he believed that God would build a great church on that property. As he was leaving, Al asked, "Will you pray about selling the property to me?"

Before the man could say anything, his wife answered, "I will see that he prays about it."

On Monday morning, Al was in his bathroom, shaving, when the phone rang. It was unusual for anyone to call that early in the morning.

"You've got to come see me immediately," the property owner told Al. "God's been speaking to me all night, and He would not let me sleep."

When Al got to the house, the owner said, "The Lord spoke to me as I have never heard Him speak in my life. I know that God wants you to have this property." Then the owner explained, "I want $100,000 and I won't negotiate the price." This was about one-third the market value of the land. He went on, "I want $29,000 cash from you as a down payment, and I will loan you the other $71,000 at 6 percent interest." The owner then gave Al 90 days to raise the down payment.

Slowly some money came in for the property, but six days before the deadline, the church had only raised $5,000. As Al prepared to pronounce the benediction on the church service that day, Susan interrupted. She explained that God wanted them to have the property and that everyone must sacrifice. Dramatically she took off the diamond engagement ring that Al had given her, walked over, and dropped it in the offering plate. A hush came over the auditorium. Then one man offered to sell his second car and give the money to the church. Two or three others stood to donate savings bonds or money, and a couple more offered cars. After the service was over, one man purchased the diamond ring from the church, and gave it back to Susan.

Malcolm Barrett, not a member of the church, had been listening to Al on the radio. He came by and said, "Let's get on our knees and pray about the rest of the down payment." When they finished, he said, "Tomorrow I will loan the church the money it needs at no interest for an indefinite period of time." This was a great miracle for Lighthouse Baptist Church.

God had done a wonderful thing in supplying the property, but would He do a second, greater miracle and provide money for the new building? Because of the example of Susan, many people in the congregation gave sacrificially, and a 225-seat sanctuary was built.

When Al returned to Nashville to plant a church, he didn't pray for hundreds or thousands of people to get saved. Instead, he prayed for one family a week. During that first year, 53 families joined the church. The church prayed for the same goal. Some-times when a new family visited the church and decided to stay, someone would tell them, "You're the family we've been praying for this week."

When Al teaches about faith, he is not simply explaining text from the Bible. Al and Susan have lived in need and expectation of miracles, so he draws from his own obedience to God. Here is Al's understanding of faith:

> Faith is allowing God to move supernaturally in a situa-tion. Faith first finds clarity as to what is God's will, then steps forward in faith so God can carry out His will.
>
> What God orders, He supplies. If it is God's will for the church to go forward, then we can trust Him to overcome any barrier or to supply any need. When I accepted Jesus by faith, He became real to me. When I accepted the Holy Spirit by faith, He filled me. When I obeyed the Lord Jesus Christ by faith, He manifested Himself to me. Faith is the supernatural manifestation of Jesus Christ in my life.
>
> I do not pray for faith—it's a gift of God. Rather I pray that this gift might become more manifested in my life.

Henson has said that praying for property, a building, a new family to join the church, or provision for Laotian refugees who came to his church, as examples, are simply steps of faith. This kind of personal growth is seen in Scripture: "from faith to faith" (Rom. 1:17). Al interprets that verse to mean we must take steps of faith daily to grow in Jesus Christ.

Fasting and praying are spiritual disciplines. So is stepping out in faith. Al has a *modus operandi* when it comes to his practice of faith:

> First I daily ask God to pour Himself and His faith into my life. Second, the more I know about Jesus Christ and the Bible, the more I can trust Him. Henceforth faith can be manifested by fellowshipping with Jesus Christ and drawing

abundant principles from the Bible. The central goal of my
life has been that I might know Him (see Phil. 3:10). In
knowing the Lord, we love Him and learn to trust Him. We
learn of the beauty and perfection of His nature and that He
is worthy to be trusted. To doubt Him would truly be fool-
ishness. And third, my faith grows in its manifestation as I
take each step of faith. God does not manifest faith in my
life just because I ask Him for it. The Lord is manifested in
my life and circumstances when I exercise faith.

## How to Pray for a Project

*The miracle for a future project is based on God's past work and on God's
past answers to prayer.* When Al was building Lighthouse Baptist
Church in Antioch, Tennessee, he knew that God was with him, so
he had the authority to ask for great things. We can follow his example and do that same thing, no matter what assignment God
has given to us.

"From the moment I went onto the back porch and saw the
lights of Nashville, I knew God wanted me to come to this city and
plant a church," Al said. "Therefore, when I began to pray for projects
such as property and buildings, I knew that God would answer even
before I asked. It was just a matter of the Lord's will and timing."

This principle applies not only to material things needed to see
our call from God fulfilled, but also to all aspects of anything God
has given us to do.

*The size of our project corresponds to the size of our faith.* Sometimes
we envision a massive project that will save a city. We mean well,
but we rush to pray and fast for the miracle needed to see it come
about. When nothing happens, or the answer is slow in coming, we
wonder why. The reason is simple: Too often we have a good vision,
but skip the necessary steps of building the faith needed as a foundation for that vision.

Fasting and praying for a miracle is something like climbing a
hill. We don't start our mountaineering ventures by scaling Mt.
Everest. We begin on flat land, graduate to a small incline, and

work our way up from there. The same is true with faith. God wants us to trust Him for small miracles before He entrusts us with big ones.

Our early prayers can be called foundation-building or conditioning prayers. The first prayer of faith is to believe in God and accept His Son as Savior. Without this prayer, we cannot have faith. As new believers, we often have relentless zeal to seek God wholeheartedly. We beam when we see God answer even the simplest prayer. As we grow in our relationship with Christ, so does our faith. When we keep alive that "first love" faith we experienced when we received Christ, we see the size of our vision and answered prayers grow. As a result, step-by-step, we get to the place where we are able to trust God for big things.

Ask yourself, "What small answers to prayer am I getting daily?" Then ask, "Have I had enough small answers to prayer to stimulate my faith to ask for bigger answers to prayer?" As you enlarge your faith, always remember what God's blessing is all about.

*The blessing of God is upon people, not necessarily places or projects.* To have a great answer to prayer, we must have allowed the Lord to transform us internally into the image of Jesus, becoming humble servants of a great God. Al challenges us: "When you are in proper relationship with God, He will bless you and bless your ministry; any success you have in outward things is because of your personal inward success of walking with Christ."

## Your Notes

_____

_____

_____

_____

_____

_____

_____

_____

_____

# PART IV

# Fasting for Breakthrough

*He uses our problems as building materials for His miracles....*
*This was my first lesson in learning to trust Him completely.*
CORRIE TEN BOOM

# Overcoming Addiction and Restoring All That Was Lost

Dion Henderson is a talented artist. He also has a past as a gambler, addicted to the lure of the illusive big pot of gold at the end of the rainbow.

In the summer of 2010, at age 69, Dion found himself in shambles. He was separated from his wife for a second time, renting an upstairs room in the house of an elderly woman, and unable to free himself from his gambling habit. As Dion tells it:

> I am not talking casino, the track, high-stakes poker, or online sports betting. My addiction of choice was the lottery, playing the so-called game of "lucky numbers"—three and four digits, day and night drawings. For 26 years, I played the numbers every day, always looking for the big hit that would solve all of my financial problems.[1]

Dion's addiction was not as glamorous as some of the high-stakes bets against the odds to take home a pile of loot. However, the consequences of his number-playing addiction were the same: misery, despair and financial devastation. His life was a daily game of lies, deceit and schemes. His friends and relatives were looked upon as assets from whom he could borrow money. He made up very convincing stories explaining why the loan was needed, and he spared no one. He even preyed upon members of his church, letting them believe the money was for household purposes. He would boldly accept loans that he had no idea how he would repay.

Without his wife's knowledge or blessing, he took out signature loans with finance companies and maxed out personal
credit cards with cash advances. He was on a first-name basis
with the payday loan outlets. Electronic household items were
put up as collateral to secure loans from pawnshops. His struggle to maintain an all-is-well façade before family, friends, co-
workers and church members became all-consuming, and the
line between what was appropriate conduct and what was not
began to blur. He formed inappropriate relationships with people and compromised his integrity. He began making cash with-
drawals from his 401(k) account—and continued doing so until
it was finally depleted.

For Dion, all of this was justified, because he just knew that
someday he would hit the big one.

As Dion continued to nurture and sustain the sinful pit he
was in, he soon found himself of a mind that nothing was off
limits. He began taking money out of his mother's checking account. This put her under a great deal of stress and no doubt
contributed to her suffering a stroke. The Bible describes how
sin blinds, binds and grinds (see Judges 16:21). "I was blinded to
all things and became someone that I didn't even recognize,"
Dion said. "I lost sight of what was important: my parents, wife
and family, and fellow believers. I was bound to a lottery game of
chance and worn down to misery, despair and hopelessness."

At one time, Dion had attended Gamblers Anonymous (GA)
meetings. His lack of commitment to the program was evidenced
when he showed up at GA meetings with number slips in his
pocket. Another time, Dion turned to psychiatry. The psychiatrist concluded that when Dion had returned from Vietnam, he
had traded his drug habit for an addiction to running. When he
got older, the habit was transferred to gambling. He learned from
the psychiatrist that he had a disorder known as an addictive personality, which meant he was prone to compulsive behaviors.
However, knowing his problem did not solve his problem.

Pastor Keith Gardner, of Calvary Chapel Breath of Life in
Maryland, told Dion, "The remedy to your so-called problem is

not a 12-step program or psychiatric diagnosis. . . . The answer is to fully surrender your life to almighty God, who has a wonderful plan and purpose for your life."

Pastor Gardner continued, "You cannot genuinely worship a God you do not trust; you clearly put your trust in the lottery before putting your trust in God." Gardner reminded Dion of the first of the Ten Commandments: "You shall have no other gods before Me" (Exod. 20:3).

Calvary Chapel has a Christian rehabilitation program, called U-Turn for Christ, for people struggling with addiction. Many addicts experience low points in their lives, but continue in their habits because they have yet to hit rock bottom. At U-Turn, they call that period "hammer time." The addict gets out the jack-hammer and digs a wider, deeper hole *to get to rock bottom.*

Dion realized that he had come to the end of himself when the Lord began to speak to him in and through his sin. Dion remembers that it was not uncommon for him to barely miss hitting the number five or more times during a week. He recalls:

For example, if I played 965, the number would come 964. The next day, I would play 488, and it would come 489. If played 818 and 1941 on Sunday, it would come 819 and 1942. Week after week this would occur, always one number off. I knew it was not just bad luck or a coincidence, but the Lord. I would be inside my car, beating the steering wheel and screaming, "C'mon, give me a break. Why am I always off by one number all of the time?" Crying out to an omnipotent, holy, sovereign, almighty God, creator of the universe and all therein, asking why He was taunting me and making it so difficult for me to hit a lottery number. The jackhammer had indeed hit rock bottom.

In October 2010, Dion read my book *The Daniel Fast* and decided to take extreme measures to confront his gambling addiction.[2] The first step in fasting was to make a vow to God. Dion told the Lord that he wanted to honor Him with his body and soul. He wrote down his commitment:

> I will not play the numbers. I will abstain from all solid food. I will drink only pure water with lemon and maple syrup. I will study God's Word, and I will begin and end each day in prayer.

On October 23, Dion surrendered everything to Christ and began his Daniel Fast. He kept that commitment to God for 21 days. During the fast, he wrote out three prayer requests: (1) that an ongoing court case related to his employment be heard and resolved; (2) that God help him find a good executor for his brother's estate, so that his nephew could receive his rightful inheritance; and (3) for the necessary provisions to get him into U-Turn.

During the first week of his fast, Dion's wife, Barbara, notified him that a date had been assigned for his case to be heard. During the second week of his fast, he located the assets belonging to his brother and secured them in a safe bank account to be disbursed to his nephew.

Around the seventeenth day of his fast, Dion went to the Lord with praise and thanksgiving. As he began to express his concern about getting into U-Turn, Dion had a feeling of quiet peace. He sensed a still voice of God saying to him, "I have taken away your bondage from you." It was only then that he realized he had *not* played the numbers for almost three weeks, and even better, he had no conscious thought about numbers as part of his daily routine. It was as if playing the numbers had never existed. Dion walked in and out of stores, passing lottery terminals—but was not even aware of the lottery machines. Not even a tug on his heart. Dion gives his testimony:

> I knelt in wonder and amazement at what the Lord had done. His love, presence, peace and revelation filled my entire being. I became mindful of Psalm 46:10: "Be still, and know that I am God." I could sense God speaking to me: "I got you. You got a late start becoming a believer, and you wasted more time until you fully surrendered. Now you are 69 years

old, with more years behind you than you have in front of you. Do not be fearful or anxious, be strong in faith, be obedient to My Word, stay in My will, and trust that I will provide to fulfill My plan and purpose for which you were created. I love you and I want you to finish well."

Dion was giddy with joy, but he still wanted to go to U-Turn for Christ. Barbara asked him, "Why do you feel a need to still go to U-Turn for Christ when your habit has been taken away by Christ? Your addiction no longer exists."

When he arrived at U-turn for Christ, they asked the same question: "You're not in recovery, withdrawal, or have the desire to gamble. Why are you here?"

Dion felt that the Lord was drawing him to U-Turn to honor Him and bring Him glory. He testified, "If I could convince one person that a fully surrendered life to Christ would give them victory to be delivered from whatever was their addiction of choice, then my time would be worth it." The idea of bondage took on new meaning for Dion while he was in U-Turn for Christ: "I no longer referred to bondage as a sickness, disease, disorder or personal wiring, but as sin—just plain ol' sin hated by almighty God."

Dion fasted again and sought the Lord for three additional requests: first, that God would heal his marriage; second, that God would keep his mother in good health so he could visit her in Seattle; and third, that he could glorify God with his artistic talent.

While Dion had been addicted to gambling, his marriage was broken, and there was little, if any, contact with his wife. Barbara would call him to say, "Dion, there is a letter here for you. I'll put it under the mat; pick it up tomorrow." The locks on the doors had been changed, and he was not allowed in the house.

After Dion's fast, and the change in his life, Barbara called to invite him to come to the house to talk. Her son, Jantzen, had told her about the healing. He also told her that her reaction to Dion had not been in keeping with biblical teaching on what makes a godly wife. Barbara apologized and asked for Dion's forgiveness. In turn, he sought her forgiveness. Over the years, he had dragged her through his gambling addiction and all its ugly consequences. After their reconciliation, Dion testified, "There were no tears, but a heartfelt response of God's love and approval right there in our midst."

Mrs. Tatum, the owner of the house where Dion had been living, surprised him with an Easter present. She had purchased a ticket for him to fly to Seattle to visit his mother. She also promised that when he returned, renovation work on the garage would be complete—it would become a studio where he could produce his art. God was faithful in answering all of the prayer requests Dion brought before Him while fasting. Dion testifies:

> As I move my life forward in God's will, I pray daily for His guidance, wisdom, discernment, understanding and protection. I thank Him continually for setting me free, and for His love and presence in my life. The mountain of debt is still there (however being reduced monthly), but I wake up in peace, being in His will. I know that the Lord is faithful and will work out all things for good (see Rom. 8:28).

## Your Notes

_____

_____

_____

_____

_____

_____

_____

_____

_____

_____

_____

_____

_____

11

# Confronting Evil and Casting Out Demons

The young man who talked with me wore a suit and tie. There was no trace of tattoos, and he did not have a history of drugs, nor did he live in a rebellious drug culture.

This man told me that he had a demon—a person—in him that communicated with him. Outwardly, the young man did not show what I thought were the traditional signs of demon possession. He did not have any physical disease or traits of possession; neither did he have any obvious mental disorders or split personality—nothing that would indicate a problem. He seemed normal—other than the fact that he claimed that he had a person inside his body that communicated with him.

"Can you help me?" the young man asked. "Can you cast out a demon?"

All I knew about demons was what I had read while preparing to write a theology textbook.[1] I had never actually talked to a person who was demon possessed (at least not to my knowledge). I had never talked to someone who had been delivered from a demon, nor had I talked at length to anyone who could actually cast out a demon.

Because I want to help people, I agreed to meet with the man, but only after I had fasted and prayed. I wanted to be spiritually ready for any possibility. If I had known the agonizing warfare I would go through, I am not sure I would have accepted the assignment. I certainly would have prayed and fasted much more deeply than I did. What I did was go through a one-day routine fast. I didn't eat the evening meal, nor did I consume food the following day.

ELMER L. TOWNS

When the young man and I met, he was again dressed neatly, had his hair combed, and appeared to be normal. I was not really sure what I was going to do, so I asked God to lead me and to protect both of us.

I placed my hands on the man's head and prayed, "In the name of Jesus, and through the power of His blood, I pray for the demon to come out of you . . ."

"UUUGGG . . . UUUGGG . . ." was the only sound that came from the man. Then he collapsed to the ground, striking his head violently on the floor. I was immediately concerned that he had suffered a concussion.

His body moved, struggling with something unseen to my eyes. The "UUUGGG . . . UUUGGG . . ." sounds continued unabated.

I panicked, much as I would have if I had seen someone shot or in a terrible car accident. My mind went blank, and I couldn't think rationally. What was I encountering?

More "UUUGGGs" came forth, but I couldn't comprehend a syllable of it. Then green saliva began to trickle out of the corner of the young man's mouth.

At first I didn't know what to make of the green saliva. I was afraid to touch it, thinking it might be something from a demon—something evil or poisonous. The green liquid didn't gush as a man throwing up vomit. Yet the stream was a little more than spittle that might come with a cough or a sneeze. I later learned that the green saliva was stomach acid. When a person goes through deep emotional revulsion, something reaches into the depths of the stomach, scrapes the stomach lining of acid used to digest food, and repels it out through the throat and mouth. Not a pretty picture, I know.

I had seen *The Exorcist*, the movie in which actress Linda Blair played a young demon-possessed girl who was spitting up similar green fluids. The young man grunting on the floor in front of me was not in a movie; this was real. Very real. There was a deep internal struggle going on within the man.

Later I would learn that this condition is called a paroxysm. The word "paroxysm" is from Old French and means to provoke.

A paroxysm is defined as "a fit, attack, or sudden increase or re-currence of symptoms (as of a disease)."[2]

In this case, when the condition of the young man was "pro-voked" by the name of Jesus Christ and the power of His blood, there was a violent reaction, resulting in his passing out. (Though he had not fainted in the normal sense of the term, I could not talk with him, nor could he talk with me, while the struggle raged between him and the demon. Later he told me that he had been aware of what was happening and what I was doing.) This parox-ysm was the symptom of the possession itself.

How did I react? I felt intimidated and threatened. Honestly, I was scared to death—perhaps more scared than I'd ever been in my life. I could only turn one place. I asked, "What would Jesus do?"

When Jesus met a demon-possessed man in Gadara, he asked, "What is your name?" (Mark 5:9). The demon answered Jesus—how could a demon not be accountable to the Son of God?

With Jesus' example as encouragement, I decided to ask the same question. I looked straight at the young man, trying to look through his closed eyes and into his soul, and said, "Demon, what is your name?"

It's a frightening thought that a human being would attempt to talk to a being in the spirit world. So I didn't think about it; I just did it. I didn't hear a clear answer, but I heard something. As a matter of fact, I heard two things.

First, I heard the young man continuing to grunt: "UU-UGGG . . . UUUGGG . . ." I could see his lips move, as the green stomach contents continued to seep out of his mouth.

But I also heard something else coming from the chest of the man. It sounded to me like a deep, guttural voice—like the demon was trying to answer my question. Was I hearing a demon? It could have been something from the spirit world, or it might have sim-ply been the sound of the man's stomach growling or rumbling.

Standing in the presence of something evil was surreal and ter-rifying. I felt like a man who had fallen off a cliff and was hurtling toward death myself. My mind shut down and my emotions took over. My recessive urges took command, and I was brutalized by the concept of satanic power. It was as if a rattlesnake were wrapped around my neck, poised to strike.

"Oh God, help me," I pled.

I don't know whether I prayed these four words out loud, or if I just thought them. But my whole faith was clinging to God at that moment, desperate for divine protection. The hair on the back of my head and arms stood at rapt attention, like soldiers ready to meet an advancing enemy. I knew I wasn't fighting the young man before me. I was there to help him. So what was I fighting?

I went back to my original prayer. With all my heart, I again said, "In the name of Jesus and by the power of His blood, come out of him . . ."

The young man continued to gag the word, "UUUGGG . . . UUUGGG . . . UUUGGG . . ."

For several minutes, I continued to plead the name and blood of Jesus Christ, and the young man repeated his one unintelligible word. I didn't try to talk to the demon again, nor did I try to understand the sound that I had heard from his body cavity.

The situation was beyond my control and in God's hands. I had felt this way once before, back in my college days. I was driving on a cold day. My wife and young daughter were in the car with me. We came to a dangerous stretch of road, and suddenly the car was sliding down a long, icy hill; no matter how hard I applied the brakes, I couldn't correct the slide. I could see a pileup of cars a quarter-mile down the hill. They had skidded into each other, and I feared that we were going to be the next vehicle added to the pile. All the way down the hill, I prayed, "Oh Jesus, help me . . . Oh Jesus, help me . . ."

The Lord did help me on that occasion. Around 50 feet from the pileup, my car unexpectedly veered toward the edge of the road, and caught gravel and dirt. We came grinding to a stop about 5 feet from the wreck. No one was hurt, and we got out of the car.

Just as I was beginning to breathe easier, I looked up to see the headlights of an oncoming truck—later I learned that it was a garbage truck—bearing down on the pile of wrecked cars. The garbage truck was caught on the same slippery slope as the rest of us had been. I prayed again, "Oh Jesus, help me . . ." but the garbage truck smashed into the back of my car, ramming it into the others.

Then the situation got worse. A police cruiser came sliding down the same hill; it smashed into the garbage truck, pushing my car further into the pile. All of my praying did not stop the growing pileup of cars.

I felt the same way as I prayed over the young man with the demon. I experienced the same helpless sensations you feel when you are sliding down an icy road where your brakes won't hold, and you face the inevitable collision ahead. Nonetheless, I kept praying for the young man, just as I had prayed on that snowy night, "Oh God, help me . . . Oh God, help me . . ."

The conflict seemed to play itself out. After a while, the young man stopped gagging and spitting up green saliva. I stopped praying. When the young man opened his eyes, he stood up from the floor.

## Calling in Reinforcements

I phoned Doris Wagner, the wife of C. Peter Wagner, who has been a long-time friend. Doris had written a book about how to cast out demons.[3] She and Peter had been missionaries in Bolivia, South America, where they had dealt with demons and spirits. God had led them into a Spirit-filled ministry, and they had been in situations of praying for people possessed by demons. I told Doris what I had done, what I had prayed, and how I had reacted. I remember her laughing—not at me, but at the situation. Doris understood. She had been through that same experience.

I told her about asking the demon's name.

"Don't talk to the demon, and don't let him speak to you," she instructed. While Jesus did converse with demons on some occasions, He generally did not allow the evil spirits to speak (see Mark 1:34). "Make the demon obey you; it's the first step to casting him out," Doris advised.

At this point, I had to learn the difference between what the Scripture *describes* and what it *prescribes*. The Bible *describes* many things that happen, but just because the Bible tells an actual story does not mean we are to do the same thing. When Jesus asked the demon his name, that story *describes* what happened, so we know— but in this case, we are not meant to follow Jesus' example.

I followed Doris's instructions, fasting to prepare for a second meeting with the young man and a second conflict with the demon. Since this exorcism took place more than 20 years ago, I don't remember whether I fasted for one day or three days. But I did fast.

I met the young man again approximately two weeks later. Almost the identical things took place the second time. Again I put my hands on his head and prayed, "In the name of Jesus and the power of the blood of Jesus Christ . . . come out of him."

The young man again went through a paroxysm and fell to the floor. A second time, his eyes rolled back as though he were having a seizure, and green slime began to trickle out of his mouth.

I kept my hands on his head, praying in the name of Jesus Christ and by the blood of Jesus Christ for the demon to come out of him.

After 10 minutes of praying, I felt that nothing was happening. It seemed to be futile. When I stopped praying over him, his eyes opened, and again we got up and cleaned up the green slime.

With the young man present, I phoned Doris Wagner long-distance and again described the attempted exorcism. Over the phone, Doris and the young man agreed to meet, approximately three weeks later, in her husband's office at Fuller Theological Seminary in California. They were to meet at 2:00 PM on the day after Thanksgiving.

The young man bought a $100 commercial bus ticket that gave him free travel anywhere in the United States for 30 days, and he headed west. He arrived at the Pasadena bus depot at approximately 1:45 PM on Friday afternoon. It was only a short walk to Peter's office, and at exactly 2:00, he walked in to meet the prayer intercessors.

There were six ladies and one man, in addition to Doris. They prayed over the young man for more than two hours; in a later conversation with Doris, I learned that there had been as many as seven demons inside of him. Even though he had been raised in a Christian home in Jamaica, West Indies, the demons had come into him when he was a young man and had taken over part of his life. Doris testified, "That was one of the hardest exorcisms that I had ever gone through, but it was wonderful to know that God can deliver the demons, and can restore a young man for Christian service."

## Some Questions and Answers About Demons

*What is demon possession?* The word "possession" means that an evil spirit or demon inhabits or takes control of the body and soul of a person, in order to influence the person to carry out the evil purposes of the demon. Sometimes the purpose of the demon seems to be good or along humanitarian efforts, as we can never know the full evil intent of the demon. Sometimes the demon's purpose is outright evil, self-destructive and violent. At other times, the demon brings great mental and physical suffering to the one he possesses.

The word "possession" means that an evil spirit or demon inhabits or takes control of the body and soul of a person, in order to influence the person to carry out the evil purposes of the demon.

### Should We Use the Phrase "Demon Possession"?

Technically the phrase "demon possession" is not found in the original Greek language of the New Testament. The phrase is used in the *New King James Version*, specifically in Mark 5:16: "Those who saw it told them how it happened to him who had been demon-possessed." It would be more accurate to say that a person is *demonized* by the demon. That is, he or she is terrorized, manipulated or controlled by a demon. As a result of the English use of the term "possession," there has been some misconception.

To be technically correct, we should use the word "demonized." I have used the phrase "demon possession" in this chapter because it is commonly used and understood by most people.

### How Is a Person Demonized?

Demon possession occurs when God allows a demon to gain control of a person's mind and body. But demon possession only occurs when a person volitionally rejects God or chooses to give himself to a demon and his master.

Demon possession is the opposite of the filling of the Spirit. How can a person be filled with the Holy Spirit? He comes to know the Word of God and what the Holy Spirit can do in his life, and he brings his life into conformity to the Word of God, getting rid of all sin and any attitude that would block the work of the Holy Spirit through him. At the crux of the filling of the Spirit, the person *yields* and prays for the Holy Spirit to enter his life and take control.

The opposite action takes place when a person is demonized. A demonized person learns about Satan and his demons. The person makes a choice to give himself to the demon to satisfy his sinful desires. The person begins to seek evil things, takes on evil attitudes, and eventually gives himself or herself over to evil. The person in essence rejects God. Then in the act of *yielding*, the person gives his life and body over to the demon to take control.

In both demonization and filling of the Spirit, there is partial control. This means that the more you yield your life to the Holy Spirit, the more He can use you. More of the Holy Spirit's influence can flow through your life. The same is true with the demonized person: The more he yields to the demon, the more the demon controls his life and works an evil purpose through him.

I sometimes explain that if you only yield 10 or 20 percent of your life to God, He will only use that much of your life. If you yield 80 or 90 percent of your life to God, He can use you greatly. Henry Varley, a British evangelist, told Dwight L. Moody more than 100 years ago, "The world has yet to see what God can do with and for and through a man who is fully and wholly consecrated to Him."[4] Moody shook America and Britain with the gospel because he sought to be completely yielded to God.

Similarly, the amount a person yields to demons determines how much he can do for evil. The more a person yields to demonization, the more satanic, miraculous things he can accomplish. Remember, there are satanic miracles and there is satanic power.

### Can a Demon "Possess" a Believer?

Part of the problem with this concept goes back to the phrase itself, "demon possession." The term suggests a demon actually lives in a believer—and that believer belongs to the demon. The question is easier to resolve when we use the verb "demonize."

A demon can influence or harass a Christian. A demon can even do his work through a Christian. But the demon cannot possess what God possesses. Two spirits cannot live in the same body (see Jas 3:9-18). Because the Holy Spirit indwells a true Christian, he or she cannot be possessed by demons. The believer is sealed with the Holy Spirit (see Eph. 4:30) and is held in protective custody until the believer arrives in heaven. However, there are people who call themselves Christians, but have never allowed the Holy Spirit to possess and control their lives. These people can be demonized.

Demons can influence or harass a Christian and even do their work through a Christian. But they cannot possess what God possesses.

Believers are not immune to the external attacks of demons. Paul reported, "Wherefore we would have come unto you, even I Paul, once and again; but Satan hindered us" (1 Thess. 2:18, KJV). On this occasion of Paul attempting to go to Thessalonica, the devil controlled the circumstances so that Paul was not able to journey there. Whereas demon possession or demonization implies internal control, demons can also work through external influence and/or harassment, so believers need to guard against these things.

## How Do Demons Get to People?

The way demons influence people is often complex and sometimes difficult to understand.

One time I was at a church in Rio de Janeiro, Brazil, and I heard a group of people praying over a demon-possessed person in the back of the auditorium. In Portuguese, they were yelling out commands at the demon, and several of the people were praying at the same time. I did not want to go back and join the crowd, because I wrongly thought that if the demon came out of the person, seeking a home, the demon could jump into me. The problem with that approach is that demons do not enter a person who does not voluntarily yield to the demon or to temptation.

John Nevius, a Christian missionary in China more than a hundred years ago, described the state of being demonized:

> The supposed demoniac at the time of "possession" passes into abnormal state, the character of which varies indefinitely, being marked by depression and melancholy; or vacancy and stupidity amounting sometimes almost to idiocy, or it may be that he becomes ecstatic, or ferocious and malignant.
>
> During transition from the normal to the abnormal state, the subject is often thrown into paroxysms, more or less violent, during which he sometimes falls on the ground senseless, or foams at the mouth, presenting symptoms similar to those of epilepsy or hysteria.
>
> The intervals between these attacks vary indefinitely from hours to months, and during these intervals the physical and mental condition of the subject may be in every respect healthy and normal. The duration of the abnormal states varies from a few minutes to several days.

The attacks are sometimes mild, and sometimes violent. If frequent and violent the physical health suffers.

During the transition period the subject often retains more or less of his normal consciousness. The violence of the paroxysms is increased if the subject struggles against, and endeavors to repress the abnormal symptoms. When he yields himself to them the violence of the paroxysms abates, or ceases altogether.

When normal consciousness is restored after one of these attacks, the subject is entirely ignorant of everything which has passed during that state.

The most striking characteristic of these cases is that the subject evidences another personality, and the normal personality, for the time being, is partially or wholly dormant.

The new personality presents traits of character utterly different from those which really belong to the subject in his normal state, and this change of character is with rare exceptions in the direction of moral obliquity and impurity.

A differentiating mark of *demonomania*, intimately connected with the assumption of the new personality is that with the change of personality there is a complete change of moral character.

Many persons while "demon-possessed" give evidence of knowledge which cannot be accounted for in ordinary ways. They often appear to know of the Lord Jesus Christ as a Divine Person, and show an aversion to, and fear of, Him. They sometimes converse in foreign languages of which, in their normal states, they are entirely ignorant.

There are often heard, in connection with "demon-possessions," rappings and noises in places where no physical cause for them can be found; and tables, chairs, crockery, and the like are moved about without, so far as can be discovered, any application of physical force, exactly as we are told is the case among spiritualists.[5]

**What Are the Stages of Demonization?**
In the initial stage of demon influence, the person is *obsessed* with the demon, or they are overly *obsessed* with sin and temptation.

In the second stage, called *possession*, the person stops resisting the demon or temptation or sin. At this point, the person involuntarily gives himself to do the purpose of evil.

In the third stage, *subjection*, the person may continue to remain healthy and normal for the most part, but he is in subjection to the demon. When paroxysm occurs, he passes into an abnormal or subnormal state.

In the fourth stage, *voluntary obedience*, the person is trained in the way of evil. He or she becomes accustomed to doing the work of the demon and becomes its voluntary slave. These people may be called soothsayers, necromancers or sorcerers. In the case of women, they are called "w-po" or witches.

## Steps for Casting Out Demons

What are the steps involved in liberating a person from demons? The following is a description of the actions and attitudes required to be victorious in this type of spiritual warfare:

> First, casting out demons is not something the exorcist does by his power; it is in the power of God. He must begin by recognizing the blood of Jesus Christ that cleanses from sin and is the only basis for helping anyone spiritually. The exorcist must be sure he has confessed all sin and is in fellowship with Christ.
>
> Second, there must be a choice by the patient (the demonized person) that he wants to be rid of the demon.
>
> Third, during the exorcism there must be an exposure of the demon as a demon. Most demon possession is hidden and observers do not perceive the person as demonized.
>
> In the fourth place, the person has to decide whether he is going to follow God and be free of the demon, or if he is going to yield to the demon and remain in his possessed state. Just as God does not heal those who do not

want to be healed, God will not cast out the demon for those who do not want the demon cast out.

Fifth, the role of the exorcist is to share faith, strength, and wisdom with the person who needs help. The role of the exorcist is to witness what God can do in building up the faith of the person who is demon possessed. Then the demonized person can make a decision.

Sixth, ultimate exorcism is not in the power of the person who is helping, nor is it in the power of the patient; but in the power of God who wrestles directly with Satan. The demon is cast out by the blood of Jesus Christ.

Seventh, it is by faith that a person is free from the demon.[6]

# Your Notes

# 12

# Rising Above Fear and Gaining a Healthy Reverence

I was scared both the first and second times I fasted, but for different reasons. The first time I fasted, I was afraid for my reputation. If I fainted because I didn't eat, what would people think? I was afraid I couldn't make it through. The second time I fasted, God showed me the miracle of His answer, and that terrified me. The hair stood up on the back of my neck, and I shivered all over, because I could have messed up what God had intended.

The first time I remember fasting in a legitimate way was in the fall of 1971. Liberty University was in its first year. Classes were convening in the facilities of Thomas Road Baptist Church; the new college was constantly broke. As a matter of fact, for the first year, Liberty didn't own one piece of furniture. Its financial sheets showed zero net worth.

Liberty operated under what is called "shared services." Every asset of Thomas Road Baptist Church was shared with the University. It was like a mother giving birth to a child. The mother gives everything for the life, health and prosperity of her child. That's the way the people of Thomas Road felt about the new college.

But the church wasn't that rich, and we usually spent more than we took in. That meant the college had to do the best it could with meager funds. At that point, Thomas Road Church had never brought in a million dollars in one year. Believing that we should reach that level, Jerry Falwell called a weekend fast to raise one million dollars.

"Jerry, we don't need a million dollars," I rationalized.

I showed him our budget for the first year, which called for $152,000 to $158,000 in revenues and expenses. I reminded him, "I am very frugal with money. I can finish this year in the black, and spend less than we budgeted."

Falwell corrected me: "Elmer, you'll see the day when a million dollars is not enough to keep this college going."

I'm not sure I believed him then, because I didn't have the vision to see what would happen. In 2012, it takes almost $2 million a day to keep Liberty University operating. But we needed Falwell's foresight as a steppingstone to get where we are today.

When the fast was called, a million dollars was a farther reach than any of us had ever attempted. I wanted a million dollars, and I prayed diligently for it. But at the same time, I didn't have the faith to believe we would get that much. There is a big difference between desiring money and having the confidence that God will send it.

Besides that, I had never fasted—at least, not seriously and properly. I was not sure I could go a whole day without eating. I remember my mother telling me to eat so I wouldn't get sick. I had this image of teaching class and throwing up in front of my students. Or worse than that, I would grow weak and faint. Such behavior would be embarrassing. I was supposed to be a spiritual leader.

I prayed, *Lord, help me get through this fast.*

I prayed that prayer a dozen times or more.

Falwell had called for a Yom Kippur fast. That meant we would not eat the meal on Sunday night, or breakfast on Monday, or lunch on Monday. We would wait until the sun went down on Monday before we ate again. We were to spend mealtime in prayer.

Since I was co-founder of the college and its academic leader, my integrity required that I fast. My walk with God demanded that I do it properly and not cheat.

For 24 hours, I fasted, and I kept praying, *Lord, help me make it through.*

When Monday night came, I was amazed: I had made it. The only accomplishment of my first planned fast was that I made it through. I didn't accomplish anything spiritually, but I learned a lesson: I could do it! As a matter of fact, it was easy and I had no physical repercussions.

Once I had successfully fasted, it was much easier to do it again. Approximately six months later, I decided to fast for a personal problem. I still owned a house in greater Chicago, where I had lived before Falwell asked me to join him in Lynchburg. The monthly payment was $420, due on the fifteenth. I also had a payment for almost the same amount due on the first day of each month for my new home. I found myself stretched between the first and fifteenth of each month.

"Ruth," I said to my wife, "let's fast on the fifteenth day of the month to ask God to sell our house in Chicago."

We both spent the fifteenth day of the month not eating, but spending our meal times in prayer for God to sell the house. The day passed, and nothing happened. There was no answer to our prayer. I forgot about fasting until the next month, when I was preparing the $420 payment check. Ruth and I again fasted on the fifteenth day of the second month. Still nothing happened.

Each month for the next four months, we fasted, and nothing happened. The real estate market in Chicago was down.

At about this time, my realtor, who is a Christian, asked me to pray because he had a possible buyer for our house. I didn't tell him that Ruth and I had been fasting, but I assured him we would pray. Our house sold approximately a year after our first fast. I went to the closing in greater Chicago. We got the price we asked, and I sat in the lawyer's office, ready to sign the papers.

The buyer, whom I had not previously met, mentioned casually, "I started looking at your house a year ago, and kept looking at other houses, but something drew me back to your house." I really wasn't paying attention to what he said. "I looked at your house on my wife's birthday," he added.

For some reason I replied, "And when was that?"

He told me it was on the sixteenth day of the month Ruth and I had first fasted and prayed. My mental response system panicked. My mind went black. I didn't know how to respond to him, but instantly I knew God had worked a miracle, and He was showing me what He had done. Inwardly I thought, *That's one day after we fasted the first time.*

My mouth went dry. I didn't think this man was saved, so I was not sure he would have understood about prayer and fasting. I began to shake uncontrollably with fear—the kind of fear you feel after your car skids down a mountain on an icy road: You're safe, you didn't hit anything, but you tremble after it's all over.

I thought, *What if Ruth and I hadn't fasted? What if we had missed God's miracle?* I couldn't talk with anyone in the room until I regained my composure. After I signed the papers, I rejoiced.

## Principles for Dealing with Fear When Fasting

Three things will help you through fear when fasting. First, when you start fasting and praying, don't give up if you don't get the answer immediately. Be faithful to your vow, continuing to fast until the end. Jesus said, "This kind does not go out except by prayer and fasting" (Matt. 17:21). The original language indicates that fasting is a continuous action. When you make a vow to fast, keep fasting until you come to the end of your time-vow.

Second, if you have prayed and not received an answer, it may be time to fast. Fasting takes your request to a higher level. The sacrifice of food gets the attention of God. But it's not your sacrifice that gets you an answer; it's your faith. As I have already noted, fasting demonstrates the sincerity of your faith.

Third, I learned that it's important to fast with someone if at all possible. When you fast together, you become accountable to each other. Again, I note the Scripture: "If two of you agree on earth concerning anything that they ask, it will be done for them by My Father in heaven" (Matt. 18:19).

Fear of the Lord should be a natural reaction to God at all times. Throughout Scripture we are told to "fear the Lord." This was not only fright, but also included a negative apprehension—a sense of being scared. Jesus offered this comparison: "Do not fear those who kill the body . . . but rather fear Him who is able to destroy both soul and body in hell" (Matt. 10:28).

Because God has authority over our souls, we should fear His judgment. The writer of Hebrews puts it this way: "Therefore, since we are receiving a kingdom which cannot be shaken, let us have grace, by which we may serve God acceptably with reverence and godly fear. For our God is a consuming fire" (Heb. 12:28-29).

Balance fear with intimacy. Yes, we should fear God, but also remember that He is a loving Father, and we are His sons and daughters. We cry to Him, "Father, my intimate Daddy" (Rom. 8:15, *ELT*). We come to God with that intimacy because we are "children, then heirs—heirs of God and joint heirs with Christ" (Rom. 8:17).

## Wrap Up

Our fear can come from a feeling of divine reverence when we see the holiness of God, or it can come from a sense of danger of being punished by God, or a sense of danger from people or circumstances. Unhealthy fear makes us hide our sins, or act deceitfully. It may be because we stand condemned before God (see John 3:18). Healthy fear is respect, because "the fear of the LORD is the beginning of knowledge" (Prov. 1:7) and "the beginning of wisdom" (Prov. 9:10).

## Your Notes

# 13

# Prevailing Over Pain and Healing Sickness

On Friday, October 3, 2008, as I finished shaving, I used a Q-tip to clean some wax out of my ears. When I inserted the swab, suddenly my right ear went deaf. I could barely distinguish any sound.

My first reaction was that I had inserted the Q-tip too far into the canal and damaged my eardrum. I was scared. Had I injured myself?

I prayed for God to restore my hearing. It was the type of prayer I prayed whenever I had a physical ailment. Going to God was always my first reaction. I would seek Him for immediate healing. But prayer for my ear didn't make any difference.

I squirted some hot water into my ear, but nothing happened. I asked myself, *What is God trying to tell me?*

Then I decided to pray boldly. Just as I had laid hands on other people to pray for their healing, I laid my hands on my right ear and prayed for God to restore my hearing.

Nothing happened.

My greatest fear was related to preaching and teaching. If I couldn't hear well, eventually it would affect my pronunciation and enunciation.

My wife used a commercial product to remove earwax, and I decided to give it a try. When she inserted the solution, I could feel gurgling down in my ear, but didn't know what was happening. When I turned my head to drain the solution out of my ear canal, it seemed as though the solution didn't help—in fact, it hurt and further diminished my hearing. So I decided not to try any more home remedies.

The loss of hearing continued through the weekend. It was like when I used to swim in the ocean or a pool, and my ears would become plugged up with water. I heard people talking, but it sounded as though they were talking through a pipe or cylinder. Monday was my usual time of fasting, so I prayed, "God, restore hearing in my right ear." Nothing happened!

The following week, I asked my early Sunday morning prayer group to pray for a miracle in my right ear. Paul Johnson, an insurance salesman, said to me, "I have the same problem all the time. I get wax in my ear, and I go see Dr. Hengerer, an otolaryngologist. When prayer is not enough, go see a doctor."

The next day, I made an appointment—and that afternoon, I waited my turn to see Dr. Hengerer.

He looked at my ear with an otoscope and said, "Hum." His "hum" scared me. I had no idea what it meant. For some reason, I believed the worst. We went into the next room, where I lay down on the examining table. With a small instrument, he reached into my right ear and pulled out the biggest, ugliest blob of yellow earwax I had ever seen. He held it up for me to see and again said, "Hum."

He said, "Hum," but I wanted to say, "Hallelujah!" Instantly my hearing returned. In fact, it was never gone; it was just blocked with earwax. It seems the Q-tip I used plugged the hearing channel. The warm water solution softened the earwax and completely covered the eardrum, like a coat of paint.

God answered my prayer for the restoration of hearing in my right ear, but not by way of a miracle. God, through providence, used the human instrument of Dr. Hengerer to remove the wax from my ear. Sometimes God heals supernaturally without human help; other times, He heals through human instrumentality, using a doctor to diagnose, prescribe and apply a medical remedy to bring about healing.

## Healing Trigeminal Neuralgia

In June of that same year, my wife was having dental work done when she developed a deep, inner pain within the right side of her jaw. She and the dentist were convinced it was an abscessed tooth, but there was really another undiscovered problem. The dentist removed one tooth, and then another, but the pain persisted.

The pain became sharp and piercing. The throb spread out like an electrical shock over her entire jaw. She said that it felt like being burned, stung by an insect, or stuck with a needle. The pain extended through the entire jaw and into the back of her head.

We changed dentists, but the second dentist couldn't help relieve her pain. He recommended a third practitioner, who was just out of dental school and understood the latest pathology. But he couldn't help either.

For the first time in my life, I saw pain cause my wife to cry real tears. Her dentist prescribed an analgesic that was supposed to help, but it did not work.

She made an appointment to see an oral surgeon. But the pain went away that week, so Ruth traveled with me to New York, where I was to speak at the inauguration of the new president of Davis College in Binghamton, New York. I was scheduled to speak to the pastors, and Ruth was to speak to their wives.

We had agreed that if her pain persisted, she would drop out of the commitment. But God intervened in a wonderful way. The pain went away. She made the trip with me and was able to speak to the pastors' wives on five occasions over two days. The pain didn't give her any difficulty.

While we were there, Dan Rathmell, the executive assistant to the college president, took us out to eat at a lovely village inn outside the city. When Ruth told him about the pain she was having, he said, "I know exactly what it is; it's the same thing that my mother had. You have trigeminal neuralgia or TMJ." We had never heard of that.

Dan described how his mother suffered for almost three years before she went to the Syracuse University Hospital to see a specialist, who used a gamma knife to reduce the pain.

When Ruth and I got home, I turned to the Internet, searching for "trigeminal neuralgia" and the "gamma knife." I discovered that the co-inventor of the gamma knife was Dr. Ladislau Steiner, Professor of Neurosurgery and Radiology at the University of Virginia Medical School in Charlottesville, Virginia. He was the world's leading authority in neurosurgery and radiology, and he was located only 60 miles from our home.

I called for an appointment, but Dr. Steiner's receptionist informed me that he would only see Ruth if a physician referred her to him, and that the referral should include a complete medical exam by her family doctor. The receptionist told me, "Dr. Steiner is in Europe, and he returns next Sunday evening, but he'll call you Monday morning." I thought the timing was rather questionable, and I really didn't expect a phone call. However, Monday morning at 8:00 AM came, and Dr. Steiner called.

I described Ruth's condition to him. He asked several questions, and then he talked at length with her. When I got back on the phone, he said he wanted us to come to his office that morning.

Dr. Steiner examined Ruth, confirmed that she had TMJ, and scheduled an operation for that week. He explained that if we could not come at that time, we would have to wait two or three months for another opening in his schedule.

The operation was a complete success. The gamma knife doesn't break the skin or make an incision, but rather with the use of a laser beam it detaches the nerve that is connected to the brain stem. Thus the nerve endings in the face can no longer send a message of pain into the brain.

It was almost as though the doctor were a prophet. He said the pain would go away in 90 days. For almost 90 days, the pain persisted. Then, almost exactly 90 days after the procedure, it vanished.

So what happened? We were praying, fasting, and asking God for a solution to Ruth's predicament. She hadn't been able to function in a normal way. God in His providence sent us to New York, where we met someone who told us about TMJ. Then I phoned and talked to the receptionist, who said Dr. Steiner would phone us. When you wait on medical personnel to phone you back, it's usually several days or more, but Dr. Steiner called us almost immediately upon arriving at his office from Austria. Then within three days, the surgery was done. God worked providentially, giving us the number one authority in the world on TMJ. So God, who knows all things, put all the details together for the healing of my wife (see Rom. 8:28).

## Praying for Healing

Paul asked, "Do all have gifts of healing?" (1 Cor. 12:30). The question seems to suggest that not everyone has the gift of healing. Realize that there is a difference between the gift of healing and prayer for healing. While I agree that not everyone has the gift of healing, I believe that every Christian can pray for healing—and God will supernaturally hear, answer and heal. *Not faith healers only, but all Christians can pray for healing.*

We see in the book of Acts that some heal through the gift of healing. "The apostles were performing many miraculous signs and wonders among the people" (Acts 5:12, *NLT*). Later in that chapter, we read: "Crowds came in from the villages around Jerusalem, bringing their sick and those possessed by evil spirits, and they were all healed" (v. 16, *NLT*).

Some say only the apostles and their contemporaries could use the gift of healing, but that is not altogether true. Saint Augustine, who lived 400 years after Jesus, at one time said that the gift of healing had passed away. But then a person in his church was healed from epileptic fits, and Augustine modified his opinion, adding a new section on healing to his book *The City of God*.[1] Augustine's reversal may not have been complete, but he did seem to say that the power of prayer for healing was still valid, and that all can pray for God to heal. I agree with Augustine that God still heals today, and that He does it in answer to prayer.

However, I'm not sure about some of the "faith healers" who have magnified healing and are known for their long "healing lines." The problem is that some "faith healers" believe it is their gift of healing or power that heals. I believe that "faith healers" can still heal, but that the healing is an answer to prayer, not a result of any power or gift they have resident within them. Therefore, let's not over-emphasize "faith healing"—or under-emphasize it. Let's keep healing in its biblical place—because to believe in God is to believe in healing.

If you refuse to believe in physical healing, you give the body secondary importance, saying God works in the human spirit (the immaterial man) but not in the human body (the physical man). That's a false dichotomy. As Christians, we believe the presence of Jesus Christ lives within our bodies and shines through us to show the glory of God—in other words, we are living temples (see 1 Cor. 6:19). Our bodies are important.

Because God loves us, He cares as much about our physical lives as He does our spiritual lives. He cares about what we eat, how we dress and how we glorify Him with our physical selves. We have to discipline our bodies. But in the same way, God wants us to discipline our spiritual selves so that we give glory to Him in all that we do.

Remember that God saved us in our entirety—both body and soul. It's not just our souls that will live forever. Our bodies will, too. They will be resurrected and joined with our souls at the rapture to live with Jesus Christ forever (see John 14:1-3). Therefore, we should expect healing in our emotions, in our minds, in our spirits, and also in our bodies.

> Remember that God saved us in our entirety—both body and soul. It's not just our souls that will live forever.

## Use of Doctors and Medicine

Let's look at how our bodies get healthy. Then we can better understand how to pray for someone to return to health when they're sick. God has many ways of making us healthy. As an example, we learn how healthy appetites give us a strong body, and we also learn that certain foods or poisons will harm the body. In addition, we learn that excessive fats, sweets, and other "delicacies" can harm the body. So we come to understand that what we eat can make us healthy, or it can destroy our health.

Then God gives us doctors. James teaches us, "Every good gift and every perfect gift is from above" (Jas. 1:17). Among the many gifts given to human beings to use are the gifts of medicine and proper care by a physician. Medical doctors do many things to keep us healthy: They cut away cancers so that we can heal; they prescribe antibiotics to fight disease; and they advise us about physical routines, rest, recreation, and a variety of other topics to keep us healthy. The purpose of the medical profession is not just to treat diseases and take away pain, but also to contribute to our health.

However, it is not the doctors that make us healthy; it is God who gives us a physical body—and in the final analysis, *the body heals itself.* The doctor takes away the cause of disease or pain, and eventually, all other things being equal, our bodies heal themselves.

Obviously, God can heal apart from any medicine, but most of the time, God chooses to heal through medicine, or food intake, or the other medical contributions within the world in which we live. So how should we pray? These are four steps to pray for healing:

1. We should pray that the doctor has wisdom to properly *diagnose* our problems.

2. We should then pray for wisdom for the doctor to *prescribe* the proper medicine or antidote for our problem.

3. We must pray for that medicine to be *effective* in its intended cure.

4. On top of all that, we should pray for God to *protect* us from any infection, virus, or contagious or communicable disease that would be detrimental to our health.

There are times when we may need to pray for God to reveal to us unknown factors that cause illness. I was gripped by the story of a fellow professor at Trinity Evangelical Divinity School in the 1960s. This professor was taken severely ill and rushed to the emergency room. A number of tests were administered, but the medical staff couldn't find the cause of the problem. He went home and recovered. Two months later, the same illness struck the professor, and this time his wife had symptoms as well. Again, they went to the hospital, and a different set of tests couldn't find the source of the problem. When they returned home, they seemed to get better and overcame their problem. No one could associate a cause with their life-threatening pathology.

When some time later the whole family came down with the same symptoms, they stopped praying for healing and prayed for God to help them discover the unseen cause. Shortly after that, they discovered that their illness was related to a beautiful set of china cups they had bought on the mission field. The cups had not been thoroughly fired in a kiln to seal in the ceramic finish, and when the family added hot tea, the melted lead paint got into their systems and caused the serious health issues they had been experiencing. Prayer can help find the culprit for our physical problems.

## Faith for God's Healing

Let's not go to either extreme as we pray for healing. Some rely only on prayer and refuse any medical attention whatsoever. The other extreme is relying only on medical technology and refusing to pray and ask God to do the miraculous. Here's my advice to those who fall into this second category.

### Analyze Your Own Lack of Faith

It can be especially difficult to pray when people have severe physical problems, e.g., an advanced stage of cancer. It's hard to know how to pray for them. Perhaps the person is dealing with a long-term disability, or has a disease that medical science has said is incurable. No matter what the issue, always search your heart for the cancer of unbelief. Deal with your own lack of faith before you begin to ask God for a miracle. Remember the father who had a demon-possessed epileptic boy. This father came to Jesus and said, "Lord, I believe; help my unbelief!" (Mark 9:24). We must have faith for healing before we ask God to heal ourselves or anyone else. The father recognized his own unbelief; that's a good place to start.

### Pray for God's Will in All Things

I begin every morning by praying, "Your will be done" (Matt. 6:10); because I want God's will in everything I do, I pray that His will be done in my life every day.

Remember, it's not God's will to heal everyone. Even Jesus didn't heal everyone who came to Him. When He went to the pool of Bethesda, Jesus saw "a great multitude of sick people, blind, lame, paralyzed, waiting for the moving of the water" (John 5:3). But Jesus healed only one man who had been lame for 38 years (see vv. 5-9). When Jesus picked out one to heal, He overlooked the multitude; He picked out a man whose condition was severe and who seemed unlikely to be healed any other way.

On some occasions, Jesus cured everyone who came to Him for healing (see Matt. 12:15). Other times, the Bible doesn't report that Jesus healed "all" but that He healed "many." For instance, "At evening, when the sun had set, they brought to Him all who were sick. . . . Then He healed many who were sick with various diseases" (Mark 1:32-34). Note that of all the sick who were brought to Him, He didn't heal everyone; He only healed many.

There's an important difference between Jesus and us. Jesus healed everyone for whom He prayed, but He didn't pray for everyone who needed healing. Not being Jesus, we must understand that not everyone for whom we pray will be healed. It may be God's will for that person to be sick (see 2 Tim. 4:20). Remember that God didn't heal Paul's thorn in the flesh, but taught him many lessons through pain (see 2 Cor. 12:9).

## Steps to Pray for Healing

The most extensive biblical passage on healing is found in James 5:13-18. Note the following principles and follow them when praying for a miracle.

### 1. Pray When Suffering

James begins this passage by asking, "Are any among you suffering?" (Jas. 5:13, *NLT*). With this rhetorical question, James recognizes the frailty of human flesh.

Obviously, every person at some time has some suffering in his or her body. So, what does James advise suffering people to do? He tells them to do more than pray one time. He says, "They should keep on praying about it" (Jas. 5:13, *NLT*). The word for prayer here is *proseuchomai*, and it communicates the idea of constantly being in face-to-face relationship to God (*pros* = toward; *euchomai* = the face; therefore, *proseuchomai* = praying in a face-to-face relationship with God).

Note that the first step to healing is for the sick person to pray for himself. The sick person should not begin by calling on a pastor or anyone else to intercede for him; rather, he should take responsibility by praying for himself.

### 2. Call the Elders of the Church

"Let him call for the elders of the church, and let them pray over him" (Jas. 5:14). This is a very specific instruction. I think it means the person's pastor and/or church leadership should be called to pray for him.

Note that there is no mention of a visiting "faith healer," or even other pastors from other churches, or preachers in television or radio ministry who may have the ability to pray. Why? This step assumes a spiritual relationship between the sick person and those who come to pray for him. If the sick person has obvious sins, has issues with others in the church, is drifting toward the world, or has any other problem, the elders should know about it because they are praying about all the people under their watchful care.

God seems to tie physical healing to the prayers of church leaders. Maybe some who pray for physical healing don't get it because they leave out prayers by their local church and its leadership.

Isn't the very act of "calling" a statement of faith? So the word of faith that moves mountains (see Mark 11:22-24) begins when the sick call for elders to pray for their healing.

### 3. Examine Any Connection Between Sickness and Sin

James ties these two things together with this promise: "If his sickness was caused by some sin, the Lord will forgive him" (Jas. 5:15, *ELT*). Of course the promise to forgive sin comes before the physical result: "that you may be healed" (Jas. 5:16). Perhaps confession of sin and repentance are the conditions for God to "raise him up" (Jas. 5:15).

One of the reasons the church leaders should be called is that they may be aware of any "sin-problem" in the sick person's life. Also, they would be able to deal with spiritual restoration and then pray for physical healing. Perhaps many sick people's prayers are not answered because they have been reluctant to deal with sin in their lives.

### 4. The Sick Person Must Confess and Repent of Sins

Notice what James said: "Confess your trespasses to one another, and pray for one another, that you may be healed" (Jas. 5:16). What exactly does this mean? A sick person must acknowledge his sin, even if it's just neglecting the spiritual disciplines of walking with God. He must acknowledge his trespasses, confess them (see 1 John 1:9), and repent from them to get on praying ground. Then God is able to answer and heal the person.

### 5. The Person's Sickness May Be a Judgment of God

In the context of healing, James has written to the Church, "so that you will not sin and be condemned for it" (Jas. 5:12, *NLT*). Condemnation here is judgment by God. Could it be that the judgment on the person is their sickness? Could it be that their sin or their disobedience to the will of God has caused their illness or is the source of their sickness? Could their physical problem be God's continuing judgment?

As we saw above, we are to "confess [our] trespasses to one another, and pray for one another, that [we] may be healed" (Jas. 5:16). Why does James tie together the confession and forgiveness of sins and the healing of the body? Perhaps because the two cannot be taken apart.

### 6. The Sick Person Must Initiate Prayers

God honors a person's faith and desire to be healed. Therefore, if you are called to pray for a sick person, ask them, "Have you been praying for your healing?" You can also ask a second question: "Do you have faith to believe that God can heal you?" When you encourage faith in them, it may lead to God's healing.

When you encourage faith in a person, it may lead to God's healing.

### 7. Remember God's Timing in Sickness

Both sickness and healing are related to God's timing. God may allow a sickness to continue in a person's life, even after you pray, in order to accomplish a specific purpose. In another case, He may begin the work of healing before you pray. Perhaps a fever has already run its course, or maybe a virus or disease has been curbed. So when you begin to pray, remember that God is time-less, and that He "calls those things which do not exist as though they did" (Rom. 4:17). Long before you pray, God has been in-volved in the process, so recognize what He may be doing, and attempt to pray according to His will.

### 8. Lay Hands on the Person

Laying hands on sick persons is an important practice that's taught throughout the Bible. When you lay hands on people, you relate to them; you show them your care and physical concern, as well as a spiritual concern. In addition, when we lay hands on someone, our faith releases power for healing, even when we're not aware of what God is doing.

On many occasions, Jesus touched the sick when He healed them (see, for example Mark 6:5; 8:22-25). Paul did the same thing: "And it happened that the father of Publius lay sick of a fever and dysentery. Paul went in to him and prayed, and he laid his hands on him and healed him. So when this was done, the rest of those on the island who had diseases also came and were healed" (Acts 28:8-9).

However, just touching the person is not enough to heal him. God does not heal through the touch; He heals through the faith that is exercised by the prayer for the sick.

### 9. Anoint with Oil

Notice the instruction about "anointing him with oil in the name of the Lord" (Jas. 5:14). Can anyone anoint with oil? Or can only the elders anoint with oil? It is a reasonable question. Some say that the elders of the church must do the anointing with oil, because the Bible says, "Let him call for the elders of the church, and let them pray over him, anointing him with oil in the name of the Lord" (Jas. 5:14). Others say that any person who is a spiritual intercessor can anoint with oil, and God will use that anointing for healing.

For many years, my church practiced healing services on Sunday evenings. We would meet at 5:45 PM, 15 minutes before the evening service started at 6:00. The pastor would invite people: "If you want to have prayer for healing, come early tonight and be a part of our anointing service."

Because I had close friendships with many Pentecostals, and they are known to anoint with oil, my pastor always asked me to do the actual anointing of oil in our healing services. I don't think the one who anoints with oil has any more effectiveness in healing than others who are involved. It is probably the prayers of all the elders of the church that bring about the healing. But in my church, one person anoints for the many prayer-warriors who are present.

By contrast, I was in a South American church where I noticed that all the leaders of the church did two things. First, each of them anointed with oil, and then each of them prayed. Again, I don't think God recognizes one method over the other; He recognizes the faith of the people who pray.

When the public is involved in a healing service, I believe God blesses the unity of the many who join in prayer for the sick person. However, there have been occasions when a sick person was anointed with oil in private, and God has healed that person. Back in the late 1960s, I was Sunday School editor for *Christian Life* magazine (at that time the largest evangelical magazine in America). The editor, Bob Walker, had been a member of an independent Bible church, but had begun speaking in tongues when the Holy Spirit came upon him. He was sick in the hospital and called me to come see him and pray for him. It was a difficult trip for me, because it involved approximately one hour of travel through traffic in the city of Chicago, before there were tollways and expressways. I inwardly grumbled about going, but I went because he was the editor of the magazine and my friend.

When I walked into the room and saw the small bottle of oil on the night table next to his bed, I knew he was going to ask me to anoint him with oil. I had never done that before, and I was somewhat uncomfortable with the idea of using oil. I had never even seen it done, and I had certainly never been instructed in how to do it. I asked myself, *What will you do when he asks you to anoint him with oil?* Then I thought of the worst alternative: *What will happen if I refuse?* I remembered that anointing was done in the Bible. So I rationalized, *There's no reason not do it, right?*

Walker did ask me to anoint him with oil, and I agreed, praying for his healing as I anointed him.

Approximately a week later, I was in the office of *Christian Life* magazine, and Walker was there. He thanked me for praying for him and indicated that it was my prayer, more than any others, which had raised him up. I was reluctant to take any credit even though I had prayed in faith, asking God to heal him.

Then he instructed me, "Elmer, if I get sick again, don't doubt God's ability to heal." He continued, "Everyone who is healed in answer to prayer eventually will die. But just because we will all die, doesn't mean that God won't give temporary relief in healing." Then he went on to explain, "God is glorified in healing, and the work of God goes forward through healing."

# Wrap Up

If you believe that God can do anything He desires, then you believe in healing. There are some occasions when the servant of God must be healed to properly serve God. (Remember, we believe in and know the limited nature of being human; sickness, whether serious or minor, is inevitable for all of us.) When you believe in healing, you believe in the miraculous.

So when healing seems humanly impossible, fast to know God and learn His presence. Then you can also fast for a miraculous healing.

## Your Notes

# PART V

# Fasting for the
# Deepest Miracles

*Nothing of spiritual significance comes without sacrifice.*
JERRY FALWELL

# 14

# Seeking Divine Guidance

While an undergraduate at Liberty University, Daniel Henderson served as the student body president. When he later joined the pastoral staff at Liberty Baptist Theological Seminary, he coordinated pastoral training of undergraduates.

Because Liberty had a fasting lifestyle, as a student Daniel had fasted on several occasions. In fact, he had participated in some of the fasts mentioned in this book.

During the fall of 1981, he was faced with a challenge. His plans were to travel to the Pacific Northwest—specifically Seattle, Washington—in the spring of 1985 to plant a new church. Through aggressive outreach, Daniel had attracted a team of 13 others who wanted to go with him to help plant the church.

The Pacific Northwest seemed exciting, challenging and needy. As Daniel shared with the student body what God was calling him to do, others were attracted to his vision. This is the first law of leadership: "When followers buy into your vision, they buy into your leadership."

But Daniel did not have peace about going to the Northwest as a single man. So he joined a friend for a 21-day fast. The friend had an entirely different prayer goal, but Daniel was fasting about a wife.

Daniel had dated, but he did not have any sense of his life's mate. He was not sure that a single man should pastor a church, and as exciting as the goal of Seattle was to him, he had this inner quandary: "What shall I do?"

God answered in an unusual way. A friend asked Daniel to double-date with him on the weekend because his (the friend's) fiancée was coming to town.

"I am not dating," Dan told his friend, not wanting to explain that he was fasting. But the friend was persuasive, and he came back two more times to twist Daniel's arm to get a date for that weekend.

As Dan thought and prayed about whom he would invite to be his date, the only girl that interested him was Rosemary Brewer—a spiritual girl, daughter of a pastor, and attractive. Dan had seen Rosemary around campus, and his family knew her family.

Daniel put out a fleece, saying, "If I meet her in the next 24 hours, I will ask her out for a date." With this he put the burden on God. "If I don't see her, I won't ask her." Then he thought to himself, *The deal will be off about the double date.*

The next morning, when Daniel went to the administration building to drop off some paperwork, he found Rosemary standing in the hallway. Since he had asked God to open the door, and he had told God he would ask her for a date if he met her, he knew God was giving him this opportunity.

Daniel went up to ask Rosemary if she would be available to go on a double date on Saturday night. At the time, she had a date with another student scheduled for Friday night. She at first accepted Daniel's invitation, but later canceled the date. However, Rosemary's sister, April, said, "Oh no, you need to go out with Daniel . . ." and talked Rosemary into changing her mind again.

They went out to the Natural Bridge resort area, approximately 50 miles away from Lynchburg, Virginia. They planned on having a meal at a white-cloth restaurant, but Daniel ordered only broth, because he felt that was legal on his fast. It was a wonderful evening, and both Daniel and Rosemary enjoyed their time together.

They decided to go out again the following Monday, which was Labor Day. Dan said, "Let's go up to the Peaks of Otter, and I'll cook breakfast for you."

After breakfast was served, she realized he was not eating. He didn't want to be clandestine about it, so he told Rosemary that he was fasting, but didn't give her his reason at that time.

Over the next two weeks, they went out for several meals—and each time, Daniel did not eat because of his fast. By the end of the 21-day fast, he felt that God wanted him to marry Rosemary.

About two months after the fast was over, Daniel went to Huntington, West Virginia, to talk with Rosemary's father, Pastor Fred Brewer of Fellowship Baptist Church. He asked, "May I have the hand of Rosemary in marriage? We have fallen in love."

Fred didn't give an immediate answer. "Let me think about it a while," he said.

About a week later, Fred phoned Daniel long-distance to say, "Yes, you have my permission to marry my daughter." Daniel and Rosemary were engaged in late November, and they married the following June.

Daniel sees God's guidance in His providence. He notes, "I almost refused to go out on a double date with a friend, and so many things could have gone wrong before Rosemary and I went on that first date." When Daniel looks back on those days, "I think because I was surrendered to God's will, and trusted His providence, God sent a friend who insisted that we go out together. God arranged for me to run into Rosemary in the hallway—and from that moment on, God has directed our steps together."

## How to Pray for Divine Guidance

We all find ourselves, from time to time, faced with a big decision or otherwise in need of guidance from God. If we're not used to seeking His direction through prayer and fasting, getting started can be daunting. Following are several principles and suggestions for how to look to God and allow Him to guide our steps.

### 1. Pray Within the Will of God

Whether you are praying for a mate, or for a job, or about any other decision, always keep in mind that God has a plan for your life. Therefore, every day you should pray the Lord's Prayer, remembering to approach every decision with the petition: "Thy will be done" (Matt. 6:10, KJV).

God is able to move and guide a yielded person. So yielding to God is your first step when praying for God's guidance. Sailors say it is difficult to move a sailboat that is sitting dead in the water, with the sails folded away. However, when the wind is blowing, and the sails are up, it is easy to guide the ship smoothly under the power of the wind. In the same way, if you yield your life to the will of God, and you are attempting to do His will, it will be easier for God to guide you smoothly into His will.

Yielding to God is your first step when praying for God's guidance.

The will of God is found within the parameters of the Word of God. If you are praying for a wife, God will probably not tell you the name of woman; however, He is likely to give you some direction. According to Daniel, "Certainly I wanted a wife who was a believer, but more, I wanted a girl who was committed to do the will of God and serve Him full-time." Daniel went on to say, "There were many girls in school who fit those qualifications, but I wanted to go a step farther; I wanted a girl whose heart was compatible with me and my calling."

Daniel observed that Pastor Fred Brewer had raised his girls to think ministry. Rosemary grew up in a pastor's home, and all she ever wanted to do was marry a pastor.

### 2. When Checking Out Compatibility, Look at Future Goals

When two people have the same goals in life, it gives them freedom to take another step. However, it does not necessarily mean that they are compatible for marriage. You must look at personality, attitudes, and the way life is lived. Daniel said, "I wanted someone who was willing to follow my ministry path—which was quite radical, since I was going to plant a church."

### 3. God Gives Divine Guidance Through Prayer

Obviously, you cannot pray about all decisions. You live according to the dictates of the event and what the moment requires. But when you come to "life-turning" events and decisions, you must pray about those before they come to pass.

When my wife, then Ruth Forbes, was five years old, she accepted Christ in her Sunday School class. Shortly thereafter, as they were having evening prayers together, her mother asked her, "Ruth, what do you want to be when you grow up?"

"I want to marry a preacher..." young Ruth told her mother.

"Then we must begin praying every night for him—that God would prepare him and lead the two of you together."

So, all through grade school, junior high and high school, Ruth was praying for the man whom she would one day marry. She would pray:

*"Now I lay me down to sleep,*
*I pray the Lord my soul to keep.*
*If I should die before I wake,*
*I pray the Lord my soul to take."*

*God bless Mommy, Daddy, and David and . . . the man I'm going to marry. Make him cute and protect him. Amen.*

## 4. God Guides Through Circumstances

Daniel Henderson promised that if he met Rosemary Brewer in the next 24 hours, he would ask her out on a date. That's circumstances. Because they did meet within 24 hours, he felt God leading him in that direction. Sometimes God leads through an open door, as Paul explained: "For a great and effective door has opened to me" (1 Cor. 16:9). The will of God may be a new ministry opportunity, a new job, or any new challenge that provides a way for us to serve the Lord.

However, pray seriously before walking through an open door. Sometimes that door may have the "glitter of success," but would actually lead you away from the will of God. Families have moved when the husband was given a promotion, only to end up where there was no church influence for the children, and limited opportunities to serve God.

Realize that the devil can use an open door to pull you away from God, just as God can use an open door to draw you to Himself. How do you know the difference?

Usually when God opens a door, there is clear guidance and a deep sense of peace. Your inner confidence tells you that this is what God wants you to do. When Satan opens a door, there is generally confusion, fear of sin, and doubt. Remember, Satan is the father of doubts, and he does not want you to have confident faith in God.

## 5. Finding Guidance Through the Fleece

When a Christian places conditions on God, it's called "putting out the fleece." The expression originated with Gideon, who was praying to find the will of God. Gideon put out a fleece—the wool sheared from a young sheep before being woven into cloth—and told God, "If You will save Israel by my hand as You have said—look, I shall put a fleece of wool on the threshing floor; if there is dew on the fleece only, and it is dry on all the ground, then I shall know that You will save Israel by my hand, as You have said" (Judg. 6:36-37). God answered according to Gideon's conditions: The following morning, the fleece was wringing wet, but the ground around it was dry. Then Gideon had a second thought. Wool usually attracts dew. His fleece being wet could simply be the natural result of weather.

So Gideon prayed the opposite: "Do not be angry with me, but let me speak just once more: Let me test, I pray, just once more with the fleece; let it now be dry only on the fleece, but on all the ground let there be dew" (Judg. 6:39). Gideon prayed for supernatural results, and again God answered: The following morning the fleece was dry and the ground was wet.

Should we put out a fleece to determine the will of God? It's not something most Christians should do, and it is definitely not the only thing you should use to find God's will. The Christian must first look to God through His Word, then be yielded to God's will, and next, pray about the situation. When all of that is done, God might finally speak through a "fleece." But if a fleece is the only thing you use to determine God's guidance, be careful.

## 6. Finding God's Guidance Through Your Spiritual Giftedness

The Bible teaches that God has given to each Christian a "spiritual gift" which is an ability to serve God.[1] Peter declares, "As each one has received a gift, minister it to one another, as good stewards of the manifold grace of God" (1 Pet. 4:10). We learn two things from this verse: First, God has given gifts to everyone; and second, everyone should be ministering according to the gift that has been given to him. That is God's will.

Paul teaches the same truth: "But each one has his own gift from God, one in this manner and another in that" (1 Cor. 7:7). You have a spiritual gift from God, and it is God's will that you use your spiritual gift in ministry for His glory. For example, if you have the gift of teaching, you can use that gift in Sunday School, small group Bible studies, or any other place where you have an opportunity to teach a group or an individual.

Sometimes we don't have to go outside our own homes to use our gifts. As an illustration, every mother and father who has children has a responsibility to use their gift of teaching to guide their children in spiritual matters. God gives us an ability to match our responsibility.

Paul tells us that different people have different spiritual gifts: "Now there are diversities of gifts, but the same Spirit. And there are differences of administrations, but the same Lord" (1 Cor. 12:4-5, *KJV*). This means that God has given different gifts to different individuals, and also that people use their spiritual gifts in different ways.

People name various spiritual gifts differently, but here is the list of serving gifts I use:

| Prophecy | Giving |
|----------|--------|
| Helper | Administration |
| Teaching | Mercy Showing |
| Exhortation | Evangelism and Shepherding |

An important thing to remember about spiritual gifts is that even though many people have, for example, the gift of teaching, not everyone will get the same results with their teaching. Why is that? Because God manifests the gifts differently through different people. Paul describes it this way: "But the manifestation of the Spirit is given to every man to profit withal" (1 Cor. 12:7, *KJV*).

So, people use their spiritual gifts in different ways. One person may use his gift of teaching one-on-one. Another may teach large groups. Still another may have a pulpit ministry of teaching the Word of God every Sunday morning. "And there are diversities of activities, but it is the same God who works all in all" (1 Cor. 12:6).

You cannot ignore your spiritual giftedness—your abilities to serve God—and still find divine guidance for your life. God leads as we discover our abilities and use them for His glory.

## 7. Divine Guidance Is Confirmed by Yielding to God

Many years ago, I sat in chapel at Columbia Bible College as a young freshman searching for the will of God. A missionary speaker challenged us, saying, *"The thing that you don't want to do is God's will for you."* He mentioned people who had resisted going to the mission field, but found it was God's will when they surrendered to Him. He mentioned people who had resisted going into ministry, but surrendered to God and then found it was His will.

As I sat in chapel, I thought about the things I didn't want to do. Then I looked a few seats to my right and saw a girl I thought was loud, obnoxious, and not at all attractive. The point of that sermon popped: *The thing I don't want to do is God's will.* I followed this up with: *I don't want to marry that girl, so that must be God's will.*

For the next two weeks, I agonized in the presence of God over that girl. I resisted dating her, and I really . . . really . . . really didn't want to marry her. I tried to pray for her to become the type of girl I wanted, with the attitude and personality I wanted and even the looks I desired. I had two weeks of frustrating prayer.

At the end of those two weeks, a female missionary from South America spoke in chapel. She made a statement that was very simple, but suggested the opposite truth: "If you are yielded to God, the thing you desire to do is probably God's will." As I sat in chapel that day, suddenly the two truths merged.

When you are fighting God, the thing you don't want to do is probably God's will. When you are yielded to God, the thing you want to do may well be God's will.

I knew I was yielded to God; I had surrendered to Him and was willing to go anywhere and do anything. I looked inward and saw the young lady in a different light. We were not compatible—we didn't have the same value system, and she laughed about ministry. The book was closed! She was not the one for me.

I concluded that since I was surrendered to God, when I found the right girl, she would be the one I wanted to marry.

## 8. Your Motives Must Be Pure in Seeking God's Guidance

Jesus said, "The light of the body is the eye: if therefore thine eye be single, thy whole body shall be full of light" (Matt. 6:22, *KJV*). In this context, the word "single" means to focus in a specific direction. When you have purpose in life, and you want to glorify God with all that you do, you can find God's will. When self-interest gets mixed up with God's guidance, our eyes become blurry and we don't see the future clearly. God guides those who have a purpose in life, and whose purpose is committed to His will.

## 9. Establish Principles and Find God's Will by Following Them

Every Christian should develop a set of principles that guide every aspect of his life. These principles will give confidence to the one seeking divine guidance.

The way to find these principles is by saturating yourself with the Word of God. Those who know the Bible best—who understand God's principles—are those who have healthy, happy lives. A wise grandfather once observed, "A Bible that is falling apart usually belongs to someone who isn't." The following are a few principles that come out of Scripture:

- *The principle of Christian responsibility* (2 Cor. 6:14-18) tells us that we should not let unsaved companions make our decisions concerning life's purpose.

- *The principle of secrecy* (Matt. 6:6) tells us that the will of God is found in secret prayer as we seek His face.

- *The principle of not offending a weaker Christian* (Rom. 14:19; 1 Cor. 8:9-15; 10:31; Rom. 14:21) tells us that we cannot offend younger Christians and be in God's will.

- *The principle of mastery* (1 Cor. 6:12) reminds us not to let anything other than Christ become our ruler. We are to master our lives for Him.

- *The principle of duty* (Prov. 3:27; James 4:17) reminds us to fulfill our obligations.

- *The principle of exceptionalism* (1 Cor. 9:19-23; Phil. 4:11-12) tells us to do the best we can for God, no matter what circumstances we find ourselves in.

- *The principle of suitability* (1 Cor. 10:23) tells us that many things may be all right for others, but not for us.

- *The principle of mental toughness* (Rom. 14:22-23) tells us that after we have thoroughly examined an issue, do everything to the glory of God.[2]

As you follow these principles, you will develop Christian character, which can be defined as "habitually doing the right thing, the right way." Character is developed by obedience to the Word of God—but this is only half of an effective Christian life. The other half is spiritual power, and that comes from the Holy Spirit. When you yield for the filling of the Spirit, you receive power to overcome temptation, and to be victorious over sin.

Remember that God is more concerned about your character than your circumstances. Sometimes He will lead you through deep waters. Why? Because He wants you to develop the character you need to live in difficult times. Sometimes God leads you into the desert—because He wants you to place your trust in Him alone. Sometimes you will face a deep, dark, cold winter's night—because when you are shut up alone with God, you learn to trust Him and glorify Him in all that you do. These difficulties prepare you to fast and pray.

# A Challenge at Three Churches

When Daniel Henderson came out of seminary, he focused his ministry on Acts 6:4: "We will give ourselves continually to prayer and to the ministry of the word." He felt that if he was to be successful in ministry, he must give himself to both prayer and preaching the Word of God. God put him in three churches that cultivated desperation to know the heart of God. In each situation, Daniel felt that if God didn't do something profoundly supernatural in the church, the congregation was probably not going to make it.

### A Great Church Wounded by a Sexual Affair

The first of these churches was Los Gatos Christian Church in San Jose, California. Daniel followed Marvin Reichard, who had led the church for 28 years and built it from 60 to more than 6,000 in attendance. But in June 1988, the board accepted Reichard's resignation after he confessed to a sexual affair that he had covered up for eight years.

Reichard had been the voice of the Moral Majority in Northern California, so the liberal media gave great publicity to the affair, treating it as a scandalous event. The church was also involved in a $25 million lawsuit regarding a church discipline case. That's a tremendous amount of negative publicity and financial risk for a young pastor to face.

Daniel was only 30 years old when he was called as interim pastor of Los Gatos Christian Church. During his four years there, he basically led the church as its pastor. He not only preached the Word weekly, but also called the church to prayer. Every Monday morning, at 6:00 AM, he met with a group of men at the church to pray for an hour. On top of that, he called three all-night prayer meetings during his first year.

Daniel had learned to fast under Jerry Falwell at Liberty University, so he also called several 24-hour fasts, i.e., sundown to sundown, for God to intervene in the lawsuit (which He did), and to stabilize the church and give the congregation health and growth. Toward the end of his four years in San Jose, he called several three-day fasts for direction and provision for the ministry.

## A Stable Church Without Energy or Growth

In 1993, Daniel was called to Arcadia Baptist Church in Sacramento, California. Arcadia Baptist was a stable church running about 1,000 in attendance. Lee Toms, the founding pastor, had been there for 40 years. The church was a very traditional one, located in an old, established neighborhood. When Daniel arrived, it had predominantly "grey hair" membership. The church owed $2.5 million, which seemed a great challenge to Daniel at the time.

Daniel attended several prayer summits for pastors in the Pacific Northwest. These were three-day events where pastors went off-site without an agenda, usually at a camp or retreat center.

A prayer summit was a free flowing event. The pastors sat in concentric circles, so they could hear one another, and anyone could read Scripture, begin singing a hymn, or otherwise express their thoughts. Then the participants looked for opportunities to pray around a theme that came out of the Scriptures that were being read.

Daniel calls this experience, "Scripture fed—Scripture led."

At times during the prayer summits, groups broke up and people were sent off on their own, observing a code of silence, to meditate, pray, and seek God's will for their lives.

The prayer summits also included time spent in gender-specific small groups (men prayed with men, and women prayed with women). It was felt that in the gender-specific groups, people would be more comfortable with one another. As a result, they could share burdens, or express needs or struggles, more openly.

Daniel calls a prayer summit "Christianity in its purest form."

God had spoken to Daniel in these pastoral prayer summits, so he decided God could speak to Arcadia Baptist Church through a similar event. In January 1994, the church conducted its first prayer summit. Daniel didn't know what would happen; that type of prayer meeting was still considered "outside the box." About 100 people attended the first summit. The Lord began to move in hearts, giving many a new start in their lives. Several marriages were also rejuvenated.

Daniel also launched a series of 12 cooperative prayer meetings each week for people to come together with a passion for prayer. A Thursday night gathering, called "a fresh encounter," brought 500 to 600 together to worship through prayer.

Daniel was at Arcadia Baptist Church for 11 years. Attendance more than doubled, rising from 1,000 to 2,300. The church was able to plant three daughter churches, and today one of those daughter churches runs 3,000-4,000 in attendance. Missions giving doubled, baptisms doubled, and there was transformative renewal at Arcadia Baptist Church in Sacramento.

## A Church Struggling to Survive

Daniel's third church was Grace Church in Eden Prairie, Minnesota. He was content at Arcadia Baptist Church and planned to stay there for a long time. The pressures in Sacramento were gone. But Grace Church in Eden Prairie was in real trouble. The church had relocated to 60 acres of ground. The new 250,000-square-foot building could seat 4,200 people. The church had launched a $50 million building project, which resulted in a monthly loan payment of $189,000. A capital fundraising campaign to reduce the debt fell $10 million short. The church still owed $28 million. Some of that was needed immediately when the congregation discovered that their pastor was having an affair.

Someone on the pulpit committee got Daniel's cell phone number by an abrupt twist of communication. When Daniel was first contacted about coming to the church, he said that he was not interested. After the call was over, though, he had an inner feeling that God was going to send him to that church.

A packet on Grace Church was sent to the Henderson home, and Rosemary watched the enclosed video while Daniel was out of town. When he returned home, she said, "I have a bad feeling about this church." Both agreed that they did not want to go there, but they also agreed that they would be open to God's call. They felt that it was a "unique challenge," and that Daniel was wired and prepared to demonstrate that God could do the miraculous in that church.

When Daniel left California, it was 80 degrees at the airport. When he landed in Minneapolis, it was 30 degrees below zero, with 17 inches of snow on the ground. He immediately began meeting with people in gatherings designed to raise $10 million to cover overruns that the church had spent on the new building. Much of the money was raised in three years. With the $10 million "monkey" off its back, the church could continue making its monthly $189,000 payments.

As at his previous churches, Daniel felt that the key to his ministry was preaching the Word and praying for God to do the supernatural. On top of its building-related debt, the church had a $2 million yearly commitment to foreign missions. This was the real attraction for Daniel.

During Daniel's first month in Minnesota, the church planned a men's retreat. When Daniel arrived, he changed the name of the gathering to "Prayer Summit." More than 300 men showed up. Just as God had done before, He ignited a passion in the hearts of people at the church to pray and trust God for the supernatural. They began praying about the monthly budget, and soon it was balanced.

Beyond the prayer summits, Daniel challenged members of the congregation to go experience "Fresh Encounters" at Brooklyn Tabernacle in New York. Twice, the church chartered airplanes so 180 people could fly out for a Tuesday night prayer meeting at the Brooklyn Tabernacle. Daniel wanted to get the people of Grace Church infected with the vision of what prayer could do.

During his four years in Minnesota, Daniel scheduled three prayer summits each year. By the time he left, there had been 33 prayer summits in the church, and things had turned completely around for this congregation that had once seemed on the brink of destruction.

# Your Notes

# 15

# Accepting When God Says, "No!"

Prayer is a relationship, but sometimes our prayers presume upon God. We ask for things He doesn't do, or we ask Him to go against His nature. God cannot lie, nor will He bless something that is against the 10 Commandments. He doesn't answer foolish or non-biblical requests. So it is only natural that when we make those kinds of requests, God tells us "No," or "I don't do it that way." Sometimes I wonder if God hears some of our prayers and responds, "You've got to be kidding!"

Sometimes God says, "No" because there are physical or spiritual dangers attached to our requests. You may ask for something that would be dangerous to yourself or other people. Isn't it the duty of a parent to keep a child from harming himself and others? If we do that for our children, won't our heavenly Father do the same for us?

What about the times when we ask God to do things He can't do? It sounds harsh to say God can't do something, but God can't do certain things that are contrary to His nature. God can't make sin into righteousness, He can't make yesterday not happen, He can't make a rock that's too big for Him to pick up, and He cannot deny Himself.

So when we presume upon God with our improper or impossible requests, what would you expect Him to say? Sometimes we get a "non-answer": He doesn't even respond. This may mean that we don't know enough about the Bible or about God, or it may be that we are blinded by our sin or our ignorance. (See chapter 16, "Listening When God Is Silent.")

# Interpreting a "No" from God

Every time God says "No," it reminds us that He has certain limits. Because we tend to expect limitless answers to our prayers, these negative answers can catch us off guard. Learning how to understand and respond to a "No" from God is an important part of our spiritual growth.

### Nonbiblical Prayers

While on a 40-day fast in 1997, I had written out two requests in my journal. First, I was fasting to know God more intimately. He answered that request abundantly. Second, I was fasting for God to put President Clinton out of office. This was not a political motive; it wasn't a Republican thing. Sometime in the past I had voted for Congressman Goodlatte, a Democrat, because we shared core values. But I disagreed with the core values of President Clinton, and I felt that many of his liberal policies were hurting the United States. I had questions about his personal moral lifestyle, Whitewater politics, and the death of his close friend, Vince Foster. It seemed like there was just too much baggage for President Clinton to remain a successful president. During the first day of my fast, I prayed without any hesitation at breakfast, lunch and dinner for God to remove President Clinton from office.

On the second day of my fast, I again prayed for God to remove President Clinton from office. It was then that the Lord spoke to me, reminding me that the Bible commands all believers to pray "for kings and all who are in authority" (1 Tim. 2:2). I couldn't argue with God, so I prayed for President Clinton to be an effective president. After I had read the Scripture and prayed, there was a small doubt in my mind about whether my earlier prayer to remove him from office had been biblical.

On day three, I again prayed for God to remove President Clinton from office. At that point, I felt a negative reminder from God: "I told you yesterday not to make that request." The feeling was strong, and I felt a twinge of conviction.

On day four, I once again prayed for President Clinton to be removed from office. It was then that I received a very strong internal conviction that I should not ask for Clinton's removal, but I should intercede to God for him. I confessed my disobedience to the command God had reminded me of just a couple of days earlier—the instruction about praying for those in authority.

On day five, I wrote in my journal, "Lord, should I pray for Clinton's removal from office?"

In response, I received a direct feeling: *Do not pray against your president; rather, pray for your president.*

As far as I was concerned, God had told me, "No!" My prayer and fasting had been for the wrong thing. So for the rest of my 40-day fast, I did not bring the subject up again, nor did I pray against President Clinton. Instead, I began praying that God would use him in his office. I concentrated my prayers on knowing God intimately, and I felt that my new attitude in praying for President Clinton enhanced my knowledge of God's character.

The strangest thing happened during my 40-day fast: The name "Monica Lewinsky" was bannered in newspaper headlines and the 6 o'clock news. Then came the vote in the House of Representatives to impeach President Clinton. During this entire time, as the scandal rocked Washington, D.C., I had an inner confidence that God would not remove the president from office. Why? Because God didn't let me pray to remove him from office. In His wisdom and providence, God was using Bill Clinton for a purpose, and I didn't need to understand it. I had come to believe that my negative prayer against President Clinton had been a *presumptuous* prayer.

### Prayers to Change the Past

Another reason God may say no is that He doesn't undo history. Recently a friend of mine was waiting for a big check in the mail, and when he received an envelope, he prayed, "Lord, let the check be in this envelope." Think about the situation! The check either was in the envelope or it was not. The check either had been mailed or had not been mailed. It was too late to make that prayer. My friend should have prayed earlier, "Lord, help them remember to mail that check to me now." Then he should have prayed for no delays in the mail system. Finally, he should have prayed for patience to wait for the answer to his prayers.

My daughter, Polly, once expected God to overturn history. When she was pregnant with her first child, she told me, "I'm praying that it will be a baby boy." I reminded her that the sex of her baby had been determined at conception. God couldn't undo the growth of the child in the womb and change it from a girl to a boy. My daughter had never thought about it that way. Maybe all of us should think about the way we pray and the things for which we ask. As it turns out, my grandchild was a beautiful girl, born during Sunday School in 1988. God will not answer our prayers to tamper with history.

## Prayers God Has Already Answered

But sometimes God begins to answer even before we ask. When we pray for rain, God may have been developing weather patterns that would bring rain to the area. Consider Elijah's experience: "Elijah was a man with a nature like ours, and he prayed earnestly that it would not rain; and it did not rain on the land for three years and six months. And he prayed again, and the heaven gave rain, and the earth produced its fruit" (Jas. 5:17-18). As we have already discussed, one way to describe a miracle is as an interruption of the laws of nature for a divine purpose. Did God interrupt the weather pattern to send a drought for divine purposes?

Note how Elijah prayed for rain. First, the faith of Elijah expected God to answer his prayers. But second, Elijah expected it to rain according to weather patterns. He told his servant to go look out over the sea for rain seven times (see 1 Kings 18:42-46). The rain came when a weather front moved into the area. There was a small rain cloud, which was followed by a torrential downpour. Elijah didn't pray against history or the weather; he prayed and expected an answer according to the way it usually rains.

Now think of the women who walked through the early morning twilight to the tomb on that first Easter. As they talked among themselves, they asked, "Who will roll away the stone from the door of the tomb for us?" (Mark 16:3). They may even have prayed for that request, but the stone had already been removed, so their prayer would not have made any difference. How many times have we done the same thing? We have prayed about things that have already happened.

Then there's the story of Peter's release from prison. Herod, who had just beheaded James (see Acts 12:1-3), had put Peter in jail. The church prayed intently, because they thought Peter might be martyred just as James had been. "But constant prayer was offered to God for him [Peter] by the church" (v. 5). Prayer was offered for Peter before he was released from prison, and the church unknowingly continued to pray for his release after he was out of jail.

God's answer to prayer in this instance was dramatic: The chains fell off of Peter, and an angel told him to put on his coat; then the iron gate that led to the city opened of its own accord (see vv. 7-10). When Peter was free, he "came to the house of Mary . . . where many were gathered together praying" (v. 12). Peter knocked, and Rhoda, the keeper of the gate, recognized his voice but didn't let him in. She ran to tell the people who were praying that Peter stood before the gate (see v. 14).

They didn't believe Rhoda; maybe they thought she wouldn't recognize Peter's voice, or maybe they didn't really believe that God had answered their prayer. Peter persisted in knocking, and "when they opened the door and saw him, they were astonished" (v. 16). The church almost missed God's answer to their prayer. When we are praying, we should ask ourselves, *Has God already answered this prayer?*

When we are praying, we should ask ourselves, *Has God already answered this prayer?*

## Prayers Rooted in Desire

Sometimes we equate great desire for something with great faith, but they are not the same. Biblical faith is connected to God, and our faith must be in God Himself. Desire arises out of our minds and hearts; it's something we want. The strength of our desire can unusually be measured on a scale of 1 to 10. We have a casual desire for some things (a "1"). We have a great desire for other things (an "8" or "9"). But great desire is not the same as great faith. We must detach ourselves from our selfish desires, and yield ourselves to God's will before entering into prayer or fasting.

## "Yes, But Not Yet"

Sometimes we pray and fast, and God provides the answers we seek—but not right away. From 1961 to 1965, I was president of Winnipeg Bible College in Canada, and on many occasions the college didn't have enough money to pay salaries. Winnipeg Bible College was a faith institution that trusted God to provide money for its support. We followed the slogan, "Full information without solicitation."

I remember one occasion when I prayed all night for God to send in money for the salaries. I prayed so fervently that I convinced myself that the money would be in the post office box the next morning. But when I opened it, there were only a few letters containing small donations—nothing like the great response I had expected. At first, I was disappointed and disillusioned because I had prayed so hard. But then I thought, *Maybe God touched the hearts of people to send the money, and the mail will arrive within the next two or three days.* That idea seemed rational, but it didn't happen that way. One or two envelopes came in each day, bringing some money, but never a windfall.

That Friday, I called the faculty and staff (nine people) into my office. This was a weekly practice. We stood around my desk; the school's treasurer, Alida Netzer, had the checkbook in hand. The bookkeeper told me how much money we had. We first paid for lights, water, heat, and groceries for the students. Then I asked each of the faculty and staff, "How much do you absolutely need?" Each told me what they had to have to make it through the week. Then, if any money was left over, we divided it equally among the nine people.

On two or three other occasions, I again prayed all night—and I still didn't get my big breakthrough. I didn't get my personal miracle. I had to learn the lesson of *delayed answers*. God was going to bless the college with a miraculous supply of money, but He would not do it for another 15 years.

While I was president, the college was accredited by the AABC (Accrediting Association of Bible Colleges), and the Province of Manitoba chartered it, which meant we could transfer its academic credits to the secular universities of Canada. That was a step toward God's provision of money, but no one recognized it at the time.

Several years after I left, president Bill Eichhorst arranged for Winnipeg College to receive a stipend of $500 per registered student per year from the Province of Manitoba. This was the same stipend that was paid to all other provincial colleges, and it gave the college enough financial backing to open up classes (offering recognized academic credit) in Ontario, Saskatchewan and Alberta—especially classes in teacher preparation and counseling. Winnipeg Bible College (which later changed its name to Providence College and Theological Seminary) became the largest Christian college in Canada because of its outreach across the nation. It worked with many other unaccredited Bible colleges to give their students academic recognition and accreditation. God heard my prayers for finances for the college, but He answered in a completely different time than I ever expected.

## A Better Plan

Sometimes God may say no to your prayers because He has a much better plan for your life. After the prophet Elijah won a confrontation with the prophets of Baal on Mount Carmel, Jezebel threatened to kill him. Elijah ran away—across the nation of Israel, and then across the nation of Judah—and escaped out into the desert to protect his life (see 1 Kings 19:1-4). Then he prayed a very unusual request: "Now, LORD, take my life" (v. 4). He was discouraged and scared, and so he prayed to die. I can't help wondering why he didn't just let Jezebel catch him instead of asking

God to kill him. I'm sure she would have been happy to do it. But I'm getting off track here.

After Elijah left Beersheba, he walked deep into the desert to Mt. Sinai. He began to climb this mountain where God had revealed Himself before. He poured out to God the dire predicament he was in. It was then that the Lord met the discouraged prophet, gave him a commission, and sent him back to work (see 1 Kings 19:8-21).

God didn't take Elijah's life when the prophet asked Him to do so. It's as though God heard his request and said, "No, Elijah, I've got a better plan for you."

In fact, even after Elijah performed more miracles, anointed Elisha to take his place, and confronted the evil King Ahab, God *still* had a better plan. God led the elderly Elijah to a special place where, suddenly, "a chariot of fire appeared with horses of fire . . . and Elijah went up by a whirlwind into heaven" (2 Kings 2:11). Elijah wasn't going to die out in the desert; no, Elijah was going to be taken up into heaven without dying. Isn't that much better?

Perhaps you've been praying for a small goal, or a marginal solution to a problem, and nothing has happened. God may be telling you, "No, I've got a better plan for you."

Right after I was saved, I began praying about a cute girl in my church. I thought I loved her, and I thought she would make a perfect preacher's wife. She loved God, was faithful in church attendance, and seemed to have great Christian character.

I went off to Bible college and heard that she fell in love with a local boy and got married very quickly. My heart was broken (temporarily). I might even have blamed God: "Why did You let this happen?"

When I was in my middle age, I saw this same woman driving a rusty, old, beat-up Cadillac. Her plump arm hung out the car window, holding a beer. Her petite figure had bloomed with the years, I would guess past 200 pounds. At that time, I thanked God for not answering that prayer about her becoming my wife. Perhaps I had only selfish desires when I had wanted to marry her. I should have believed God when He said, "I've got a better plan for your life."

## "Do No Harm"

Sometimes we fast and pray for a request that would hurt another. If God says, "No" to something we are praying about, we should consider whether this might be the reason.

Once I was called to intervene in a small southern town where a church was split. People had turned against one another—family against family, and in some cases, brother against brother, and children against parents.

The problem was that the church's pastor had homosexual thoughts, and he had gone to Jacksonville, Florida, to see a secular psychiatrist about the matter. The pastor was not sure his thoughts were from Satan, or even a demon itself. He doubted he really was homosexual.

I never tried to find out whether the pastor was homosexual or not. After the incident was over, he went into an interdenominational ministry and served the Lord, along with his wife and two children, for the rest of his life.

Part of the problem was that one lady in the church heard about the psychiatrist—and before long, everyone in the church knew that their pastor had gone to see an unsaved psychiatrist. Half the church wanted to fire him because he had gone to see a psychiatrist for his problems, rather than trusting God the Holy Spirit. Some wanted to fire him because he had homosexual thoughts. Many people said, "Our pastor hasn't done anything wrong. He's just like us; he has temptations." Still others didn't know what to do.

I was asked to moderate a meeting where a vote would be taken on whether to oust this man from the pastorate. I won't attempt to describe the firestorm that broke out that evening, with people yelling at one another across the auditorium. Again, friend turned against friend, and neighbor against neighbor. The vote was very close, and the pastor was removed.

From what I saw during the rest of his life, the pastor was not homosexual, though perhaps Satan and/or demons tempted him. Whatever the case may have been, it seemed that people who called themselves Christians had been praying against their pastor.

The next time you want to pray against someone, I recommend taking several steps. First, remember that God loves everyone and has wonderful plans for their lives. You may be praying against God when you pray against a fellow believer.

Second, follow the admonition of Jesus to turn the other cheek when slapped: "Whoever slaps you on your right cheek, turn the other to him also" (Matt. 5:39).

Third, try praying good things for the person you want to hurt. Isn't that what Jesus would say? "Love your enemies, do good to those who hate you, bless those who curse you, and pray for those who spitefully use you" (Luke 6:27-28). The root problem is that those who hate another Christian don't want to pray for their good; they want to harm them. However, if their hearts are right with God, and they really seek to love and pray blessings on the person they feel has wronged them, they will, as Paul reminds us, "heap coals of fire on his head" (Rom. 12:20).

There's a fourth thing about praying against your enemies. Make sure you're not trying to step closer to God by stepping on someone else. God answers the prayers of those who are sincere and humble; if you want Him to answer your prayers, you must develop a positive attitude that will help you move His heart.

> If you want Him to answer your prayers, you must develop a positive attitude that will help you move His heart.

### Demanding a Sign

When I was a young ministerial student, I attended First Baptist Church of Dallas, Texas. I heard the great W. A. Criswell tell the following story about how he had heard the testimony of a young man who said, "God sent a ball of fire out of heaven and struck my soul. I fell on my knees and cried out to God. I prayed through until I got peace."

As a young preacher, Criswell tried to duplicate that experience of the fireball on several occasions. First he prayed for the fireball to hit him so he could be a more powerful preacher. Then he prayed for the fireball to hit his listeners so that they would be converted in the same dramatic way. But it never happened. If he had listened carefully, he might have heard God say, "No, I don't do it that way. I don't use fireballs; I use the Word of God."

Most of the time, those who asked Jesus for a sign didn't receive one (see, for example, Matt. 12:38-39). God wants people to place their faith in Him based on the Word of God.

After encountering Jesus on Easter Sunday evening, the disciples told Thomas that they had seen Jesus. The Lord had "showed them His hands and His side" (John 20:20). John goes on to say that the disciples "saw the Lord." The Greek word used here is *eidon*, which means to experience and see.

Apparently the disciples saw and touched Jesus that evening.

Thomas thought he had to have that same experience; he said, "Unless I see in His hands the print of the nails, and put my finger into the print of the nails, and put my hand into His side, I will not believe" (John 20:25).

It's a terrible thing to tell God, "I will not believe." Perhaps it's almost as bad to demand a sign from God before we will believe in Him. But the Lord Jesus was merciful. He appeared to His disciples again the following Sunday evening and immediately singled out Thomas, offering, "Reach your finger here, and look at My hands; and reach your hand here, and put it into My side. Do not be unbelieving, but believing" (John 20:27). The text is silent about whether Thomas actually put his finger in Jesus' wounds. But it does tell us that Thomas responded to Jesus with worship. Thomas cried out, "My Lord and my God!" (John 20:28).

As I mentioned before, those who demand a sign or some physical reaffirmation usually don't get it. Thomas did, but even so, notice that Jesus told him to focus on belief rather than physical proof, and He commended those who believed without an outward sign: "Because you have seen Me, you have believed Blessed are those who have not seen, and yet have believed" (John 2:29).

# Wrap Up

How many times has a student walked into my classroom to take an exam and prayed, "Lord, help me get an A"?

I believe God would tell my students, "That's not the way I do it." God expects a student to study, memorize and learn the lessons. Then, out of the fullness of his understanding, the student can pray for help in writing a complete and comprehensive exam. But when he walks in not having studied, his mind is empty, and God doesn't communicate out of a vacuum. His empty mind will be reflected in an empty exam paper.

Once I went to take an exam I had not studied for at all. I faced 100 true or false questions. I figured that if I answered all of them either "true" or "false," I could at least get a 50 on the exam, which included a lot of "stuff" I had never seen before. If I had prayed, "God help me guess correctly," God would undoubtedly have said, "I don't do it that way."

God runs the world by laws, so don't pray against the laws of learning. The next time you're tempted to pray for an A instead of studying, remember how God works. First, pray to understand what you studied, then pray for help to retain what you memorized, and then pray to properly explain what you know. After you've done all that, pray for an A. That's a prayer God can answer.

God also runs His world by the laws of time. God took six days to create the earth and universe. He didn't do it in one minute. If God allowed time to control His creative process, shouldn't you ask Him to use time to mature your thinking, to increase your insight, and to prepare you for ministry? When you dash out to preach the Word of God without proper study and without meeting God in prayer, your cup is empty; there's no water to pour out to thirsty souls. It takes time to read, study the Word, and meditate on the Scriptures. Then with a full cup you can ask God to satisfy the thirsty.

And how can you apply the laws of time to your uncle who has an infectious disease? God may not heal him immediately; physical improvement takes time. Becoming stronger takes time. Even after prayer removes the infection, it takes time to build up resistance against future disease.

Sometimes you pray for healing for an uncle, but a physician's scalpel is required to remove the cancer. Even after the cause of the illness is gone, it's going to take time for the incision to heal, for the muscles to get strong, and for the body to recuperate.

God heals—none of us should be doubters—but healing may follow the laws of time. If you ask for an instantaneous miracle, you may hear God say, "I don't do it that way." Allow God to do it His way.

## Your Notes

# 16

# Listening When
# God Is Silent

Have you ever fasted and prayed for something, but you didn't get any answer at all? God didn't say "yes," or "no," or even "wait." He just didn't answer at all. Nothing! You're not the first to get a non-answer. When you fast and pray, but don't get an answer, do you think God doesn't care or hasn't heard? Do you figure that, like the busy clerk in a cubicle, He has put you on hold? Perhaps you picture God glancing down at His divine cell phone—and pressing the button to "ignore" your call.

There can be many reasons for an unanswered prayer or fast. Let's begin our discussion of the topic by looking at a story from the life of King David. David had sinned against God when he committed adultery with Bathsheba. She became pregnant, and then David arranged to have her husband killed. God rebuked David through a message from Nathan, the prophet, and David responded with contrition: "David said to Nathan, 'I have sinned against the LORD'" (2 Sam. 12:13). But as is often the case, David's repentance didn't take away the consequences of his sin. "The LORD struck the child that Uriah's wife bore to David, and it became ill" (2 Sam. 12:15).

What David did next is what we all ought to do when nothing else can help: "David therefore pleaded with God for the child, and David fasted and . . . lay all night on the ground" (2 Sam. 12:16). For seven long, anxious days, David continued fasting without any answer from God. None of David's staff could help him; they tried "to raise him up from the ground. But he would not, nor did he eat food with them" (2 Sam. 12:17).

David's prayer and fast were not successful; the child died. God did not answer David, as sometimes He will not answer you or me. Even in his time of prayer, David knew something had happened: "David perceived that the child was dead" (2 Sam. 12:19).

When God doesn't answer your intense prayer and fasting, you have to yield your request to God. You have to stop praying. When you come to the end of your fast, yield your request and all of the circumstances surrounding it to God—and then go on with life. Notice what David did: He "arose from the ground, washed and anointed himself, and changed his clothes; and he went into the house of the LORD and worshiped" (2 Sam. 12:20).

> When God doesn't answer your intense prayer and fasting, you have to yield your request to God. You have to stop praying.

The Bible doesn't describe God's reaction to David's attempted fast to save his child. We don't get any more of an answer about that than David did. But God apparently heard David and decided to bless him, because "David comforted Bathsheba his wife. . . . She bore a son, and he called his name Solomon" (2 Sam. 12:24).

Sometimes God's silence isn't about sin. Consider this illustration from C. S. Lewis's *The Magician's Nephew* (from his *Chronicles of Narnia* series). Fifteen-year-old-Digory Kirke's mother was extremely sick, so Digory asked Aslan to heal her. Digory was desperately hoping that the lion would say yes to heal her. At the same time, he was braced for the lion to say no. But the lion said nothing. He didn't answer yes or no. Finally the lion's face bent down close to Digory, and the young boy saw a great big shining tear in the lion's eye. In that moment, Digory realized that the lion must really feel as sorrowful about his mother's dying as he himself did.[1]

Perhaps when we fast and pray for God to heal someone who is dying, and God doesn't seem to answer, it's because the natural cycle of life is taking its effect. The person is dying because it's their time to die. Perhaps God is as sorrowful as you are, even if it seems like He just isn't answering.

We've already seen how God responded to David's prayer for his sick child with silence. But that was not the first time David seemingly did not get an answer from God. David had been anointed the future king of Israel when he was 15 years old. Then David had his famous confrontation with Goliath, and won that battle and cut off Goliath's head. As the popular song laments, "Those were the days, my friend. We thought they'd never end."

David must have thought he would be a hero forever, as he listened to songs sung in his honor: "The women answered one another as they played, and said, Saul hath slain his thousands, and David his ten thousands" (1 Sam. 18:7, *KJV*). But this statement that brought so much joy to David's heart also brought him future grief. From that moment on, Saul was envious of David, and Saul's envy worked to become several attempted murders. "It was determined of his father [Saul] to slay David" (1 Sam. 20:33, *KJV*).

David fled into the wilderness and was there for 13 years, cut off from family, friends and his hometown. He couldn't even go into the house of God to worship in God's presence; David prayed continually, but God didn't seem to hear him.

"LORD . . . why do You hide Your face from me?" (Ps. 88:14). David had been promised the throne of Israel, but Saul was sitting on it. David didn't know what to do. So he prayed, "Why have You forgotten me?" (Ps. 42:9) Have you ever felt that way? It looks like David received a *non-answer* from God. There will be times when God seems to deal with you the same way, and you may find yourself asking, "How long will you forget me?" (Ps. 13:1, *NLT*)

When you want a word from God—any word—how do you pray? Perhaps you pray, as David did, "O God, whom I praise, don't stand silent and aloof" (Ps. 109:1, *NLT*). You cry out for deliverance—or for any answer—but God doesn't respond. You are in a hole, and you can't get out. Maybe God has lessons to teach you in that hole. Everyone has to go through a desert experience at some point—possibly at multiple points. Maybe God doesn't deliver because He wants you to learn what to do when no one else is around. When you are in a lonely desert, or you're shut up alone with God, perhaps God wants to teach you something about Himself.

Job was another who saw his joy turn to sorrow. The story is well known: Satan asked permission to tempt Job, and God allowed it. As a result, Job lost his children, his cattle, and almost everything that belonged to him. The lively music of his abundant life turned into a funeral dirge. So Job asked, "Where is God my Maker, who gives songs in the night?" (Job 35:10). Have you ever felt like you have lost your song—or you lost your way—and you have no friends to help you?

# Searching for Meaning in Non-answers

How do you feel when you ask your spouse or children to do something, and they don't answer? Sometimes you feel hurt; other times you get angry. Sometimes you may even be ready to lash out at them for their inconsideration. After all, don't you always answer when they ask for something? Or do you? Think about it. You probably answer most of the time, but there may be times when you didn't hear, or perhaps your mind was on something else, or maybe you responded in your mind but didn't put your thoughts into words. So let's examine why God might not answer when you call out to Him.

### Sin Is Blocking the Relationship

God might not answer because sin is blocking your relationship with Him. Do you remember the story of the formerly blind man who argued with the Jews over the miracle done for him by Jesus? The man stated, "We know that God does not hear sinners" (John 9:31). He was saying that Jesus could not have healed him if He had been a sinner. To apply that illustration, God does not hear us when there is sin in our lives.

The psalmist understood this principle perfectly: "If I regard iniquity in my heart, the Lord will not hear" (Ps. 66:18). Again the Scriptures tell us that sin blocks our communication with God: "Behold, the LORD's hand is not shortened, that it cannot save; neither His ear heavy, that it cannot hear: But your iniquities have separated between you and your God, and your sins have hid his face from you, that he will not hear" (Isa. 59:1-2, *KJV*). The phrase, "His ear is heavy," actually means, "Plugged up with ear wax." Just as we can't hear when we get wax in our ears, so our sin plugs up God's hearing.

Now, God hears everything, because God knows all things possible (omniscient), and He is present everywhere at the same time (omnipresent). Therefore, God hears every prayer. But sometimes, God does not hear to answer. As you casually watch television, an announcer may ask you a question about floor wax, such as, "Don't you want a shinier floor?" Technically, you hear the question, but you don't pay attention, because you are not concerned with floors at that moment.

So, sometimes God hears our requests, but sin keeps Him from paying attention, and He doesn't do anything. For this reason, when we have sinned, we must (1) confess our sins to God (see 1 John 1:9); (2) repent, which means determine never to do it again; and (3) ask God to cleanse us by the blood of Jesus Christ (see 1 John 1:7).

## God Wants You to Examine Your Request

Perhaps God doesn't respond because He wants us to examine our request. Sometimes if God were to quickly answer, "Yes," or, "No," we would not learn a lesson through the experience. God chooses not to respond to our request because He wants us to learn through self-examination why our prayer is inappropriate, or why we must wait; or maybe we must learn a deep lesson about God Himself. Rather than simply telling us, "No," God wants us to find out why He is not answering, so a *non-answer* has teaching value.

## You Didn't Hear What God Said

Perhaps God began answering when you prayed, but you didn't listen long enough to hear what He said. We are an impatient generation—we like instant cereal, instant messaging, instant everything. Because time is a commodity, we don't want to waste it. We want everything NOW.

Suppose you call your boss asking for a raise, or additional funds for a project. If he doesn't call you back immediately, you think he has ignored you or rejected your request. You might get irritated at the boss for not answering in a timely manner. But suppose he actually called you back immediately—only you were on the other line, and he couldn't leave you a message because your voice mailbox was full.

Could it be that sometimes God is trying to answer us, but we are so busy we don't hear Him speak? We may be occupied doing other things for God, or perhaps we have forgotten about Him, or maybe we just turned off our phones. Whatever the reason, when God tries to answer, He can't get through to us—and we assume He is rejecting us.

### God Has a Purpose in Not Answering

Even though it may seem like He is simply not paying attention, God has a purpose in everything He does. Whereas your boss might have his communication diverted because of cell phone problems—or might in fact have gotten distracted before he had a chance to return your call—God never has those kinds of problems. He knows all things at all times, including all things possible (see Rom. 4:17), and He is not forgetful or careless. If He has chosen not to answer you for the time being, He has a reason. Try to find out what that reason is.

> If God has chosen not to answer you for the time being, He has a reason for doing so. Try to find out what that reason is.

### You Put Conditions on God

Be careful of rationalizing your experiences. Sometimes we put conditions on our requests to God, and those conditions are wrong. Suppose a young man wants to date a girl, but he is a little timid. So he tells himself that he will phone her, and if she answers, it's his "sign" that he should ask her for a date. But when he phones, she does not answer. He takes that to mean he shouldn't ask her out, but perhaps she did not hear the phone, or he might have dialed the wrong number, or the call could have gotten dropped, or she might have been using the phone. The young man did not get his date because of the assumptions he made—and his quickness to give up. Perhaps the girl would have gone with him if he had been more persistent. A faint heart never won a fair maiden. So don't try to explain away a non-answer to your own satisfaction. God has a purpose.

### God Wants You to Continue Praying

Jesus said, "Ask, and it will be given to you" (Matt. 7:7). The original language should be translated, "Keep on asking..." God wants you to be persistent in your prayer.

Jesus gave the illustration of a man going to his friend in the middle of the night to borrow bread, because travelers had come to stay with him. The empty-handed man banged on the door of his friend's house, but he was turned away: "Don't bother me. The door is locked for the night, and we are all in bed. I can't help you" (Luke 11:7, *NLT*). The empty-handed man continued to pound on the door, because he needed bread—and eventually he got it. Jesus explained it this way: "Because of his persistence he will rise and give him as many as he needs" (Luke 11:8).

## Wrap Up

We must guard against responding wrongly to God when we think He is not hearing or answering our prayers. The most important thing in our relationship with God is *trust*. We must trust God when He says, "Yes!" and trust Him when He says, "No!" We must also trust Him when He says, "Wait"—and even when He doesn't seem to answer at all. You must know that God is there and that He loves you. "Without faith it is impossible to please Him, for he

who comes to God must believe that He is, and that He is a rewarder of those who diligently seek Him" (Heb. 11:6).

## Your Notes

_____

_____

_____

_____

_____

_____

_____

_____

_____

_____

_____

_____

_____

_____

_____

_____

_____

_____

_____

_____

_____

_____

_____

_____

_____

_____

_____

# 17

# Knowing God
# More Intimately

Ed Silvoso of Harvest Evangelism once invited me to fly to Mar del Plata, Argentina, to speak to approximately 14,000 pastors on the topic of fasting. When I walked into the basketball arena and saw the crowd, Ed apologized, "We only have 10,000 here today, but in my estimation it looks more like 8,000." I was not discouraged about speaking to a smaller number of people; that crowd was one of the largest gatherings of Pentecostal preachers I had ever addressed.

The preacher before me worked the crowd up to a frenzy; there were shouts of "HALLELUJAH!" and "PRAISE THE LORD!" As all those exclamations were in Spanish, I could only understand a little of what they were saying. I had been invited to lecture on fasting, not to deliver an emotional, "stem-winding" sermon like the preacher who was finishing up.

*Oh, Jesus, help me* . . . I silently prayed as I took my seat on the front row. The men in the row behind me were standing, fists pumping in the air. The benches were packed as full as people could pack an auditorium.

## Five Men Came to Pray Over Me

As I sat, five men approached me. The leader of the group said, "We have read your book on fasting . . . and have come to pray for God to use you to teach many pastors to fast."

The five men had fasted all week. They had gone from one fishing boat to another in the harbor, laying hands on nets, engines, and sonar equipment used to find fish. Argentina was in an economic recession. Other groups of Pentecostal preachers had gone through the entire area, praying over factories, businesses, banks and schools.

"We drank a glass of orange juice each morning just like you," the leader explained, "but what is V-8 juice?"

I laughed to myself. I had mentioned in my book that during a long fast, I drink a glass of orange juice each morning, and a glass of V-8 juice each evening. Apparently the American brand name didn't translate.

The men laid hands on me and prayed quietly over me. I could barely hear them over the rambunctious crowd.

As I returned to my seat, a well-dressed lady came to sit next to me. She spoke cultured English and explained that she was a Supreme Court justice in Argentina and had translated for meetings of the World Bank and the International Monetary Fund. She added that she was a believer, and she had heard that I was speaking. Then she said, "God told me to interpret for you today. Would you permit it?"

"Absolutely." I assured her that she was a gift of God and I needed her help.

## Anointed for Service

Then before me appeared a small, elderly, obviously poor lady holding a basin and a bottle of water. A clean white towel was draped over her arm.

"May I wash your feet to prepare you for ministry?" she asked.

The preacher had finished, and announcements were being made. I knew that shortly I would go on the platform. I didn't want to find myself in the awkward situation of having one bare foot, but I also didn't want to embarrass her by telling her, "No!" or "Later."

"I must go to the platform immediately," I explained. "But I receive your blessing in the spirit in which it is given." I went on to say that because of her willingness to wash my feet, God could see her heart and bless my sermon accordingly. "I receive your blessing as though you've already washed my feet."

## God Changed My Sermon

It was then that Silvoso reached over, tapped me on the knee, and said, "God spoke to me this morning about your message." Then he advised me, "You should not preach on fasting today, but you must speak on knowing God intimately."

I panicked! Immediately my mind raced through the catalogue of sermons I could preach by heart. I did not have a sermon on intimacy with God. I wanted to appeal to Silvoso that he was wrong! I had fasted repeatedly over this sermon on fasting... three or four times for a total of approximately 30 days. But then again, I knew I had to listen to the voice of God speaking through other people—not just the voice of God in my own heart. In my panic I was thinking, *What'll I do?*

I heard my name announced, and the audience began applauding. As my interpreter and I approached the podium, I was more surrendered to God than at any time in my past. I was scared of embarrassing myself. My mind was empty. I was prepared to speak on fasting, but Silvoso had said, "God spoke to me, and you are to preach on knowing God intimately."

Inwardly I prayed again, *Jesus, help me!*

I cannot preach bombastically like Pentecostal preachers do. So God sent a quiet, dignified woman to help me—one who could speak with both authority and clarity. I knew the audience would understand what I said—if I only knew what I was going to say.

*Jesus, help me!* I prayed over and over, until a thought came to me. I remembered something that I had written just a couple of weeks earlier.[1]

## As Close to God as the Angels

"If you are going to become intimate with God, you must get close to God," I told the crowd. "And no one has ever been closer to God than the two angels on the lid of the Ark of the Covenant."

I turned to a passage of Scripture probably not often preached on: "You shall make a mercy seat of pure gold; two and a half cubits shall be its length and a cubit and a half its width. And you shall make two cherubim of gold; of hammered work you shall make them at the two ends of the mercy seat" (Exod. 25:17-18).

Then I explained that the Ark was about the size of a chest, and its lid was called the mercy seat. God came down to earth to sit on a box (the word "ark" means "box"), and the lid of the box was a solid gold mercy seat. Located on the right and left sides of the mercy seat were two angels made of pure gold.

## Pure Gold Suggests Holiness

The two angels weren't just made of gold, but of *pure* gold. Gold has several degrees of purity, 24-karat gold being the purest (and therefore the most expensive!). God told Moses to make the angels of pure gold, because He wants purity in the lives of those who worship him and are close to Him.

The difference between pure gold and a lesser grade of gold is *fire*—and the hotter the purifying fire, the more dross and impurities are burned away. As the gold is heated in the fire, it melts. The sludge then floats to the top, where it is skimmed away, leaving refined gold. Because God wants those closest to Him—the ones who will receive the most attention from Him—to be holy, He uses the fire of suffering and difficulties to rid intercessors of their impurities.

Because God wants those closest to Him—the ones who will receive the most attention from Him—to be holy, He uses the fire of suffering and difficulties to rid intercessors of their impurities.

Sometimes God allows financial reverses to strike devoted believers so that they will draw even nearer to Him. Because of financial disasters in Argentina, its people cry out earnestly to God in prayer. While they are crying to God and seeking His presence, they are releasing their covetous grip on material possessions. Fire burns away the impurity of their greed.

Do you have any impurities that need to be burned away? Do you feel fire licking around the edges of an unyielded possession? Don't complain to God, or doubt Him. Don't think that He doesn't love you. Instead, let your prayer be, *O God, do Your work in my life!* Let His purifying fire upgrade you into pure gold.

When gold is first put into the goldsmith's fire, the heat burns away the dirtiest impurities, including trash and filth. The same thing happens in the Christian life. God first touches our fleshly sins—our sexual sins and other outward problems.

The goldsmith then turns up the flame, so the fire can burn away unseen impurities. Again, the same thing happens in the life of the believer. After you've been separated from your outward sins, God focuses on any inward sins that hinder your walk with Him. The fire of conviction burns away unseen impurities of attitude and desires—little things you allow to block your communion with God.

Why did God demand that the angels and the mercy seat be made of pure gold? Because He Himself was going to sit there. God is pure, so He would not sit there if the mercy seat and the angels were made of impure gold.

How pure is pure gold, and how does the goldsmith know that the gold is pure? You can't tell just by looking at it. Nor is purity determined by how long you leave gold in the fire, or by how big the flames are. Only when all the dross is gone is the gold pure; and the goldsmith will know when the gold is at that stage only by looking into the golden liquid as he would look into a mirror, to see his own face. When he can see himself in the gold, then he knows the gold is pure.

Likewise, when God looks into your soul and sees Himself, then He knows that you are pure. Why does God allow the flames of trials in your life? He's burning away dross, so He can see Himself in you.

Today, whom does God see when He looks into your heart? You—or Himself?

# Angels Were Sculpted

The two worshiping angels were to be sculpted from one piece of gold—not poured into a mold, but beaten into the proper form. "And thou shalt make two cherubims of gold, of beaten work shalt thou make them, in the two ends of the mercy seat" (Exod. 25:18, *KJV*). The angels were to be shaped and crafted by hand. The purer the gold, the easier it would be for the craftsman to sculpt them as he intended.

This reminds us that worshipers are not formed easily or cheaply. They are literally shaped by God's hands into the worshiping position. To be beaten is not the same thing as to be purified. When you are pure, you have separated yourself from sin, i.e., you are holy. When you are sculpted—or beaten with hammers—you become yielded to God and His purpose for you.

We are also reminded that all things that are poured into the same mold become identical. But when you sculpt something, it is unique. A sculptor cannot beat two images into identical shapes. Each is a little different from the other. As God forms us into worshipers, each of us is a little different from the other, even though all of us are fashioned by the hands of the same Master Craftsman.

Don't forget that while anyone can make cheap imitations by pouring liquid into a mold, it takes a master craftsman to sculpt a genuine work of art. He puts his personality and talent into what he forms. So God, the Master Craftsman, puts unique life—*His* life—and design into us when He molds us into worshipers.

Can you see the goldsmith shaping one of those worshiping angels? Is a wing not lifted correctly in praise? A few touches from the master's hand will bring it into the proper position. Perhaps the head is not bowed as it should be. A touch with the right tool—the proper hammer—will correct the problem.

What kind of hammer does God use on you? He always has the right kind of tool to use on the unique problem of pride. He might use a different hammer on greed, and an entirely different hammer on lust. Because my problems are different from yours, God will use a different hammer on me than He uses on you. He has all kinds of hammers for all kinds of problems, and He uses His tools to sculpt us until each of us is just right for worship.

If you won't allow the Lord to use His hammer on you, then something else or someone else will have to beat you into submission. If you are beaten by the world, the flesh and the devil, you can end up broken—in body and spirit—perhaps for your whole life. That's not God's plan. He doesn't beat you to crush you. No! God uses His hammer to mold you into a true worshiper. He doesn't want to break you, but to bend your heart to His will—to enable you to look more like Him. "But we all, with unveiled face, beholding as in a mirror the glory of the Lord, are being transformed into the same image from glory to glory, just as by the Spirit of the Lord" (2 Cor. 3:18).

As I shared these thoughts, the audience was still and reverent. There were no shouts of "AMEN," as there had been during the previous sermon. Like the silent morning fields waiting for the dawning of the glorious sun so they can break into the harvest, the Pentecostal pastors waited anxiously for the message God was revealing to their hearts.

## Spread Wings to Worship

The angels with outstretched wings remind us of worshipers stretching out their hands in praise to God. God consented to dwell at the mercy seat in the Tabernacle—not because Moses followed the blueprint down to the last detail, and not because of the expensive gold appointments. He dwelt there because the angels' outspread wings were praising Him. The Lord came down to live in the praises of Israel (see Ps. 22:3).

The angels on the Ark of the Covenant remind us of the importance of worship. Before you ask for something, make sure you worship the Lord first. Then He will come to you with His presence.

## The Angels Gazed on God

Here's something else about the angels who are close to God. "And the cherubim shall stretch out their wings above, covering the mercy seat with their wings, and they shall face one another;

the faces of the cherubim shall be toward the mercy seat" (Exod. 25:20). Those closest to God want to gaze upon Him. Their first glance is not to the beauty of the Tabernacle, nor do they look to see the carvings throughout the interior. No! They look intimately to God.

Note that their gaze was toward each other, but each was not looking at the other. Their gaze was upon God, who sat between them. The top, or lid, of the Ark was the mercy seat. That's the place on earth where God sat. God promises, "And there I will meet with thee, and I will commune with thee" (Exod. 25:22, *KJV*).

Prayer is how we look at God. We must be close to Him if we are to see Him clearly and know Him intimately. How close to God are you today?

Your gaze must be constant. You must see God every morning upon arising. You must see God in all your activities throughout each day. You must gaze upon God in prayer before you go to sleep at night.

## Angels Reaching Out to God

As I drew toward the close of my talk, I returned to the image of the wings of the angels stretched out in worship to God. "The cherubims shall stretch forth their wings on high, covering the mercy seat with their wings" (Exod. 25:20, *KJV*).

"When you get close to God, you lift your hands in worship to God," I said. "Your outward body reflects your inner soul. You give praise to God with your hands."

Hands were lifted heavenward all over the audience. The people's hearts were with me; 8,000 pastors and I were one. I had prayed frantically, *Jesus, help me!* He was doing it. My quiet presentation was having a quiet salutatory effect on the pastors. Their response to my message was very different from the previous loud shouts, yet both responses glorified God, each in its own way.

I did not preach long—maybe 20-25 minutes. As I came to the conclusion, I began appealing for action.

*"What shall we do?"*

I repeated the question two or three times for emphasis, getting a little bolder and louder than I had been throughout the sermon. I had just emphasized the angels' bowed heads and wings stretched out to God.

So I said dramatically, *"WE MUST FALL ON OUR FACE BEFORE GOD!"* And they did! All over the arena, people began dropping to the floor, lying in the aisles and on the floor beneath their benches. Some knelt at their benches. Others continued to sit, but bowed their heads in reverential worship.

As I saw people dropping to the floor, a very unspiritual thought popped into my mind: *I didn't mean fall literally.* At the same time, I realized it was a sacred moment. God was working in hearts.

The congregation's prayers swelled into a great chorus of praise to God. He was receiving a concert of prayer. Throughout history, God's people have prayed simultaneously, all speaking their praises and requests out loud at the same time. Whereas some may hear a loud, jumbled noise, God listens and enjoys the concert of praise from the hearts of His people as one might enjoy a symphony, with each instrument playing a different note at its appointed time, but blending in perfect harmony.

## How to Fast to Know God Intimately

When Ed Silvoso asked me to speak about intimacy with God rather than fasting, I was startled, and the message I shared was quite different from the one I had prepared. However, the two topics are not unrelated. Of all the reasons we may fast, growing in intimacy with God is perhaps the most important. Our ability to know Him at all is, in fact, a miracle of the deepest kind.

### Intimacy Begins with God's Invitation to Come to Him

We are invited to come to God to know Him and His power. "Come, behold the works of the LORD" (Ps. 46:8; see also Ps. 66:5). How do we respond when someone calls us to come to them? It begins with a listening ear—we listen to God's voice in His Word. Then we turn our attention to the one who is calling us. We focus to find out where the voice is coming from. Since God is everywhere at all times, we can come to Him from any place, at any time. But most of us have certain places where we experience God best, so we come to those places. It may be in a church, or in our homes at Bible study, or in our prayer closets.

Jesus has invited us, "Come to Me, all you who labor and are heavy laden, and I will give you rest" (Matt. 11:28). This is His call to bring our sins or problems to Him.

Jesus also calls us to service: "Come ye after me, and I will make you to become fishers of men" (Mark 1:17, *KJV*). So whether we need to find purpose through service, victory over sin, or to draw near to God in worship, we must begin our search for intimacy by coming to God.

## God Invites Us to Know Him

Another invitation God extends to us is to: "Be still, and know that I am God" (Ps. 46:10). Intimacy begins when we stop what we are doing so we can "be still." That means we come to an end of ourselves. It's then that we can begin to find the presence of God.

As remarkable as it may sound, God is knowable. Remember, we are made in His image. Because He thinks, we are rational. Because God has the emotions to love the sinner but hate the sin, so we have the emotions to love God's mercy and fear His wrath. Because God knows Himself, and we are made in His image, we can know Him.

Because God knows Himself, and we are made in His image, we can know Him.

We are commanded to know God in relation to knowing our humanity. "Know that the LORD, He is God; it is He who has made us" (Ps. 100:3). Because He created us, God understands the vast gap between Him and us.

God knows Himself perfectly, because God is perfect in all things. But we can only know Him partially, because we are limited human beings. Even though we can never perfectly know all things about God, we can know more today than we knew yesterday. We can grow in our understanding of God. That means I can be closer and more intimate with God today than I was yesterday.

## Intimacy Is Experienced in God's Atmospheric Presence

I can make a sanctuary out of a motel room. Sometimes I travel to speak, and I get to my motel late. The next morning, I'm tired when I pray, or I'm not yet wide awake; my prayers seem to bounce off the walls, or go no further than the ceiling. Then, in that moment of frustration, I remember the supernatural power of worship. Jesus told us, "The Father is seeking worship" (John 4:23, *ELT*). That means God goes to the places where people are worshiping Him in order to receive their worship.

In the movie, *Field of Dreams*, Iowa farmer Ray Kinsella heard the phrase, "If you build it, he will come."[2] We can apply this insight to seeking God's intimacy: "If you worship the Father, He will come to receive it."

Therefore, whenever I am praying and feel that I'm not getting through to God, I begin worshiping Him with His many names.[3] Then I feel His presence. Note the phrase, "I *feel* His presence." He was always there, but worship changes me and equips me to experience God's presence.

I call this God's atmospheric presence. Just as I can feel moisture in the air when it's raining, so I can feel God's presence with me when I pray and worship. Sometimes we can walk into a church service and feel the presence of God among the people—in stark contrast to the empty or dead feeling we get in some other church services.

## Intimacy Is Based on Christ's Indwelling

On Easter Sunday, 1951, I experienced a special intimacy with God that I had not previously felt. I had been feeling discouraged, even though I had been saved for a year, and Christ lived within me. At about 9:00 that morning, I was waiting for my ride to Sunday

School. At the time, I taught in a small Presbyterian mission, called Capital View Community Chapel, outside Columbia, South Carolina. My ride was approximately 30 minutes late that morning. While I waited, I meditated on the meaning of Galatians 2:20, especially the phrase, "Christ lives in me."

For the first time, I identified with Christ's resurrection on the first Easter of history. That morning I experienced His life in my heart. I experienced His fullness, and for the first time I felt His "atmospheric presence." As I stood in the warm sun, waiting for my ride, I volitionally yielded anew to God, asking Jesus Christ to give me victory. Jesus had never gotten discouraged, and I wanted to live above discouragement. I wanted not only faith that could trust God for money, but also faith that would not worry about anything. I wanted to trust Him completely.

What I experienced was His intimacy. I did not kneel in prayer, nor did I close my eyes. I simply talked to Jesus and yielded everything to Him. I asked Him to live His life through me. That morning, for the first time in my Christian life, I fully experienced the meaning of the Resurrection.

The previous year, when I was still unsaved, Easter had simply been an historical fact. Now I had come to know personally the One who was raised from the dead—and He was not only sitting at the right hand of God in heaven, but also alive in my heart. I would discover later that my life and faith would be tested as I grew in Christ. But that morning I did not have a care in the world, because I felt one with Christ.

## The Intimacy of Double Transference

Jesus promised, "You in Me, and I in you" (John 14:20; see also John 15:4-5,7). When we become Christians, it is more than mental agreement with Scripture, and it's more than asking God to forgive our sins by the blood of Christ. Salvation is in the Savior, and we must ask Christ to enter our lives. "As many as received Him, to them He gave the right to become children of God" (John 1:12).

The first intimacy happens when Christ indwells our lives. This is the "I in you" part of the promise. The second stage is "You in

Me." This means that I am in Jesus Christ; therefore I can be as close to the Father as Jesus is. Today, Christ sits at the right hand of the Father in heaven. That's pretty close! The intimacy that Jesus has with the Father is available to me as I dwell in Christ.

The first intimacy is experiential: "Christ in me." The second is non-experiential; the believer is positionally "in Christ."

Just because being "in Christ" is non-experiential does not mean we do not have an experience as a result of that truth. You cannot be "in Christ" without having "Christ in you." Likewise, when you experience Christ in your life, the result will follow that you are "in Christ." Those who try to take the mystery out of this doctrine take the supernatural out of Christianity.

Watchman Nee argues that the believer is placed "in Christ" as he accepts "Christ in him."

> But if God has dealt with us "in Christ Jesus" then we have got to be in Him for this to become effective, and that now seems just as big a problem. How are we to "get into" Christ? Here again God comes to our help. We have in fact no way of getting in, but, what is more important, we need not try to get in, for we are in. What we could not do for ourselves God has done for us. He has put us into Christ. Let me remind you of 1 Corinthians 1.30. I think that is one of the best verses in the whole New Testament: "Ye are in Christ." How? "Of him (that is, 'of God') are ye in Christ." Praise God! it is not left to us either to devise a way of entry or to work it out. We need not plan how to get in. God has planned it; and He has not only planned it but He has also performed it. "Of him are ye in Christ Jesus." We are in; therefore we need not try to get in. It is a Divine act, and it is accomplished.[4]

In identifying the believer's position "in Christ," Paul also hints further at the intimacy that exists between the believer and his Lord. As the unborn child grows in his mother's womb, he is very much a part of his mother, while at the same time being a distinct and unique person. In the same way, when we are "in Christ," we are profoundly connected to our heavenly Father while retaining our individual personalities. This concept involves a greater intimacy than most believers ever experience.

### Developing a Hunger for God Through Fasting

Daniel Henderson (see chapter 14) says fasting not only makes us physically hungry, but also creates a hunger to know God intimately. He states, "I have found that fasting recalibrates vision, appetite, desire and focus. I can really trace back my own hunger for the Lord and my desire for prayer as being regularly linked to the times of fasting in which I set aside those moments to be with Him. Fasting is a time to focus my appetite on Him. Hunger for God really challenges us spiritually, more than any physical thing."[5]

### Fasting to Empty Yourself

When you fast, obviously you stop taking in food—which is what usually provides the energy you need to live. At the beginning of a fast, you live off the food that's stored up in your body. The food in your stomach will supply energy for about a day. Fasting will cause hunger pangs, similar to the fuel gauge in your automobile that tells you the tank is almost empty. However, unlike your car, your body doesn't stop running when its regular fuel supply runs out. Instead, you then start to get energy from the stored fat in your body. So when you fast for several days, you live off your fat, which means you lose weight. That's good if you're overweight, but it can be disastrous if you're anemic (which is why you should consult a doctor before starting an extended fast).

By definition, you physically empty yourself when you fast. This is part of the point. The hunger pangs you feel should alert you to seek God all the more. But what about emptying yourself spiritually? The longer you remain on a fast, the more you demonstrate your sincerity and desire to have God's presence in your life. "[The Lord] is close to all who call on Him sincerely" (Ps. 145:18, *TLB*).

God will not hear you just because you stop eating. To think you'll get your prayers answered because you don't eat is legalism. But the symbolism can be meaningful. As you allow your physical body to empty itself of food, make an intentional effort to empty your soul before God. If you honestly pray and seek Him, you can be filled. When you come to God empty—of food and of self—then He can fill you.

> Turn to Me, says the Lord, with all your heart while there is time. Empty your hearts, not just your stomachs. Fast with weeping and mourning. Don't just tear your clothing to impress Me, rather tear your hard hearts. Return to Me, Your Lord and God . . . who knows if I will give you mercy and a blessing instead of a curse? Perhaps I'll give you abundant blessings (Joel 2:12-14, *ELT*).[6]

### Fasting as You Wait on God

You can learn many things while you are waiting. For example, if you want to learn human nature, stop everything you're doing and watch people. The great thing about waiting is that you see many things you would miss if you had not been intentional in waiting and watching. When you wait on God, you will discover many things you've never known before. Fasting provides an excellent opportunity to wait on God to experience His goodness. Those who continue to wait before God will learn that "the LORD is good unto them that wait for him" (Lam. 3:25, *KJV*). Waiting is also a time to learn about worship, reverence and trusting. Waiting is a school where we can learn about God Himself.

Have you ever been given a gift but couldn't open it right away? You were told you had to wait until Christmas to open the gift, or you had to wait until your birthday. Waiting makes you focus on the contents of a package. But waiting also teaches you to think about the giver. It binds you to the one who is giving the gift. As you quietly wait on God, enter into His goodness and His presence. Then waiting becomes meaningful because you get something for it. You get God. *Lord, bind my heart on You.*

When you learn the secret art of waiting, you will find the heart of God. Someone has said that we become holy when we learn to wait, because we become like God. "The LORD wait[s], that he may be gracious unto you" (Isa. 30:18, *KJV*). Waiting is a quality of God. We become like Him when we learn to wait. *Lord, I want to be like You.*

As we talk about *waiting*, the implication is that we are waiting for the right time. Sometimes God waits to answer your prayers, because now is not the right time. Maybe you need to learn more lessons. Maybe circumstances need to change. When you pray for a friend or relative to get saved, it may take time for God to bring a soul winner into that person's life to share the gospel—or it may take time for that person to be convicted of his or her sins. Timing is everything with God.

If God could wait 4,000 years until the fullness of time to send His Son into the world (see Gal. 4:4), surely He's not going to hurry up for you. Remember, you can't hurry God the way some of us try to hurry a slow waiter in a restaurant or a child who is grudgingly getting ready for school. As you are waiting, remember that when God prepares to give you something, He will do it on His timetable, not yours.

God wants us to learn the lesson that He is everything. So, the next time you are waiting on God, remember that right around the corner may be the greatest thing you've ever received in your life. It may be that God Himself will be there. *Lord, I'm waiting.*[7]

## Wrap Up

Your soul can know God because your heart has spiritual eyes that can see Him. You will come to understand God and His will for your life as you see Him because of your fast.

Your soul's spiritual ears can hear God; as you listen, you will become familiar with His voice. Fasting can turn your attention to God to hear Him more clearly and learn what He wants you to know.

Your spiritual fingers can touch God, so that you know He's there when you reach out to Him through prayer. Fasting will give you assurance of your relationship with God.

Your spiritual nostrils can sense the beauty of God's perfume and allow you to smell the aroma of His spiritual food. In fasting, you enjoy the fragrance of His Person as you anticipate the smell of the heavenly feast He has prepared for you.

Your spiritual taste can be satisfied by knowing God. Just as food pleases the physical taste and strengthens the body, so can you "taste and see that the Lord is good" (Ps. 34:8)—bringing satisfaction to your life and strength to your soul.

Receive the benediction of Christ: "Blessed are your eyes for they see, and your ears for they hear" (Matt. 13:16).

When God touches your life, you must surrender to His divine purpose. Some are becoming evangelists to win souls. Some are becoming teachers to instruct newborn babes in Christ. Some are becoming pastors to care for the lambs in God's flock. Some are becoming intercessors who can wrestle with the enemy in spiritual warfare. But whatever they are in the process of becoming, each one must yield to the hands of the Sculptor.

## Your Notes

_____
_____
_____
_____
_____
_____
_____
_____
_____

# When Charles Needed a Miracle (continued)

Have you ever thought about the events in your life that stifled your faith in God? In the winter of 1978, I read the book *Coma*.[1] It was a gruesome story about a person who was stealing the body parts of coma patients and selling them. The story was not about how victims became comatose, or whether any of them were healed. It was about criminal intent involving coma patients.

In case you're not familiar with the technical definition of the term (as I wasn't before reading this book):

> Coma, from the Greek word *koma*, meaning deep sleep, is a state of extreme unresponsiveness, in which an individual exhibits no voluntary movement or behavior. Furthermore, in a deep coma, even painful stimuli (actions which, when performed on a healthy individual, result in reactions) are unable to effect any response, and normal reflexes may be lost.[2]

So what did I learn about comas from the book? First, I learned that coma victims were not usually restored to life; as a matter of fact, coma victims were generally considered as good as dead. Second, I learned that coma victims cannot respond to people around them. Therefore, I was conditioned to believe that God couldn't heal a comatose patient.

When Jerry Falwell told me that Charles Hughes was in a "coma," the news triggered the negative thoughts I had from the book I was reading. I wasn't even finished with the book, but I knew a coma was not good. I was pretty sure no one ever recovered from a coma.

"Quick!" Falwell told me to gather everyone in my department around my desk and to kneel down and pray for Charles's recovery. Then he said, "Get the switchboard to alert every departmental superintendent to pray for Charles' healing—now!"

I did as Falwell directed, calling the switchboard and then personally dialing two or three other departments. I dialed as fast as I could, but in my heart I knew it was hopeless. As far as I was concerned, Charles was dead.

While sad, I also felt some positive emotions; for instance, I was glad David Musselman was not injured. I could praise God for His protection and deliverance of this young man.

Within two minutes, my whole staff had gathered around my desk, and we did as Falwell asked—we knelt and prayed. I forget who prayed first, and I really didn't pay attention to anyone else who was praying. I remember that there were tears. In some voices you could feel the urgency, while in other voices you could sense fear.

I heard my staff say things like, "Please don't let him die," "Heal him now," and other heartfelt requests.

I prayed, too, but thoughts of a coma took away the faith I needed to believe that what I was asking was possible. I was controlled by the words of a popular novel, not the Word of God. I was guided by what humans thought, not by what God could do. I prayed a passive prayer: "Lord, if it be Your will, heal Charles." At other times in my life, I would pray with great faith, but not that day. Others had faith. I didn't.

Falwell flew home to conduct a prayer meeting at Thomas Road Baptist Church. Before saying anything else, he gave us an update on Charles's condition, explaining the severity of the damage: "Charles's head has a large gash on the top, and he is on every life-support available."

Falwell instructed us to divide into groups of two—dyads—or groups of three—triads. All of us were to pray out loud with at least one other person and claim healing. I was sitting on the platform and knelt with Falwell at a pulpit bench. I knew that he would pray with great faith, but I knew my faith was weak.

Before we divided into small groups, Falwell announced, "I believe Charles will be healed, and because of this I am going to make a faith-statement now."

I wondered what Falwell would say.

He continued, "I believe Charles will be healed, and next May he is going to be our commencement speaker for Liberty University."

I could have fallen off the pew onto the floor. I couldn't believe my ears. Falwell had just said the opposite of what I believed. In my heart, I knew there was no way that Charles was going to live; that is, if the medical reports I had heard were true. I said under my breath, "You'll be embarrassed when Charles dies!"

But Falwell went on. "We must say what we want from God in faith, because God has promised to hear and answer," he told the congregation. Then he read Mark 11:23: " For assuredly, I say to you, whoever says to this mountain, 'Be removed and be cast into the sea,' and does not doubt in his heart, but believes that those things he says will be done, he will have whatever he says."

I'd like to say that Falwell's reading of the Scriptures helped me to believe, but it didn't. As I later learned, Falwell quite often exercised "Say-It-Faith statements."[3] He said what he wanted God to do, and he asked in faith for it to happen. That was great for Jerry Falwell, but it didn't work for Elmer Towns.

We knelt to pray, and I spoke first: "Lord, you know I don't have faith to pray for Charles's healing. I want him to be healed, and I pray that You would heal him—if it's Your will—through a miracle." I should acknowledge that there have been several occasions on which I have asked for a miracle when I didn't believe God would send a miracle. It seemed like the proper thing to ask, and it's the thing I wanted—but I didn't actually believe that it would happen.

My mind was so boggled by the event that I can't remember how Falwell prayed that evening. I do remember him returning to the pulpit to announce that we were beginning a fast. At this point, I had already participated in several one-day—Yom Kippur-style—fasts in which we had fasted from sundown to sundown.

Falwell announced to the audience that we were beginning just such a fast that night. "I don't know if you ate before you came to church this evening," he said, "but as of right now, we're starting a one-day fast." He explained if we had not eaten, we should begin fasting immediately until the following evening. For those who had eaten, he invited them to join the fast to miss breakfast and lunch the following day.

"Praying is more important than eating," Dr. Falwell reminded all of us. He also reminded us that it's not the fast that heals anyone. It is faith that heals; fasting just motivates us to greater faith.

My own faith, as I have already confessed, was weak when it came to believing that God would heal Charles. But the 4,000 of us who heard and heeded Falwell's call to fast and pray that night must have had enough faith among us to get God's attention, because He gave us what we asked for. Charles did not die.

Kathy Hughes (Charles's wife) later shared her remembrance of those difficult days after the accident:

> The first four weeks in Carlisle, the doctors were more concerned about the stress ulcers that resulted from the trauma to his body. They could not get the bleeding under control and had re-opened the same incision that they used to remove his spleen three times. This last time, they were going to have to remove 98 percent of his stomach, but they determined that he would die on the table if they did that, so they sewed him back up to die. He received more than 40 pints of blood. It was then that Dr. Hughes rallied all to go to the prayer chapel. After that night of begging God to spare his son's life, the bleeding miraculously stopped, never to be a problem again.
>
> After four weeks, he was stable enough to fly by air ambulance to the University of Virginia Hospital in Charlottesville. We were later told that for the sake of the family, he was sent there to be closer to home when he died. Immediately upon his arrival at UVA, they did surgery (two burr holes in the front top of his head) to relieve the

pressure on his brain. He remained another six weeks in a coma.

When he was well enough to leave the hospital, he still could not feed himself or bathe himself, and he could barely talk. They wanted to send him to a nursing home until a space opened up in Rehab for him, but I refused. For me, it was the hospital or home. They reluctantly let him go home. Charles went back for a follow-up visit two or three weeks later, and they were so impressed with his progress that they said it was nothing short of miraculous—and that if he continued to do so well, he would not need to go to Rehab (he never did go to Rehab).[4]

Jump forward to May 1979. The students were seated, waiting for the graduation ceremony to begin. For the service, the university had set up a temporary platform in the back of the dining hall parking lot, because that was the largest paved area on the campus. More than 3,000 folding chairs were set out, and there was a hint of rain in the air. It wasn't warm; rather, the rain was chilly.

In the back of the chapel, Falwell met with his vice presidents, preparing for the entrance onto the parking lot. Charles sat in a chair as he waited to exit the chapel.

"You need a wheelchair, Charles?" Falwell asked.

"No, sir, I want to do this on my own; I want to walk." And walk he did.

There were umbrellas throughout the crowd, but none of the graduates had umbrellas. They just let their robes protect them from the moist air and the cool wind.

I didn't march with the procession that day. I was writing a story to share the miracle of Charles's healing. I walked through the crowd, interviewing different people. I even had a camera slung over my shoulder to take a few pictures. I kept praying, *Lord, help me write this story accurately. Help me tell of Charles's healing so people will believe in Your power—so people will give praise to You.*"

I put my camera to my eye to take a picture of Charles walking up the platform stairs, but I couldn't see to focus my camera.

Taking out a handkerchief, I found myself wiping my eyes rather than the viewing lens. Then I wiped my whole face. I realized I was weeping because I was seeing a miracle I hadn't believed could happen. I saw God do something, and He got all the glory.

Charles's sermon that day was not a great one. As a matter of fact, some of his sentences were incoherent, and his words tumbled out one over the other. Charles had been a fluid preacher, perhaps the best of all the Liberty ministerial students. He had preached at two or three of the largest churches in America; even as a sophomore in college, the power of God was upon him. He preached at Temple Baptist Church in Detroit, Michigan, to a crowd of more than 5,000—and the altar was filled with people seeking salvation.

But on this day, his words were slurred and tumbled over one another. He spoke like a young boy yelling to warn people of fire; at other times, he'd start a sentence over again.

I don't think anyone got much out of Charles's words that day. Whatever message was in his heart, it didn't reach the ears of the audience. But Charles's sermon was one of the greatest any of us had ever experienced. It was not the words he said; it was his life as he stood before us. It was not the sermon; it was the miracle of healing we saw standing before us—preaching.

Here's how Jerry Falwell described the process that brought us to that miraculous moment:

> I told everyone Charles would live if we deeply fasted and prayed from the depths of our hearts. I was so sure that God would answer our prayers that I announced Charles was going to speak at Liberty's graduation next year. Charles lived and was restored enough to bring a powerful message at the 1979 graduation. Liberty had previously had well-known speakers such as Dr. W. A. Criswell of First Baptist Church, Dallas, Texas, and Dr. Charles Stanley, pastor of First Baptist Church, Atlanta, Georgia, but to me the greatness of that message was not what Charles said, but the testimony of his healing as he stood before the audience that day.[5]

There had been 4,000 students in the prayer meeting that night when we first heard the details of the accident and Charles's condition. Most of these students had fasted for their school-mate's healing. Now they saw with their own eyes God's answer to their prayers. They heard with their own ears the voice of a man speaking as though from the dead.

God listens and answers when many interces-sors agree together in sincere, united prayer.

Charles helped his father plant a church in Pensacola, Florida, in 1980. The next year, they planted another church in Titusville, Florida. Charles served on the staff at Titusville's Temple Baptist before going on to pastor Glen Fork Baptist Temple in Glen Fork, West Virginia. Then he returned to Lynchburg to be on staff at Thomas Road Baptist Church. He eventually completed his M.A.R, M.R.E., and M.Div. degrees. Then Charles pushed on to become the first graduate of Lynchburg Christian Academy to go all the way through the University and receive a Doctor of Ministry de-gree from Liberty Baptist Theological Seminary.

Where do you think Charles ministers today? He's not in a classroom or a counseling ministry, nor is he working in any office at Liberty University. Charles is a full-time campus pastor for prayer and leads what may be the only full-time prayer ministry in any school in America at the Prayer Center at Liberty University.

## Praying for Severely Injured Victims

There is great power in prayer, and sometimes—as we have seen in Charles's story—prayer accomplishes things that medical science cannot. However, that does not mean that we should neglect or hinder proper medical care, or that we should pray wildly without applying reason to our requests. Following are some principles to keep in mind when praying for someone who has suffered a serious injury.

## Do Everything Medically Possible First

First, *do everything medically and physically possible for the accident victim before you begin praying, calling for others to pray, and/or trying to marshal spiritual activity.* Some might disagree and say prayer should come before doing anything else. But at a time when Jesus faced grave danger, He told His disciples, "Watch and pray" (Matt. 26:41). In this instance, prayer came after watching. The disciples' main duty was guarding and watching for Jesus; their second responsibility was to pray for Him.

Always, let's do first things first. Remove the person from any situation that could cause further damage, such as a burning car or the middle of a busy intersection. By doing everything you can for the victim, you are paving the way for the victim's rehabilitation and future health. Once you get the victim into an ambulance, or to the hospital, or under professional care, then you can devote your mind to prayer. But if you haven't done all you can do physically for them to survive, it might not be possible for you to do all you can do in prayer to help them spiritually.

## Remember Your Obligations

*Remember that you have an obligation to survivors, witnesses and those with you.* If you begin praying for the victim to be healed before you stop the bleeding, or before you remove them from danger, you may damage your testimony to those who see what you are doing. They will expect you to first help the person physically.

## Pray for Those Giving Care

*Pray for doctors, nurses, and emergency personnel who are giving medical aid to the victim.* Pray for them to make the correct diagnoses, and to do all things correctly. Pray that they will have wisdom to properly prescribe medication and use "life-saving" instruments. Praying for medical personnel may be just as important as praying for the recovery of the injured.

## Don't Pray for the Unreasonable

*Do not pray for restoration of organs or limbs by creative miracles.* I remember once hearing a preacher pray for a man to see through his glass eye. God does the miraculous, but He doesn't do the unreasonable. A glass eye doesn't have all the functions and properties of a physical eye, and a glass eye cannot be tied to the optic systems of the nerves and brain for any person. While the preacher's desire to help a man see is commendable, this was probably a prayer he shouldn't have made. He did not make a good impression on me, nor did he have a good testimony to the friends with me.

Then the preacher went even further. He prayed for the glass eye to become a regular physical eye. Again, the preacher was asking for something that's not even supernatural. Yes, God does impossible things (see Matt. 17:20; 19:26), but He doesn't do the absurd.[6]

God heals and stops cancer—and He does sometimes cure blindness. But if a person has lost a limb, you can't pray for that limb to be recreated. The act of creation has ceased; God does not add creative miracles to His agenda today. "So the creation of the heavens and the earth and everything in them was completed" (Gen. 2:1, *NLT*). The *King James Version* says, "God ended his work which he had made; and he rested . . . from all his work which he had made" (Gen. 2:2).

Let's first consider what this verse doesn't mean. It doesn't mean that God got tired, so He had to take a break and stop working for a while. God is omnipotent and has all power to do all things. The word "rest" means that God stopped His creative activity. It doesn't mean that He stopped working in the world. He lets this universe proceed according to the laws He's established.[7] God still works providentially (see Rom. 8:28), but He has ceased His creative work. So when a hand is cut off, it might be surgically repaired and re-attached, but you can't pray for another hand to be regenerated by a creative act.

There are several miracles that will only ever happen once. Let's remember the miracles and praise God for His greatness, but let's not ask God to do it again. The very nature of some supernatural miracles is non-reproducible: Creation, the virgin birth, the incarnation, Jesus' resurrection from the dead, and His second coming to earth.

## Pray with the Person

*Finally, pray for the person in his or her presence.* I have heard of instances where a sick person did not hear anything spoken in the hospital room or surrounding him, but when somebody prayed out loud in front of him, he heard everything that was said. Your prayers may reach God, but the sound of your voice may also encourage the victim—and their positive attitude may give them a will to survive. That in itself may lead to restoration.

# APPENDIX A

# What Is Fasting?

## Definition

### What Is Fasting?

Fasting is a spiritual discipline involving abstention from some or all food for a certain time limit for a divine purpose. Some feel that when one withdraws voluntarily from the enjoyment or necessity of food, that person is obeying God and the Scriptures; hence, that person grows in faith. It is not their abstinence from food that gives them an answer to their prayer; it is their faith in God (see Heb. 11:6) and their relationship with Him.

### Fasting and Dieting

Fasting is not the same thing as dieting. While there can be many physical and/or health benefits from abstaining from food(s) and/or certain liquid drinks, spiritual fasting has a supernatural element. First, it is a vow to God.[1] Second, it is a spiritual experience in the presence of God. Third, it has a divine purpose.[2]

### Origination of Fasting

The Hebrew term for fasting (*tsom*) was originally associated with an emergency or distress; people lost their appetites because of personal anguish or fear. When we rush to the hospital because a loved one has had an accident, we lose our hunger for a hamburger at lunchtime. The body no longer craves food. All we want to do is fix the problem. When a problem is too big for a person to fix by himself, that person may fast and pray until an answer is achieved.

Fasting was originally commanded for all of God's people on the Day of Atonement, i.e., a day of repentance and seeking forgiveness of sin. "On the tenth day of the seventh month of each year, you must go without eating to show sorrow for your sins" (Lev. 16:29, CEV). Today, a one-day fast is often called by its Hebrew term, a Yom Kippur fast. Many believers fast from sundown to sundown, following the designation for a day that God gave in Genesis 1:5: "The evening and the morning were the first day." During mealtime on the Day of Atonement, the Jews fasted and prayed instead of eating.

A Yom Kippur fast skips the evening meal of the first day, and breakfast and lunch of the second day. A conscientious Jew does not break his fast until the sun goes down on the second day. Christians follow this example.

Spiritual fasting has been used in the Christian Church since its beginning (see Acts 13:2-3). However, until recently, there had been few books written on fasting in the Western Church in the past 100 years. The topic has returned to the forefront in the past few years.

## Six Ways to Fast

There are probably as many ways to fast in our modern times as there are ways to pray—the following six methods of fasting are suggested guidelines.

The *normal fast* or *juice fast* involves going without food for a definite period during which you ingest only liquids (water and/or juice). The duration can be 1 day, 3 days, 1 week, 1 month or 40 days. Extreme care should be taken with longer fasts, which should only be attempted after obtaining medical advice from your physician.

The *absolute fast* allows no food or water at all, and must be short. No one should attempt an absolute fast longer than three days. A person will die if they go longer than seven days without water. The average body is 55 percent to 80 percent water, and must be replenished on a regular basis.

The *Daniel fast*, also called a *partial fast*, omits certain foods or incorporates a schedule that limits eating. It may consist of omitting one meal a day. Eating only fresh vegetables for several days is also considered a partial fast.

A *rotational fast*, also called a *Mayo Clinic fast*, consists of eating or omitting certain families of foods for designated periods. A person may observe an absolute fast for one day to cleanse his bodily system. Then for the next week, he eats food from only one food group or food family. The various food families are rotated to determine what illness may be attributed to certain families of food.

The *John Wesley fast* was practiced by Wesley, the founder of Methodism, prior to a Methodist Conference where the ministers gathered for retreat, revival, and preparation for continual ministry. Wesley and the other leaders consumed only bread and water for 10 days prior to the conference to prepare themselves spiritually for teaching the pastors.

The Bible describes a *supernatural fast*: "[Moses] was there with the LORD forty days and forty nights; he neither ate bread nor drank water" (Exod. 34:28). God did a supernatural miracle for Moses in this fast; a person normally dies if they go without water for more than 7 days. No one should attempt a 40-day fast without water.[3]

## References

Elmer Towns, *The Daniel Fast* (Ventura, CA: Regal Books, 2010).

_____, *Knowing God Through Fasting* (Shippensburg, PA: Destiny Image, 2002). This volume is suggested for its spiritual benefit of developing an intimate relationship with God.

_____, *Fasting for Spiritual Breakthrough* (Ventura, CA: Regal Books, 1996). This book shares practical verses about fasting and has been on the bestseller list for Regal Books for the past 15 years. To order the book, contact Regal Books (www.regalbooks.com or 1-800-4-GOSPEL).

# APPENDIX B

# The Miraculous Bible

A belief in miracles is indispensable to belief in a real living God. And a belief in the miracles found in the Bible is indispensable to believing that the Bible is a living book that came from God. Indeed, the Bible is miraculous in the writing of the original manuscripts by inspiration, miraculous in its content, and miraculous even today in its impact and influence on those who read it.

Everything about the Bible is supernatural, including the way the original autographs were conceived, written and inspired. Since a perfect God wrote the Bible through limited human beings, it must be concluded that the Bible is a perfect book, even as it reflects the limitations of its authors.

Today we use the phrase "dual authorship" to indicate that holy men of God wrote a holy book, but the Holy Spirit also wrote the Bible. Human authors scribed with their limited knowledge, limited vocabulary, and even limited use of grammar. God guided them so that what they wrote was perfect—without error (see 2 Tim. 3:16).

The word "inspired" means "God-breathed." God breathed His Spirit into the words of the Bible as it was being written, making it His book. The Holy Spirit is in the words of Scripture. Therefore, those who read and believe the Bible can be transformed by God's Spirit, who lives in the book.

We believe that God has inspired every word of the Bible, down to its minutest detail—such as the dotting of an *I* or the crossing of a *T*. Why do we believe that? Because Jesus promised, "Till heaven and earth pass away, one jot or one tittle will by no means pass from the law till all is fulfilled" (Matt. 5:18). Jesus personally guarantees the accuracy of the Bible.

ELMER L. TOWNS

To believe in the Bible is to believe in Jesus, and the reverse is also true; to put confidence in Jesus is to trust the Bible.

Following the same reasoning, to reject the Bible is to reject Jesus, and those who reject the Son of God do not have eternal life (see 1 John 5:11-13).

Archeology continues to confirm the accuracy of the Bible. Every time an archeologist's spade uncovers ancient treasures, it verifies the message of the Bible. It seems that every time liberal claims are made—asserting that there are mistakes in the Bible, or that there are no places like Jericho, or that there are two Isaiahs or two Daniels—the opposite has been demonstrated.

The Bible predicted that Jesus would be born in Bethlehem of a virgin; that He would do miracles; that He would ride into the city of Jerusalem on a donkey, be betrayed for 30 pieces of silver, and be crucified on a tree; and that He would cry out in death, "My God, My God, why have You forsaken Me?" (Ps. 22:1). The liberals say that all those statements were written after the fact, many years after Jesus lived. If the liberals are correct, then Jesus is not who He said He was—the Son of God.

But two startling scientific facts demonstrate that the liberals are wrong. First, the Septuagint—translations of the Hebrew Bible into Greek—was completed during the period from 275 BC to 100 BC. Therefore, we know that the Old Testament was written more than 200 years before Jesus was born. We have those manuscripts. We can touch them, read them, and say with authority that the liberals are wrong.

Then a little shepherd boy discovered the first of the Dead Sea Scrolls. These scrolls were copies of the Old Testament, written approximately 400 years before Jesus was born. I have been to Jerusalem, visited the Shrine of the Book, and actually read some of these documents.

How did God do this miracle? The Bible had approximately 40 authors, who were separated by 1,500 miles, wrote over a period of 2,000 years, and came from different vocations—writers included lawyers, fishermen, herdsmen, and a medical doctor. Yet with all of the possibilities for error and contradiction because of so many sources, the Bible has one theme, one thrust, and centers around one person, i.e., the Lord Jesus Christ. Forty humans working independently could not possibly be as consistent in their writing as were the authors writing Scripture under the divine inspiration of God.

Not only is the Bible supernatural in its writing, but it is also miraculous in its influence on people. No other book has transformed as many men and women as has the Bible. When prostitutes, thieves, murderers and addicts read the Bible—when these individuals meet Jesus Christ through the pages of Scripture—they are transformed by the message of the Bible. Why is that?

The Bible regenerates; those who receive and believe its message are born again (see John 3:5; 6:63-68; Heb. 4:12; Jas. 1:18; 1 Pet. 1:22-23). The Bible gives power to break addiction; it gives new desire to live a godly life; it gives new purpose to serve others; it motivates its readers to share the gospel with unsaved people; it connects people to God in prayer, worship and communion; and it guides believers in their daily lives. When Scripture touches people's lives and they want to live for God, they sacrifice self-motivated pursuits and are even willing to die or be a martyr for the Lord who loved them first by dying for them.

The Bible is miraculous in its perseverance throughout history. In AD 303, the Roman emperor, Diocletian, issued a decree to destroy the Scriptures. However, only a few years later, the message of the Bible captured Constantine and he became a follower of Jesus Christ. When Constantine became Caesar, he declared Christianity a religion of Rome, and the Bible's influence continued its march across the known world.

Rulers have tried to corral it by laws, infidels have tried to prove that God—its Author—doesn't exist, liberal theologians have tried to deny biblical revelation, opponents have tried to argue that it's not inspired, and skeptics have tried to explain away its message. Yet, the Bible stands as strong as ever, its revelation as powerful as ever and its influence as wide as ever.

The Bible has supernaturally persevered because its Author, God, protects it, guides it, and continues to miraculously use its message of transformation and regeneration.

ELMER L. TOWNS

We do not have the original documents written by the authors of the Bible, but we have what no other ancient manuscript has—abundant support.

There are seven copies of Plato's works, eight copies of Herodotus' history, nine copies of Euripides's plays, and five copies of Aristotle's writings. There are very few original copies of ancient manuscripts that are accepted by universities and studies as true. But there are more than 40,000 copies of the Bible that are studied and protected. Why so many? Because God wrote the Scriptures through human authors, has supernaturally preserved His Word, and continues to use its message to save individuals from eternal hell. Why? Because God so loves people that He sent His Son to die to forgive their sins and give them eternal life (see John 3:16). God has protected the Bible so that people would have the opportunity to hear that message and call on Jesus Christ for salvation.

Just before his death, Sir Walter Scott was taken into his library and seated by a large window where he could view the scenery. As he sat there, he called to his son-in-law to "get the book" and read to him. During his lifetime, Scott had built one of the world's largest private libraries, so his son-in-law asked the logical question: "From what book shall I read?"

Scott's reply was simple: "There is but one."[1]

Yes, there is only one book that stands above all the rest: God's book. Critics can criticize all they want, but in the end the Bible stands in its beauty and authority. The Bible is miraculous because it is God's Word.

# APPENDIX C

# Biblical Words for Miracles

There are four words used in the Bible to describe the supernatural. First, a *miracle*, as described by C. S. Lewis, is "an interference with Nature by supernatural power."[1] Second, a *sign* is a supernatural visual event that authenticates a man sent from God and verifies that his message comes from God. Third, *wonders* are miraculous acts of God that verify His self-revelation as the Creator and Controller of events. Wonders are usually done in the sky or heavens and generally do not occur by themselves, but are connected to miracles, signs, and the work of God. The fourth is an active *work* of God, which is something He performs that may be unexpected from a human perspective, but is expected for a deity to do. Jesus said, "My Father has been working until now, and I have been working" (John 5:17).

| English Word | Modern Greek | Original Greek | Short Definition |
|---|---|---|---|
| miracles | *dunamis* | δύναμις | interruption of the laws of nature |
| signs | *semeion* | σημεῖον | that which authenticates |
| wonders | *teras* | τέρας | a marvel, wonder, or supernatural event |
| works | *ergon* | ἔργον | supernatural results (i.e., God's workmanship) |

One verse describes all four of these actions: "God also bearing witness both with signs and wonders, with various miracles, and gifts of the Holy Spirit, according to His own will [works]" (Heb.

2:4). According to the definitions above, the verse could be para-phrased, "God gave witness by authenticating His message to the world, so that people marveled when they saw His supernatural intervention in the laws of nature, as He performed the works that only God can do" (*ELT*).

## Miracles

A miracle is beyond human possibility; only God does miracles. So when you fast for a supernatural healing, it's not what you do, nor is it even your faith. A miracle is a manifestation of God's power.

The word "miracle" describes (1) the power, strength or inherent ability that resides in God who acts, (2) the influences that come from the Person who has the source of power, (3) the innate ability of God to do what is required at the time, and (4) the demonstration of the Person's ability.

*Dunamis* is used 119 times in the New Testament. It is translated as "miracle(s)" 7 times in most translations. It is otherwise translated as "power," "mighty work," "mighty," "ability," "powerfully" and "miraculous power." *Dunamis* is the word from which we get "dynamite": a blasting compound that generates explosive force. Following are a few examples of the use of this term in Scripture:

- Miracles caused amazement in Simon (see Acts 8:13).
- Unusual miracles (see Acts 19:11).
- Miracles attested Jesus Christ (see Acts 2:22).
- Some have spiritual gifts to do miracles (see 1 Cor. 12:10,28).

## Signs

The word "sign" has several meanings: (1) to signify or make known the nature of a thing; (2) a visual means of information, direction or explanation; (3) a mark or token; (4) to distinguish from others; and (5) a biblical sign authenticates a man or a message as belonging to, or coming from, God.

John describes the miracles of Jesus as signs. "Truly Jesus did many other signs in the presence of His disciples" (John 20:30). Jesus authenticated Himself by His sign-miracles, which were then written down so that readers today could witness them and be saved: "But these [signs] are written that you may believe that Jesus is the Christ, the Son of God, and that believing you may have life" (v. 31).

The word *semeion* ("sign") is used throughout the Bible:

- The sun and stars are signs (see Gen. 1:14).
- Moses did signs to authenticate his message to Pharaoh (see Exod. 4:9,17,30).
- Signs caused the disciples to believe in Jesus (see John 2:11).
- Signs were an outgrowth of ministry (see Mark 16:17).
- Signs authenticated an apostle (see 2 Cor. 12:12).
- Satan shall do signs (see 2 Thess. 2:9).

## Wonders

The Greek word for "wonder" is *teras* and refers to the results or response of those who see or experience a miracle or supernatural sign. A wonder usually relates to the expected response when God does the supernatural: People marvel. In the Bible, wonders are usually attached to miracles or signs:

- God did wonders before an unbelieving Pharaoh (see Exod. 3:20; 4:21; 11:10).
- Israel praised God because of wonders (see Exod. 15:11).
- Joshua expected God to do wonders (see Josh. 3:5).
- The psalmist worshiped God for His wonders (see Ps. 77:11).
- Wonders will accompany Christ's second coming (see Acts 2:19-20).
- Wonders are attached to signs and miracle (see Acts 2:22; Heb. 2:4).
- Satan can do wonders (see 2 Thess. 2:9).

# Works

The fourth word used to describe the supernatural is *ergon* ("works").
While this word occurs 188 times in the Greek manuscript, it does
not always mean a supernatural work of God. *Ergon* can mean:

1. business, employment, or craft of one's hand;
2. the enterprises one undertakes to do;
3. the accomplishment of skill, training, and discipline
   that is usually done with the hand, but can be a work of
   the mind or emotions;
4. an act, deed, or accomplishment of effort or determination; and
5. occupation, job, or employment.

*Ergon* is the opposite of uselessness or idleness. A person works
when they expect a return for their efforts.

The word *ergon* describes the task that Jesus came to do on
earth, almost as a human might describe the labor he does for a living. Jesus did the work of the Father (see John 5:36), and both Jesus
and the Father work (see John 5:17). Jesus also refers to one of His
miracles as a work (see John 7:21).

At one point, a crowd asked Jesus to give them the ability to do
the work of God. "What shall we do, that we may work the works
of God?" (John 6:28).

Jesus answered that the beginning of one's work for God is believing. "This is the work of God, that you believe in Him whom He
sent" (John 6:29). Therefore, our faith is the basic prerequisite for
doing anything miraculous in serving God. *Ergon* appears fre-
quently in the New Testament narratives:

- Unbelief hinders the work of God (see Mark 6:5).
- Jesus did the Father's work on earth (see John 4:34).
- No one can do God's work without faith (see John 6:29).
- Jesus finished the work the Father sent Him to do (see
  John 17:4).
- Believers can do the works of Jesus (see John 14:12).

Biblical Words for Miracles    237

- The Holy Spirit sent out missionaries to do God's work (see Acts 13:2).
- Some refused to do God's work (see Acts 15:38).

# Wrap Up

Only God can do miracles, and those who think they can do the supernatural through any inherent ability of their own are misguided. However, God wants to do the supernatural through His yielded servants today (see John 14:12; Mark 16:17). Those who would do the supernatural must begin with faith (see John 6:29).

God does miracles for a variety of purposes; if we want to see miracles happen, we must pray according to the will and work of God. There were many occasions on which Jesus was asked to do miracles, but He didn't do them just to satisfy the curiosity of the crowd (see John 6:30-36; Matt. 12:38-39).

Sometimes a miracle confirmed that a speaker was sent from God; at other times, a miracle authenticated the message that was given. These were called sign-miracles.

When miracles were done, people often marveled or showed great joy. This is the *wonder* aspect of a miracle. Sometimes wonders are attached to the supernatural phenomena done in heaven.

Not everyone will do miracles, nor should everyone pray for miracles. It is said of John the Baptist that he "performed no sign" (John 10:41). John had a greater task than to authenticate his message by miracles. The message of John the Baptist was "Jesus." The Father authenticated Jesus when He said, "This is My beloved Son, in whom I am well pleased" (Matt. 3:17). The Holy Spirit authenticated Jesus when "He saw the Spirit of God descending like a dove and alighting upon Him" (Matt. 3:16). We should have John the Baptist's attitude when seeking the supernatural: "He must increase, but I must decrease" (John 3:30).

ELMER L. TOWNS

# APPENDIX D

# Nine Different Purposes for Fasting

Shelly Seager and her husband, Dave, were students at Liberty University. As Shelly, my secretary at the time, was typing the manuscript for the book *Fasting for Spiritual Breakthrough*, she and Dave tried a fast of their own.[1]

Dave had just graduated, and he had interviewed for a job in Harrisburg, Pennsylvania. Shelly described this position as "an opportunity of a lifetime." So they agreed to fast, something they had never tried before. They fasted for 24 hours and spent much time in prayer. The morning after Dave had spent extra time in prayer about his dream job, the long-distance call came from Harrisburg. They offered him the position.

Of course not every circumstance in life can be "fixed" by fasting, but God can be touched when His people obey the command to fast and pray.

Richard Foster, the author who has awakened so many people to the spiritual disciplines, observed at one point that there had not been a major book on fasting for a hundred years.

Why? Perhaps people these days are so much into "feel-good religion" that they don't want to be bothered with any thought of hunger or self-denial. Perhaps our confidence in activity, such as splashy evangelistic programs, has made us forget the spiritual side of God's work. Perhaps the widespread promise that "you can have it all" has blocked all thought of sacrifice and discipline.

Isaiah 58 provides principles for genuine biblical fasting. Rightly used, these types of fasting can help us touch God for those things for which we pray. Notice what God says about fasting:

Is not this the fast that I have chosen? to loose the bands of wickedness, to undo the heavy burdens, and to let the oppressed go free, and that ye break every yoke? Is it not to deal thy bread to the hungry, and that thou bring the poor that are cast out to thy house? when thou seest the naked, that thou cover him; and that thou hide not thyself from thine own flesh? Then shall thy light break forth as the morning, and thine health shall spring forth speedily: and thy righteousness shall go before thee; the glory of the LORD shall be thy reward (vv. 6-8, *KJV*).

This passage mentions nine objectives of fasting. When we properly fast, we can claim the promises that God makes in Isaiah 58:6-8. Each of the nine results has been given a title to help identify in your mind the results you seek.

## The Nine Results of Fasting

1. To loosen the bonds of wickedness, i.e., to break sin's addiction (The Disciple's Fast);

2. To undo heavy burdens, i.e., to solve problems (The Ezra Fast);

3. To let the oppressed go free, i.e., for revival and soul winning (The Samuel Fast);

4. To break every yoke, i.e., to overcome discouragement or despondency (The Elijah Fast);

5. To give bread to the hungry and provide the poor with housing, i.e., to care for the needy (The Widow's Fast);

6. To allow light to break forth like the morning, i.e., to make decisions and gain insight (The Saint Paul Fast);

7. To cause health to spring forth speedily, i.e., for healing and physical health (The Daniel Fast);

8. To cause righteousness to go before them, i.e., for testimony and influence (The John the Baptist Fast); and

9. To cause the glory of the Lord to be their reward (or "rear guard," *NIV*); i.e., for protection from evil (The Esther Fast).

The following nine fasts are not the only results of fasting available to the believer, nor are they totally separate from each other. Nor do I want to suggest that any one fast is the only way to fast for a particular problem. These suggested fasts are models to use and should be adjusted to your own particular needs and desires as you seek to grow closer to God. The following is a brief overview of the nine fasts.

## 1. The Disciple's Fast

*Purpose*: "To loose the bands of wickedness" (Isa. 58:6)—freeing ourselves and others from addictions to sin.

*Key Verse*: "This kind goeth not out but by prayer and fasting" (Matt. 17:21, *KJV*).

*Background*: Jesus cast out a demon from a boy whom the disciples had failed to help. Apparently they had not taken seriously enough the way Satan had his claws set in the youth. The implication is that Jesus' disciples could have performed this exorcism had they been willing to undergo the discipline of fasting. Modern disciples also often make light of "besetting sins" we could cast out if we were serious enough to take part in such self-denying practices as fasting—hence the term "Disciple's Fast."

"I have a sexual addiction," a person told me at the church altar. This person had been to several counselors, had come to the altar several times, and tried everything suggested. This person was serious about being released from the problem.

"Have you tried fasting?" I asked.

"No."

I took this person through the steps described in the Disciple's Fast as a means of breaking bondage. This person wanted me to pray and fast with him, but I refused. Some addicts want to depend on the faith of others, rather than developing their own faith to break addiction. I told this person that once they began fasting, that I would later join him. Twice this person fasted and there was no breakthrough. Then I joined in the Disciple's Fast, not to be a substitute for his responsibility, but I wanted to come alongside and add value to this person's life. I wanted to support him in his struggle to be free in Christ.

Many Christians are helpless victims to a besetting sin (see Heb. 12:1). This is not your average sin of neglect or momentary lapse. This is not even the sin of rebellion where God says, "Thou shalt not," and the person says, "I will" in God's face. A "besetting" sin is habitual sinful behavior or attitudes that victimize you. A besetting sin puts you into bondage.

When you are a victim of a besetting sin, you do not clench your fist in the face of God and transgress His purpose; you are helpless and broken because of your sin. A besetting sin makes you a slave and takes away your will. You cry out "I can't help myself!" as one person once said, "I am forced to play a game where I always lose, and I can't quit playing. I hate the game . . . I hate playing . . . I hate life."

Thanks to the Disciple's Fast, a person's addiction can be broken and he can enter freedom in Christ.

## 2. The Ezra Fast

*Purpose*: To "undo the heavy burdens" (Isa. 58:6)—inviting the Holy Spirit's aid in lifting loads and overcoming problems that keep ourselves and our loved ones from walking joyfully with the Lord.

*Key Verse*: "So we fasted and entreated our God for this, and he answered our prayer" (Ezra 8:23).

*Background*: Ezra the priest was charged with restoring the Law of Moses among the Jews as they rebuilt the city of Jerusalem by permission of Artaxerxes, King of Persia, where God's people had been captive. Despite this permission, Israel's enemies opposed them. Burdened with embarrassment about having to ask the Persian king for an army to protect them, Ezra fasted and prayed for an answer to his problem.

Everyone has problems and hard times. Job, in the oldest book of the Bible said, "Man who is born of woman is of few days, and full of trouble" (Job 14:1). Because of the nature of the world, everything that is made will break. Every person eventually will get old and feeble. Every business will collapse if not attended. Houses must be painted, cars must be tuned up, fields must be replanted every Spring, and everyone faces problems that must be solved. Again, Job understood this: "Man is born into trouble as surely as the sparks fly upward" (Job 5:7, *NIV*).

The Ezra Fast is for those difficult problems that won't go away. It's when we fast for a problem and God sends an answer. The Ezra Fast is for those who have prayed, so now they fast and pray for an answer from God.

### 3. The Samuel Fast

*Purpose*: "To let the oppressed (physically and spiritually) go free" (Isa. 58:6)—to identify with enslaved people everywhere, and to pray for God to bring people out of the kingdom of darkness into salvation.

*Key Verse*: "So they gathered together at Mizpah, drew water, and poured it out before the LORD. And they fasted that day, and said there, 'We have sinned against the LORD' " (1 Sam. 7:6).

*Background*: Samuel led God's people in a fast to celebrate the return of the Ark of the Covenant from its captivity by the Philistines. As a result of their fast, God sent revival to Israel.

The Samuel Fast for evangelism and revival has been applied throughout Church history. Before Jonathan Edwards preached his famous sermon, "Sinners in the Hands of an Angry God," he

244 Fasting for a Miracle

spent the previous 24 hours in an absolute fast. Many credit this sermon as the beginning of the first Great Awakening that shook America and England.

### 4. The Elijah Fast

*Purpose*: "To break every yoke" (Isa. 58:6)—conquering fear and other emotional problems that would control our lives.

*Key Verses*: "He himself went a day's journey into the desert . . . He arose and ate and drank; and he went in the strength of that food forty days and forty nights" (1 Kings 19:4, 8).

*Background*: Although Scripture does not call this a formal "fast," Elijah was struggling with negative emotions. Elijah deliberately went without food as he fled from Queen Jezebel's threat to kill him, and as he struggled with his own negative emotions. Before Elijah's self-imposed dep-rivation began, God sent an angel to minister to him in the wilderness, and after the fast was completed, God spoke to Elijah directly and gave him a new mission (see 1 Kings 19:9-18).

The Elijah Fast is designed to break emotional habits of despon-dency or discouragement. A young man at the church altar told me he couldn't stop cursing. He said he had a bad habit—that it was just rooted in his subconscious.

"Do you want to stop cursing?" I asked.

"Yup." His answer didn't reflect a deep desire to stop.

I explained the Elijah Fast to him, telling him that when he took control of his body by denying it food, he was also taking control of his inner life.

"Your self-denial of food will tell God you are serious about changing your mouth," I told him.

I was not sure he was serious, nor was I sure he could break the cursing habit. But later he reported that he had fasted—which he had never done before—and that only a few times had he slipped and let a curse word out.

Two years later, when he graduated from the university, he told me God had completely delivered him from a filthy mouth.

## 5. The Widow's Fast

*Purpose*: "To deal thy bread to the hungry" (Isa. 58:7, *KJV*)—caring for the poor and providing for the needy.

*Key Verse*: "The jar of flour was not used up and the jug of oil did not run dry, in keeping with the word of the LORD spoken by Elijah" (1 Kings 17:16, *NIV*).

*Background*: God sent the prophet Elijah to a poor, starving widow—ironically, the widow went without food to provide food to Elijah. Today, we may choose to do without food so we can give the money we save by not eating to humanitarian causes.

A pastor in Chiapas, Mexico, had made a practice of distributing Bibles door-to-door. The people in his area were hungry for the Word of God. When they received a Bible, they would immediately sit down with it to read and learn God's message to them.

When the pastor ran out of Bibles to deliver, he did without food and spent his salary to purchase more Bibles. Three days later, some of the people realized that the pastor had not been coming to the market to buy food. While he did not enter a formal fast in the traditional sense, this pastor followed the prescription for the Widow's Fast. Within his own admirable value system, he had chosen abstinence for the good of others and service to God. Scripture provides several illustrations of widows who did without food so others could eat. Today, the Widow's Fast entails practical abstinence when an individual or family gives up food or a meal to contribute to meeting the physical needs of others.

## 6. The Saint Paul Fast

*Purpose*: To allow God's "light [to] break forth as the morning" (Isa. 58:8, *KJV*)—bringing clearer perspective and insight as we make crucial decisions.

*Key Verse:* "And he [Saul, or Paul] was three days without sight, and neither ate nor drank" (Acts 9:9).

*Background:* Saul of Tarsus, who became known as Paul after his conversion to Christ, was struck blind by the Lord while he was in the act of persecuting Christians. Saul not only was without literal sight, but he also had no clue about what direction his life was to take. After going without food and praying for three days, Paul was given both his eyesight and a spiritual vision for the future.

A ministerial student once fasted before accepting a position as an associate pastor in a large and prominent church. Like Saul on the road to Damascus, the student needed guidance from God about what he should do. During the fast, God shut the door to the potential position in the student's mind. He lost his burden for the church that had issued him an invitation.

A month later, the senior pastor at that church resigned, and the board asked for the resignations of all staff members. Before the Saint Paul Fast, the student was flattered by the prospect of ministering in a prominent church, but when he retreated into a quiet place and fasted to focus on the will of God, the insight he received proved to be providential. If the student had accepted the call to that church, he would have been released within a few months of arriving there.

We all face major decisions in our lives, so all of us will need the Saint Paul Fast at some time. These kinds of decisions redirect our entire life—maybe even our destiny. A decision about what person to marry, for example, can make us or break us. In many other ways, we stand at a fork in the road and must make the decision to turn either to the left or the right.

If we knew everything that lay ahead on each road, the decision would probably be easy. If we knew the good things that would happen, the decision to move forward would be easier. If we knew the dangers ahead, we might be discouraged and turn back. But we don't know either of those things. If we follow the Saint Paul Fast, God will cause His "light [to] break forth as the morning" (Isa. 58:8, *KJV*). If we focus on God's will instead of our own when we face such major decisions, He will bring us clearer perspective and the insight we need to make crucial decisions.

## 7. The Daniel Fast

*Purpose*: So "thine health shall spring forth" (Isa. 58:8, *KJV*)—seeking healing or physical wellbeing.

*Key Verse*: "Daniel purposed in his heart that he would not defile himself with the portion of the king's delicacies, nor with the wine which he drank" (Dan. 1:8).

*Background*: Daniel and three of his fellow Hebrew captives kept themselves from pagan foods and became healthier than others in the king's court. Today, God can heal in response to prayer and fasting. Sometimes healing comes from an improved diet, and at other times God heals supernaturally.

God heals in many different ways. He heals when a disease or infection is stopped or reversed. He heals by a physician's correct diagnosis and prescription of medication, or by surgery that removes the cause of the illness, or by a change in the patient's physical routine. God can heal by supernatural intervention or by divine providence—working His will by directing the circumstances of life.

Fasting plays many roles in healing. God may heal supernaturally in response to a fast (see chapter 3, "Challenging Cancer and Changing God's Mind"). Fasting can also lead to God's guidance, so that the sick person adjusts his life to find healing.

Then too, fasting may result in a vow to adopt a healthy lifestyle. Some might vow a life-long abstinence from alcoholic beverages, or choose to break other "risky" food habits that are not necessarily healthy. The person finds health by keeping his vow.

## 8. The John the Baptist Fast

*Purpose*: That "thy righteousness shall go before thee" (Isa. 58:8, *KJV*)—enhancing our testimony and our influence for Jesus Christ.

*Key Verse*: "He shall be great in the sight of the Lord, and shall drink neither wine nor strong drink" (Luke 1:15, *KJV*).

*Background*: John the Baptist took the "Nazarite" vow that required him to avoid (or fast from) wine and strong drink. This was part of John's purposefully chosen lifestyle that set him apart as a special testimony for the cause of Christ.

A woman in a certain church spread lies about the church's pastoral ministry and integrity. The church's board did not capitulate to her demands, but fasted once a week for the testimony of the church and the pastor. When the woman threatened to sue the church over alleged damages, and the threatened lawsuit was publicized in the local newspaper, the board thought its worst fears were realized and that God hadn't honored their fast.

Then the board received letters from leaders at two other churches, saying that the woman had "pulled the same stunt" in their churches. Unfortunately, the other churches had given in to her demands and paid her off. The newspaper printed these letters, and the lawyer who had threatened to sue the church changed his mind and refused to represent the woman. He suggested that the church had a legal complaint against her, although he stated that he couldn't get involved. The church board did not sue her. The Lord had honored their John the Baptist Fast, so they entered into another fast for the woman's spiritual health.

### 9. The Esther Fast

*Purpose*: That "the glory of the LORD will be your rear guard" (Isa. 58:8, *NIV*)—seeking God's protection from the evil one.

*Key Verses*: " 'Fast for me. . . . I and my maids will fast . . . [and] I will go to the king.' . . . He was pleased with her." (Esther 4:16; 5:2).

*Background*: Queen Esther, a Jewess in a pagan court, risked her life to save her people from threatened destruction by Ahasuerus (Xerxes), King of Persia. Before appearing before the king to petition him to save the Jews, Esther, her attendants, and her uncle, Mordecai, all fasted in order to appeal to God for His protection. Today, the Esther Fast will protect us from evil and satanic influences, as well as from physical danger posed by other human beings.

Jerry Falwell was a friend of mine. During the meteoric growth of the Moral Majority he headed, he received several death threats, as his enemies vented their hatred toward him.

I was with Falwell in the summer of 1982, when he visited Australia. More than 1,000 Moral Majority opponents rushed the National Legislative Building in Canberra, the capital. The evening news described their actions as a "National Disgrace." Never before had the Parliament been threatened like that.

The following Sunday afternoon, a mob showed up at the Sydney Civic Center to protest Falwell's presence. Only a few uniformed patrolmen were present to keep the mob behind police barricades. As I watched, a thousand people plunged through the barricades and broke down the revolving door at the front of the building. I did not know that we wouldn't be killed. The second door held, and the rally was cancelled.

After that experience, I tried raising the preventive wall of The Esther Fast as I prayed for the safety of Jerry Falwell and other crusaders for God. Of course, outsiders can't tell whether God has protected those for whom I have fasted. The world might say they just experienced "lucky breaks," but we who have wrestled with the evil one know what happens when we yield our circumstances to God. We know that The Esther Fast is effective.

## Wrap Up

I have great visions for this new book on fasting. Like a parent giving birth to a new baby, every author sees something special in his book and hopes that it will change the world—or at least change lives. I believe that this new book, *Fasting for a Miracle*, can make a difference in the life of every Christian who learns to fast—to fast properly, and to fast for results.

E L M E R   L .   T O W N S

If every Christian fasted, the results could shake our culture like a windstorm bending a sapling. By fasting, Christians would demonstrate that they live differently, that their faith is imperative, and that the Almighty works in their daily lives.

If every church fasted, they would move forward in evangelism, reach out in feeding and helping others, and see God pour out His presence on His people.

# APPENDIX E

# Nonbiblical Miracles

Have you ever thought, *Why are there so many false miracles that are claimed by almost all religions (non-Christians and pseudo-Christians)?* Similarly, *Why are there so many false revelations ("God spoke to me")?* Could it not be possible that there are false miracles and revelations because there is one real miracle worker (God) who does authentic miracles for His purposes?

Just as there can't be a shadow without light shining through a real object to make the shadow, there must be true miracles that are mimicked by false miracles. And there would be no "knock-off" drugs to imitate the real drugs if the real drugs didn't exist. Could it be that there are so many false religions because there is a truer one? Therefore, we can't conclude that there are no true miracles because there are so many false ones. On the contrary, we must say the opposite: There *are* true miracles because there are so many false ones.

Different groups make various claims concerning miracles for different reasons. The following list reflects an attempt to systematize reported experiences into self-explanatory categories. These categories are not hierarchical (meaning the events become supernatural, or more powerful in performance, as you continue down the list), but represent different expressions of miracles by different people.

### Nonbiblical Signs and Wonders
1. Counterfeit Miracles
2. Psychosomatic Miracles
3. Holistic-Healing Miracles
4. Confession Miracles

5. Stimulated Miracles
6. Pseudo-Miracles
7. Deceptive Miracles

The following consideration of signs and wonders is necessary because some have indiscriminately accepted and promoted every testimonial of miraculous occurrences. But all miracles are not true miracles. Others have gone to the opposite extreme of denying the existence of any miracles. If we are careful in our analysis of miracles, and we assume the possibility that both authentic and false miracles exist, then we can explain the false in at least seven ways. The following categories of nonbiblical miracles recognize that some reported phenomena may not be genuine, and every genuine miracle may not necessarily be a direct act of God. Satan does miracles, and a heathen witch doctor may do the supernatural by the power of demons.

### I. Counterfeit Miracles

There are signs and wonders that are in fact miracles, but have their supernatural source outside of God. This type of miracle recognizes Satan as "an angel of light" (2 Cor. 11:14). Evangelical writers tend to interpret a miracle by the devil in terms of his ministry of counterfeiting the works of God. This is an area often overlooked by writers on mysticism; however, as Roger Bastide observes:

> Side by side with divine mysticism is Satanic mysticism. According to the theologians it allows two degrees. When a demon torments a soul from without it is a case of obsession, but when he completely masters the soul it is a case of possession. This demoniac mysticism presents the same characteristics of passivity and of violence as the others, but the two are distinguished by their efforts. While divine mysticism brings joy, consolation and moral progress, demoniac mysticism induces nervous disorders, spiritual torture and the disposition for sin.[1]

The question might legitimately be asked: Can such an explanation for signs and wonders realistically be applied to an evangelical experience described by its participants in terms of biblical phraseology? For some observers of such movements, the answer is undoubtedly yes. Sir Robert Anderson cites the writings of Robert Baker, historian of the Catholic Apostolic Church, and adds his own comments concerning the nature of the "charismatic" experience of that group, noting:

> I have been much confounded by the fact occurring in this instance, as also in most others of the public testimonies of preaching; that Christ was preached in such power, and with such dearness, and the exhortations to repentance so energetic and arousing, that it is hard to believe the person delivering it could be under the delusion of Satan. Yet so it was, and the fact stands before us as a proof that the most fearful errors may be propounded under the guise of greater light and zeal for God's truth. "As an angel of light" is an array of truth, as well as holiness and love, which nevertheless Satan is permitted to put on, to accomplish and sustain his delusions. It is yet more mysterious, and yet not less true, that the truth so spoken was carried to the hearts of several who, on this day, hear it, and these services were made the means of awakening them, so far as the change of conduct and earnest longing after Christ from that day forward can be an evidence of it.
>
> As an angel of light. These words recur as a refrain throughout the "*Narrative.*" Many a one will exclaim: "How could a movement which denounces the devil and all his works, and which promotes piety and honors Christ be Satanic?" But this ignores the solemn warning of our Divine Lord, "They shall deceive, if it were possible, the very elect." A moment's thought might satisfy us that the false could never deceive the elect if it did not simulate all the characteristics of the true—honor paid to Christ, a high tone of spirituality, and a beautiful code of morals.[2]

How can a believer tell a counterfeit miracle? Moses dealt with the issue of counterfeit supernaturalism in Deuteronomy. A miracle from God will:

1. Be in the Lord's name (see 18:22).
2. Not recognize false gods (see 13:2-3).
3. Stimulate love for the Lord (see 13:3).
4. Be consistent with the Word of God (see 13:4).

## 2. Psychosomatic Miracles

An area of the non-miraculous signs and wonders finds its explanation in the psychosomatic orientation of the healer or the convert. Dr. S. I. McMillen defines the psychosomatic phenomenon as the power of the mind over the body, noting:

> These cases illustrate the most intriguing subject in modern medicine. With every passing year, we obtain a wider comprehension of the ability of the mind (psyche) to produce varied disturbances in the body (soma), hence the term psychosomatic. Invisible emotional tensions in the mind can produce striking visible changes in the body, changes that can become serious and fatal.[3]

Aware of this phenomenon, George W. Peters stresses the need to differentiate between miraculous and psychosomatic healing:

> One must distinguish between faith healing and divine healing. Divine healing comes through the gracious intervention of God. It may come with or without medication; it may come suddenly or gradually. Faith healing rests mainly on the individual's psychological make-up and his personal relationships. It is principally a matter of psychology and suggestion. No doubt, many healings in healing campaigns are of this nature; they have little to do with the Gospel and divine intervention.[4]

A psychosomatic healing may be described as non-miraculous because God does not intervene directly, but is it an indirect work of God? If a person has an "illness" that is not real and is healed of that "illness," do we call it a non-real miracle or a non-real intervention by God? The illness may not be real by medical definition, but there is a reciprocal influence between body and mind that gives a real effect of pain even though there is no adequate cause.

### 3. Holistic-Healing Miracles

The area of holistic medicine may be a consideration in reported signs and wonders. The fundamental premise of holistic healing is that the body can and will heal itself of disease when positive mental health and corrective action are taken by the sick. This includes a positive attitude toward wanting to be healed. Because of the radical nature of evangelical conversion, it is to be expected that lifestyle changes on the part of the new convert will affect other areas of life, and this could include bodily functions. The man with an ulcer, who gains the peace of God internally and for religious reasons abstains from the use of alcohol and caffeine drinks, will also be treating his ulcer and will likely experience healing. The widespread application of this typology of healing is evidenced in Dr. Carl Jung's conclusion:

> Among all my patients in the second half of life—that is to say, over thirty-five—there has not been one whose problem in the last resort was not that of finding a religious outlook on life.[5]

### 4. Confession Miracles

The fourth type of sign and wonder is also non-miraculous. This type involves a testimony from a participant who knows the sign is nonexistent, but feels pressure from an evangelist or friend to experience a sign. This is a catch-22 statement of faith. A person must "say" he is healed as a statement of faith so God will heal him. He knows he is not healed, but he claims something he doesn't have so he can get it. Catch-22 usually occurs when a sick person has for some time sought healing without success. If the illness is psychosomatic, he may well be healed because of a change in the mind-body relationship previously described by Dr. McMillen. But the sad example is the case of the individual who "confesses" a healing from a serious disease but dies shortly thereafter. Others simply continue to suffer.

### 5. Stimulated Miracles

Another type of non-miraculous sign may be the result of some form of stimulus, such as drugs or other physical or psychological stimuli (music, hypnotic suggestion, brainwashing, and so on). Many drug-oriented religious sects use drugs as part of their religious experience and report visions and new revelations while under their influence. While this sort of stimulus and its effects are widely known, fewer people are aware that the influence of music, physical posture, behavior, and special diets can also result in a physical response. In his study of a revivalistic sect in Jamaica, Joseph Moore noted a direct relationship between the practice of hyperventilation and the entering of a possession trance state.[6] Similarly, M. J. Field was able to explain the unique religious experience of at least one sect in Ghana in terms of hypoglycemia caused by prolonged periods of fasting.[7]

### 6. Pseudo-Miracles

A pseudo-miracle is promoted not for ulterior motives but largely out of ignorance involved in the reported sign and wonder. This is apparently the explanation of the remarkable report of people being raised from the dead during the widely publicized Indonesian revival in the late 1950s. After interviewing those reportedly raised from the dead and those who raised them, George W. Peters concluded:

> The reports from Timor that God raised some people from the dead have startled many American Christians. I do not doubt that God is able to raise the dead, but I seriously question that He did so in Timor. In fact, I am convinced that it did not happen. Let me explain:
> I visited a man known in the community as having been raised from the dead. I met a woman who reported that her

infant daughter of four months had been raised. I talked to the woman who was said to be responsible for having brought back to life two people, and to the man who claimed to have been instrumental in raising two people from the dead, a boy of twelve and a man of forty to forty-five years old.

In my questioning, I kept the sentiments of the people in mind. Their absolutist beliefs will not respond to questions of doubt. I was also aware of the fact that their word for death may mean unconsciousness, coma, or actual death. I also knew of their traditional belief in the journey of the soul after death from the body to the land of the ancestors.

I had to explore the experiences of these people while they were in the state of death, how far they had "traveled," so to speak, between death and resuscitation. It became apparent that death takes place in three stages according to their beliefs. In the first stage, the soul is still in the body; in the second stage, the soul may be in the home or immediate community; and in the third stage, the soul takes its flight to the beyond and the land of the ancestors. Not one of the dead persons believed his soul had completely departed to the region beyond. That is the region of no return.

Those who claimed to have experienced resuscitation and immediate restoration were people who had died suddenly. Several children who had died after suffering prolonged illnesses had more gradual restorations.

I noted several interesting facts regarding the experiences reported during the state of death. One man told me that his soul had been so near his body during his state of death that he was able to hear people come near his body. However, he was not able to speak or move. He was able to relate experiences during his state of death. After some questioning, his wife added, "My husband was not absolutely and totally dead." This led to some further probing and lengthy discussions.

The mother whose infant daughter was raised was quite sure that her soul had not left her body, for she had been dead only about half an hour. An older man was able to describe his condition after dying. While dead he had promised God that if he could ever live again he would confess his sins and pay back the money he had stolen from an evangelist. He was sure that this theft had caused his sudden death, and so was the evangelist who brought him back to life. Thus the stories went. Two younger boys, one four and another eight, were not able to recount their experiences while dead. However, they were sure that they had not yet left the earth.

I shall leave any judgments about these miracles to the reader. I went away satisfied that according to their usage of the word death, and their concept of death, they had experienced resuscitation. According to my concept of death, no such miracles happened: I learned again the value of seeing words and concepts from the people's point of view and interpreting them according to their mentality and understanding.[8]

## 7. Deceptive Miracles

Some alleged signs and wonders have been humanly faked or deceptively reported. In any analysis, it must first be determined if the miracle is genuine; if it is not, then the source or motive behind the deception must be accounted for. Not every reported miracle is miraculous, and some who report them have been found to have less-than-pure motives. In the fall of 1971, leaders in the controversial Children of God sect tapped phones at a French Canadian church camp where they were holding a special conference. As new converts to the cult made calls home for money, notes were taken and later became the basis of "prophecies" given in public meetings. Undiscerning converts regarded these prophecies as evidence of God speaking to them through the sect leaders.[9] This is but one of many such abuses and must be considered as a possible explanation in evaluating a particular manifestation of a sign and/or wonder.

# Some Different Types of Prayer[1]

### Abandonment, Prayers of
When we don't know what we want God to do in our situation, so we yield the outcome (and ourselves) to Him.

### Asking Prayers
When we make a petition to God and specifically ask Him to answer our request.

### Beginning Prayers
Initial prayers we say to God when we first enter into a relationship with Him.

### Blind Obedience, Prayers of
When we determine to follow God regardless of whether we get answers to our prayers and no matter what the consequences.

### Brokenness, Prayers of
When we are convicted of our sin and become emotionally upset as we pray.

### Commitment, Prayers of
When we commit ourselves unreservedly to the answers for which we are praying.

### Continual Prayers
A state in which, through our intimate relationship with God, we remain in continuous fellowship with God as we progress through the day.

### Crucifixion, Prayers of
When we repent of and put to death a sin, attitude or practice by promising not to do it again.

### Deliverance, Prayers of
Interceding for God to give us victory over sin or unwanted practices in our life.

### Desperation, Prayers of
When we need an answer from God immediately because of an emergency or life-threatening problem.

### Faith, Prayers of
Praying with the firm belief that we will receive the things for which we ask.

### Fellowship Prayers
When we join together with others to pray in oneness of spirit (also known as *Communion Prayers*).

### Forsaken, Prayer of the
Searching for God in prayer when we think He is not hearing our petitions.

### Geographical Praying
Praying in places in which we feel the atmospheric presence of God or in which we previously received answers.

### Healing, Prayers of
Prayers of faith that raise up the sick and restore them to health.

### Hunger, Prayers of
Prayers in which we eagerly seek to enjoy God's presence.

### Hypocritical Prayers
When we pray publicly in order to bring glory to ourselves instead of sincerely speaking to God from our hearts.

## Identificational Repentance, Prayers of

Prayers of our troubled spirits, in which we choose to confess the unrepented transgressions of others (including the sins of past generations) and accept the consequences for those sins.

## Injustice, Prayers Against

When we use prayer as a weapon to purposefully intercede against the evil we encounter in this world and to right the wrongs therein.

## Intimate Prayers

Prayers in which we enjoy intimate fellowship with God.

## Introspective Prayers

Prayers in which we search for the sin in our life.

## Lord's Prayer

A model prayer that Jesus gave to us (see Matt. 6:9-13 and Luke 11:2-4). The Lord's Prayer contains all of the elements that are necessary for effective prayer.

## Meditative Prayers

Meditating in God's presence without making audible requests or even carrying on a conversation (also known as *praying without words*).

## Minutia Prayers

Praying about even the little details of life.

## Praise, Prayers of

When we focus on God in prayer to compliment Him for who He is and what He has done in our lives.

## Prayer Excursions

When a group of people go to a specific location that is in need of prayer.

## Prayer Journeys

When people go from one destination to another while praying for the specific needs of those along their routes.

### Prayer Walking

When individuals or groups walk around their neighborhoods to pray for the people who live there: "Praying on-site with insight."

### Praying in Jesus' Name

An act by which we can enter into a relationship with Jesus Christ, take full advantage of His death on the cross as payment for our sins, and accept Him as the Lord over our life.

### Praying in the Spirit

Allowing the Holy Spirit to make requests through our prayers to God the Father.

### Prevailing Prayers

Continually interceding in prayer until we receive an answer from God.

### Redemptive Prayers

Interceding in prayer for the salvation of others.

### Resting in Prayer

Passively surrendering in God's presence as we rest in the Lord.

### Solo Prayers

Praying individually for God to meet our needs.

### Transformational Prayers

When we open our hearts to God's power and allow Him to transform our lives into the likeness of Christ.

### Victory Prayers

When we claim God's triumph over any internal or external conflicts in our life.

### Vowing in Prayer

When we make a commitment to be faithful to God no matter what comes our way.

### Warfare Prayers
Struggling against evil influences through prayer so that God can bring us the victory.

### Worship Prayers
When our whole focus of prayer is to worship or magnify God.

### Written Prayers
When we recite the prayers of others or write out words that God has placed on our hearts.

# APPENDIX G

# Fasting for Supernatural Guidance

The Lord has promised, "I will guide you with My eye" (Ps. 32:8). We also have Jesus' assurance that "when He, the Spirit of truth, has come, He will guide you into all truth" (John 16:13). I believe these promises mean that the Spirit of God will help us understand the spiritual nature of truth. So, how exactly does God respond to my fast for insight and supernaturally guide me to understand His truth?

### Guidance Begins When Spiritual Blindness Is Removed

We begin our spiritual journey toward God in blindness, because the gospel is veiled. "If our gospel is veiled, it is veiled to those who are perishing, whose minds the god of this age [Satan] has blinded" (2 Cor. 4:3-4). Spiritual blindness prevents the unsaved person from seeing and understanding spiritual truth. Notice what truth is concealed: "Lest the light of the gospel of the glory of Christ, who is the image of God, should shine on them" (v. 4). Unsaved people are unable to understand the truth about Jesus Christ. God does a miracle when the Holy Spirit takes away spiritual blindness: "The Spirit of truth . . . will guide you into all truth" (John 16:13). God makes truth known by removing spiritual blindness.

C. S. Lewis defines a miracle as an interference with the laws of nature for a divine purpose.[1] The Holy Spirit doesn't put something in our minds that's not there, i.e., He doesn't fill up a vacuum in our brains. No! The Spirit of truth removes our inability to understand what we are observing. Therefore, as we study God's

Word to know His plan for our life, the Holy Spirit takes away our spiritual blindness so we can more fully understand His Word.

### The "Indwelling" Christ Reveals Truth to Us

When we became Christians, we invited Jesus Christ into our lives, resulting in His indwelling presence within us (see Gal. 2:20). Paul reinforces this truth by praying that the Ephesians would understand spiritual truth: "That Christ may dwell in your hearts ... [to] be able to comprehend with all the saints what is the width and length and depth and height" (Eph. 3:17-18). One of the promises of Christ within us is to show us His truth and help us to understand how to live. But most importantly, Christ helps us to know Him better. "We know that the Son of God has come and has given us an understanding, that we may know Him" (1 John 5:20).

### The Scriptures Guide Us into Spiritual Understanding

God promised that He would guide us through Scripture: "Your word is a lamp to my feet and a light to my path" (Ps. 119:105). Because the Bible was given to show us what to believe and how to live, it is a book to guide our daily lives. God uses Scripture to reveal His will to us.

### The Holy Spirit Guides Us into Spiritual Understanding

The Holy Spirit will guide us to understand our experiences so we will grow in our faith. As we study the Bible and try to understand its meaning, we have the Holy Spirit to lead us: "As many as are led by the Spirit of God" (Rom. 8:14). As the Spirit is leading us, He also confirms truth to us: "The Spirit Himself bears witness with our spirit" (Rom. 8:16).

# Endnotes

**Prologue: When Charles Needed a Miracle**

1. Liberty had 12 teams made up of students preparing for evangelistic ministry. They went to local churches to conduct weekend rallies.

**Chapter 2: . . . for a Miracle**

1. C. S. Lewis, *Miracles* (New York: HarperCollins, 2001), p. 5.
2. A law is an extension of the person of God, and His power to control or run the universe. A law is more than a written expression on the books; it is the standard of actions, enforced by a controlling authority, and, so far as is known, is invariable under its given conditions. Law has power, force, life and consequences, so that violating a law leads to the implied consequences of its power.
3. *Holman Christian Standard Study Bible* (Nashville, TN: Broadman & Holman, 1999), p. 96.
4. *Merriam-Webster*, s.v. "miracle," http://www.merriam-webster.com/dictionary/miracle (accessed March 1, 2012).
5. However, I have heard of individual believers or churches who prayed for the removal of dirt or a mountain, and it happened.
6. God used miracles when He changed direction or introduced a new message for His people.

**Chapter 3: Challenging Cancer and Changing God's Mind**

1. Vernon Brewer had one of the greatest ministries at Liberty University as a vice president and dean of students. He poured his life into many students, and they loved him. Even though he enforced the rules, and disciplined some students, they all loved him and learned many positive lessons from him. Vernon was considered a spiritual giant on campus.
2. The entire list of Christian classics Falwell read was: *Power Through Prayer* by E. M. Bounds; *The Christian's Secret of a Happy Life*, by Hannah Whitall Smith; *Your God Is Too Small*, by J. B. Phillips; *Spiritual Maturity*, by J. Oswald Sanders; *God's Way of Holiness*, by Horatius Bonar; *Spiritual Secret of Hudson Taylor*, by Dr. and Mrs. Howard Taylor; *Abide in Christ*, by Andrew Murray; *The Saving Life of Christ*, by Major W. Ian Thomas; *Bone of His Bone*, by F. J. Huegel; *The Pursuit of God*, by A. W. Tozer; *The Kneeling Christian*, by an unknown Christian; *Prayer: Asking and Receiving*, by John R. Rice; *Crowded to Christ*, by L. E. Maxwell; and *The Pilgrim's Progress*, by John Bunyan.

**Chapter 4: Fighting for Finances and Seeing the Biggest Miracle Ever**

1. Adapted from Jerry Falwell and Elmer Towns, *Fasting Can Change Your Life* (Ventura, CA: Regal Books, 1998), pp. 18-20.
2. For more information, read Jerry Falwell and Elmer Towns, *Capturing a Town for Christ* (Old Tappan, NJ: Fleming H. Revell, 1973).

**Chapter 5: Confronting Terror and Prevailing Over Danger**

1. A. E. Elmore, *Lincoln's Gettysburg Address: Echoes of the Bible and Book of Common Prayer, first edition* (Carbondale, IL: Southern Illinois University Press, 2009), p. 146.
2. "National Day of Prayer," http://en.wikipedia.org/wiki/National_Day_of_Prayer (accessed May 30, 2012).
3. Anson Stokes, *Church and State in the United States*, vol. 2 (New York: Harper and Brothers, 1950), p. 38.

4. "Abraham Lincoln XVI President of the United States: 1861-1865, Proclamation 97—Appointing a Day of National Humiliation, Fasting, and Prayer, March 30, 1863," The American Presidency Project, http://www.presidency.ucsb.edu/ws/index.php?pid=69891#ixzz1wRx3LKBT (accessed May 31, 2012).

### Chapter 6: Repenting Leads to Revival

1. I heard this story in 1984 from J. Edwin Orr, world-renowned authority in revivals, and professor of awakenings at Fuller Theological Seminary in Pasadena, CA. Orr taught a course at Liberty Baptist Theological Seminary in 1984, and he related this story from his research. There are seven biographies of Jonathan Edwards, and his role in revival is mentioned in many other documents. Some have doubted this story, but its facts could be hidden in some of those documents.

2. Elmer L. Towns, *The Christian Hall of Fame* (Grand Rapids, MI: Baker Book House, 1971), pp. 71-72.

3. Paul R. Dienstberger, *The American Republic: A Nation of Christians* (e-book, © 2000), chapter 6: "The Noonday Prayer Revival." http://www.prdienstberger.com/nation/Chap6ndp.htm (accessed May 8, 2012).

4. Edward Hindson, *Glory in the Church* (Nashville, TN: Thomas Nelson, Inc., 1975). The foundation for this story is found in the Postscript, pp. 118-126, "The Story of the Lynchburg Revival," by Jerry Falwell.

5. Jerry Falwell and Elmer Towns, *Fasting Can Change Your Life* (Ventura, CA: Regal Books, 1998), pp. 239-240.

6. Ronnie W. Floyd, *The Power of Prayer and Fasting*, 2nd edition (Nashville, TN: B&H Publishing Group, 2010).

7. Laurie Goodstein, "In Hope of Spiritual Revival, a Call to Fast," *The New York Times*, February 8, 1998, http://www.nytimes.com/1998/02/08/us/in-hope-of-spiritual-revival-a-call-to-fast.html?pagewanted=all&src=pm (accessed May 8, 2012).

### Chapter 7: Kneeling with Soldiers and Praying for Salvation

1. The Romans Road to Salvation is: (1) All have sinned (see Rom. 3:10,23); (2) the penalty of sin is death (see Rom. 5:12; 6:23); (3) Christ paid the penalty (see Rom. 5:8); and salvation comes through faith (see Rom. 10:9-10,13).

### Chapter 10: Overcoming Addiction and Restoring All That Was Lost

1. The personal dialogue throughout this chapter was documented by Barbara Henderson via email, July 9, 2012.

2. Elmer L. Towns, *The Daniel Fast for Spiritual Breakthrough* (Ventura, CA: Regal Books, 2010).

### Chapter 11: Confronting Evil and Casting Out Demons

1. Elmer L. Towns, *Theology for Today*, (Fort Worth, TX: Harcourt Custom Publishers, 2004), pp. 389-418. Many of the conclusions about demon possession that I present in the "demonology" section of my book are based on John L. Nevius, *Demon Possession* (Grand Rapids, MI: Kregel Publications, 1973). I feel that this book, written more than 100 years ago (originally copyrighted in 1899) by a Presbyterian missionary to China, is the best I've read on demon possession.

2. *Merriam-Webster's Dictionary*, s.v. "paroxysm." http://www.merriam-webster.com/dictionary/paroxysm (accessed May 9, 2012).

3. Doris Wagner, *How to Cast Out Demons: A Guide to the Basics* (Ventura, CA: Regal Books, 2000).

4. John MacArthur, "What Does It Mean to Be Filled with the Spirit?" *Grace To You*. http://www.gty.org/resources/positions/P04/what-does-it-mean-to-be-filled-with-the-spirit (accessed May 9, 2012).

5. Towns, *Theology for Today*, pp. 410-411.

6. Ibid., p. 417.

## Chapter 13: Prevailing Over Pain and Healing Sickness

1. See Elmer L. Towns, *How To Pray When You Don't Know What to Say* (Ventura, CA: Regal Books, 2006), p. 139.

## Chapter 14: Seeking Divine Guidance

1. There are many spiritual gift inventories available to find your spiritual giftedness. Visit www.elmertowns.com and look on the toolbar under "Resources" to find the Spiritual Gift Test I use. Larry Gilbert of Church Growth Institute has another fine spiritual gift inventory, entitled *Team Ministry Spiritual Gifts Inventory*, that may be found at http://www.churchgrowth.org/cgi-cg/gifts.cgi?intro=1.
2. Elmer Towns, *A Fresh Start in Life Now that You are a Christian* (Roanoke, VA: Progress Printing, 1976), p. 30.

## Chapter 16: Listening When God Is Silent

1. C. S. Lewis, *The Magician's Nephew* (New York: HarperCollins, 2000).

## Chapter 17: Knowing God More Intimately

1. See Elmer L. Towns, *Prayer Partners* (Ventura, CA: Regal Books, 2002), pp. 57-60.
2. Quote from *Field of Dreams*, a 1989 American fantasy-drama film directed by Phil Alden Robinson and adapted from the novel *Shoeless Joe* by W. P. Kinsella. For more information, see http://en.wikipedia.org/wiki/Field_of_Dreams (accessed June 1, 2012).
3. Many times I begin worship with the many names and titles of God the Father (more than 100 names), God the Son (more than 700 names), and God the Holy Spirit (126 names). These names are listed and discussed in my three books on the three Persons of the Trinity. These books are available free on my website; go to www.elmertowns.com, click Books Online on the tool bar, and search the list for *My Father's Names*, *The Names of the Holy Spirit* and *The Names of Jesus*.
4. Watchman Nee, *The Normal Christian Life* (Radford, VA: Wilder Publications, 2008), p. 22.
5. Jerry Falwell and Elmer L. Towns, *Fasting Can Change Your Life* (Ventura, CA: Regal Books, 1998), p. 127.
6. The material in this section is adapted from Elmer L. Towns, *Knowing God Through Fasting* (Shippensburg, PA: Destiny Image, 2002), pp. 17-19.
7. Ibid., pp. 38-42.

## Postscript: When Charles Needed a Miracle (continued)

1. Robin Cook, *Coma* (New York: Signet Classics/Penguin Group USA, 1977).
2. *The Free Dictionary by Farlex*, s.v. "coma." http://medical-dictionary.thefreedictionary.com/Coma (accessed March 20, 2012).
3. Elmer Towns, *Say-It-Faith* (Carol Stream, IL: Tyndale House Publishers, 1983).
4. Personal written account from Kathy Hughes concerning Charles's miraculous recovery from a devastating accident (via email, July 9, 2012).
5. Jerry Falwell, *Building Dynamic Faith* (Nashville, TN: Word Publishing, 2005), pp. 130-131.
6. As we discussed in chapter 15, God won't make yesterday not happen, nor can He make a stone so heavy He can't lift it. He can't make Himself cease to exist.
7. Remember that the definition of a miracle is "an interference in the laws of nature for divine purposes."

## Appendix A: What Is Fasting?

1. Elmer Towns, *The Daniel Fast* (Ventura, CA: Regal, 2010), pp. 23-26.
2. Towns, *Fasting for Spiritual Breakthrough* (Ventura, CA: Regal, 1996).
3. Ibid., pp. 23-24.

## Appendix B: The Miraculous Bible

1. As quoted in Elmer L. Towns, *Concise Bible Doctrines* (Chattanooga, TN: AMG Publishers, 2006), p. 23.

**Appendix C: Biblical Words for Miracles**
1. C. S. Lewis, *Miracles* (New York: HarperCollins, 2001), p. 5.

**Appendix D: Nine Different Purposes for Fasting**
1. The material in this appendix is taken from Elmer Towns, *Fasting for Spiritual Breakthrough* (Ventura, CA: Regal Books), 1996.

**Appendix E: Nonbiblical Miracles**
1. Roger Bastide, cited in George W. Peters, *Indonesia Revival: Focus on Timor* (Grand Rapids, MI: Zondervan Publishing House, 1975), p. 72.
2. Sir Robert Anderson, *Spirit Manifestations and the Gift of Tongues* (New York: Loizeaux Brothers/Bible Truth Depot), p. 3.
3. S. I. McMillen, *None of These Diseases* (New York: Pyramid Books, 1968), p. 58.
4. Peters, *Indonesia Revival*, p. 74.
5. Carl G. Jung, *Modern Man in Search of a Soul* (New York: Harcourt, Brace & Co., 1933), p. 261.
6. Joseph G. Moore, "Religious Syncretism in Jamaica," *Practical Anthropology* (1965) 12:64.
7. M. J. Field, *Search for Security: An Ethno-Psychiatric Study of Rural Ghana* (Evanston, IL: Northwestern University Press, 1960), p. 59.
8. Peters, *Indonesia Revival*, pp. 58-63.
9. Douglas Porter, "The Children of God," *Evangelical Baptist* (March 1975), p. 9.

**Appendix F: Some Different Types of Prayer**
1. In the "Principles of Prayer" section of the *Prayer Journey Bible* notes (Shippensburg, PA: Destiny Image Publishers, 2011, pp. 1965-2111), I compiled a list of 549 ways to pray. The prayers listed here are just a few of those ways.

**Appendix G: Fasting for Supernatural Guidance**
1. C. S. Lewis, *Miracles* (New York: HarperCollins, 2001), p. 5.

# About the Author

**Elmer Towns** is vice president of Liberty University and dean at Liberty Baptist Theological Seminary, which he co-founded in 1971 with Jerry Falwell. He has taught the Pastor's Bible Class at Thomas Road Baptist Church in Lynchburg, Virginia, for 27 years. Elmer is a Gold Medallion Award-winning author, and his books include *Fasting for Spiritual Breakthrough*, *Fasting for Financial Breakthrough*, *The Daniel Fast for Spiritual Breakthrough*, *When God Laughs*, *How to Pray When You Don't Know What to Say* and *What's Right with the Church*. He and his wife, Ruth, have three grown children.

For more information about prayer and fasting, visit:

**WWW.ELMERTOWNS.COM**

# A LIFE TRANSFORMED
# BY A FAITHFUL GOD

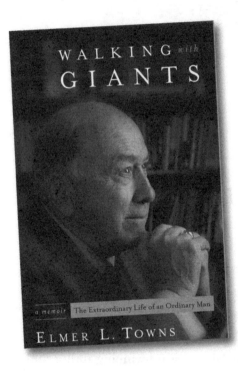

**Walking with Giants**
Elmer L. Towns

The ministry of Elmer Towns has spanned more than half a century and is well known to many in the Church. But what events and encounters in his early years shaped and prepared him for the extraordinary opportunities to come? *Walking with Giants* is Elmer Towns's story, in his own words, from his struggles as an adolescent to accepting salvation to pastoring his first congregation at the age of 19. You will read about the doors God opened for Elmer and his friend Jerry Falwell to found Liberty University and about the school's incredible growth over the past 40 years. Above all, you will see the faithful hand of God at work for His glory in the life of an ordinary man—and know without a doubt that He can work in you, too.